AMERICA UNDERCOVER

Adventures of the Unknown Humorist

May the "Schwartz" be with you!

GARY SCHWARTZ

Gary Schwartz

HARD SHELL

PUBLISHING

Mukilteo, Washington

Publisher's Note: Many of the products and services mentioned in this book are trademarks of their respective companies. Every effort was made to identify these trademarks with initial capitalization. Should there be any omissions in this respect, we shall be pleased to make the necessary changes in future printings.
The names in the narrative portion of this book are real. They were included to credit those who made the author's journey positive and meaningful. We regret any misspellings.

A Hardshell Publishing Book
PO BOX 1630
Mukilteo, Washington 98275
Copyright © 1997 by Gary Schwartz

Library of Congress Catalog Card Number: 97-93545

ISBN: 0-9649558-4-9

Printed by Complete Reproduction Services
November, 1997
Santa Ana, California

10 9 8 7 6 5 4 3 2

Dedication

This book is dedicated to:

My wife *Debbie*, for standing by me for six difficult years.

David Anderson, my friend, writing coach and editor, who has stood by me for 32 years.

And *myself*, for having the wisdom to know that without them there would be no book.

Acknowledgments

The greatest pleasure I had with my first book, *ADVENTURES IN THE SLOW LANE: Tales From the Other Side,* was meeting most of the people who bought it. They gave me the encouragement and financial opportunity to publish this one. Each of them deserves recognition for taking such a risk. This is my way to say thank you. Several names aren't included because the idea to collect them didn't occur until several weeks after publication — and, in the manic moments of a sale, I sometimes forgot to get them. And in a couple of instances, I lost my address book in which they were written. I sincerely apologize to them and to those whose names I've inadvertently misspelled — either because I couldn't read their writing or my own.

 A sincere thank you to: (Please turn to pages 275-285)

And **Helen Ibach**, who encouraged me to become an author and join her in the difficult and rewarding business of books. **Dave Shaw**, a customer I met on the San Juan ferry who lives in Rochdale, England, who gave me occasional kicks of literary inspiration through e-mail, to help finish this project. And **Dan Hunter** and **Dr. Nancy Brainard**, for their assistance in proofreading and editorial guidance. And **Russ Smith**, who computerized the tire tracks and little car on pages 1-86.

And a *very* special thanks to the following for unselfishly permitting me to sell my book at their places of business: **Eddie Davis, Mike Olson, Tom Bradley, Karim Qureshi, Melissa Hsu, Art Schwartz, Steve Bader, Steve Koeplin, Karen Pederson, Jim Baugher, Bob Goodman, Oren Combs, Paul Williams, Oscar Blaser, Rod Skulrod, Dean Duvall, Dirk Heuser, Jerry Fulk, Rich Ehni, Jim Wire, Michael Teggart, Dave Mischel** and **Dan Diedrichs.**

And the **Hovander brothers**; Jeff, Cory, Scott and Derek, for use of their cabin and the solitude it provided when needed for this project.

Introduction

Many people have asked why I sell my books in such an unusual manner. Survival is the simple answer. But there's a lot more. I wasn't really sure until I searched my clouded soul for answers as deeply as I searched across America for sales. That question spawned so many good and bad feelings, the best, and perhaps only way I could answer, was to write about it. So I did.

AMERICA UNDERCOVER: Adventures of the Unknown Humorist, is about my journey from near suicide to success. Under the cover of anonymity and the mystical tortoise shell symbolic of my syndicated newspaper column *Life in the Slow Lane*, I crossed America to sell books. More importantly, I learned about myself and others and how we're all alike and so different at the same time. I hope to inspire and encourage those who feel lost and afraid, with the wish that they too, can find their own paths to happiness.

For those I met who already have, and for those who could only smile at me with warm encouragement rather than laugh at my sales antics, I hope they receive some satisfaction in these pages. They helped me join them on that mountain peak where I'm now able to glow with a sense of victory and new hope for my future.

It's no secret that humor is a good antidote for pain. Therefore, in the first portion of this book, I've revealed serious aspects of my background so you'll understand why the collection of satirical essays and tales may be somewhat off-the-wall and a little cynical.

People's names in the first section are real. My intention is to acknowledge their positive influence on my journey.

Table of Contents

AMERICA UNDERCOVER

<u>MORE</u> Adventures of the Unknown Humorist
PART ONE: *In Pursuit of Trivia*

Table of Contents

Table of Contents

Part Five: *Politically Incorrect*

Part Six: *Healthy Sicknesses*

Table of Contents

Part Seven: *Almost Serious Reflections*

Acknowledgments *275*
Names of people who bought the first book

AMERICA UNDERCOVER
Adventures of the Unknown Humorist

The Author's Diary

Boxes filled with books arrived on a cold and rainy January day, 1996. I hadn't been excited like this since the idea was just a spark in my mind. I had labored nine months to produce this first book — and it sure was a beauty!

While the UPS driver was stacking the boxes in the garage, I supervised as quickly as he could work. He left, exhausted, and I went into the house where Debbie was waiting for our celebration.

I held a copy of my accomplishment in one hand and sipped some fine wine with the other. I felt warm inside, and it wasn't just the grapes. This was a crowning moment for both of us. I wanted to rest. We *needed* to rest. We had planned a ski trip to unwind, and now we could go.

"Nobody can say I don't have substance anymore," I said to Debbie very quietly. I ran my fingers slowly across the smooth cover of the book. "I wish my parents could see me now."

It had been a long and stressful adventure so far . . . and yet, it was just beginning. I was ready to prove that I was the strong and confident man I once was — or at least, thought I was. Now I would become a famous author and get the respect I deserved. But after three glasses of wine, I started to cry.

"I'm not sure I'm strong enough. What if I can't sell the books? What if I don't become famous? What if I die too soon, just like my father? What if I just need more wine?"

Debbie didn't know how to answer.

———————

I had lost everything four years earlier in Los Angeles — my job, a fiancé, my house, my savings and a lot of those who I thought were friends. A heart attack and bungled surgery at the VA hospital had left me lingering on thoughts of suicide. I was very angry, but couldn't afford Doctor Kevorkian. But I did have a gun.

Instead, I moved north for a fresh start and to avoid the big-city peer pressures I had always felt but could never quite live up to.

I had visited Washington several times before. The ample helpings of green foliage, clean air, water and snow-capped mountains served up by the Northwest, were always a welcome change from the diet of crowded streets, crime and polluted air in the city I had once bragged about as my hometown.

I arrived in May of 1991. I survived the first lonely months because I met Cory Hovander. He was a class act living on a no-class budget at the time. Still is — he manages an RV park and is still 12 years younger than I am. He had the exuberance and enthusiasm I once had and was a positive influence then, as he is now. He was impressed that I could match his obnoxious cussing and swearing, and that I knew who the Beatles were. I was impressed with him because he was impressed with me.

I told Cory's friends about the rich and famous people I knew and the important work I had done in public relations. No one cared and I continued feeling isolated and unconnected. Cory tried desperately to save me. He took me to important places like Billy Bob's Tavern where I felt foolish because I don't drink much and my cowboy act was never credible. When I got excited seeing a sexy, drunk cowgirl wearing a Stetson, I had to pop a nitroglycerin tablet to keep from falling off the stool — two of them if one of the so-called ladies got too close. My heart was in bad shape.

I was adapting fairly well in spite of Cory's good, but misguided intentions. My rural wardrobe was growing, and I was beginning to understand the language. Then, all of a sudden, I met Debbie and her 8-year-old son, Rain, in the food area of the Everett Mall. (*My favorite place in* any *mall*). This was no cowgirl! She was shy, intelligent and naturally beautiful. I popped two of the nitroglycerin tablets when she wasn't looking, then bribed Rain with a handful of quarters to use at the video arcade — I only had three hours to impress his mother before the place closed.

I told Debbie my best exaggerated stories of professional and athletic feats and of all the women who weren't wise enough to catch me. But I was truthful with her about my fears that no employer, senior athletic team or woman would want me now — I was merely a broken-hearted, chest-scarred, downtrodden and very unemployed man with little confidence and even less money.

She didn't say much at that first meeting. She must've been listening to the upbeat intercom music instead of paying attention to me. We were married three months later in Santa Fe, New Mexico. Debbie's parents and Rain had little time to reason with her, but her foolishness was later my salvation.

I was still having heart problems that prevented me from doing those things men are supposed to do. (*I've always hated yard work and jobs anyway.*) So when she suggested a second surgery to repair the first, I reluctantly succumbed to the saw, scalpels, tubes and needles. It was worth it. The hospital food was better this time.

I felt good. I worked out and lost weight. Then I went on an interview to get the high-paying public relations job I had promised her. But I got caught in a lie. The interviewer asked what the titles were of the book and two screenplays I hadn't really written. Embarrassed and ashamed, I convinced Debbie I could syndicate my column in 100 newspapers instead of getting a traditional job.

She said "okay," but not very convincingly.

I fell far short of my goal after two years of tedious work. The task was harder than I had thought. I began losing confidence again and felt unworthy of Debbie's admiration. My desperate pursuit of self-esteem had reversed into a severe depression. I had no job — I was worthless. No matter how much I begged her to reassure me that I was okay without a job and had fallen short of my syndication goal, she wasn't convincing with her weak affirmations. Although I had some success, I felt she was like my mother — it wasn't good enough.

Early in 1995, I didn't care anymore. The few remaining happy spirits I had, died. One day I screamed violently at Debbie to give me the gun I had asked her to hide, anticipating what I might do with my self-destructive thoughts. She refused. I began trembling violently.

"Give me the gun! Give me the gun, damn it!" I was terrified by my deranged thoughts of violence toward her if she didn't. "Get out of the house! Now! Hurry."

She left and I fell, mentally and physically exhausted, onto the bed, crying. I began psychiatric therapy the next day.

After several sessions, Dr. Noel suggested I review my past successes and dwell on them instead of on my failures.

"You just won first place for humor writing in the state newspaper competition," said Debbie. And I recalled winning other writing awards in school and business since the sixth grade. Dr. Noel reminded me how much I liked to talk in our sessions and said "you're very good at expressing yourself." And I remembered I had been pretty good at giving inspirational speeches and coaching children in T-ball and basketball.

But what inspired me most were two comments I found in my high school yearbook while reviewing my past. One was from a classmate in a creative writing class and the other by a colleague on the school newspaper. "Your stories have in them real talent . . . I'm counting on you to be among guys like Alfred Hitchcock . . . . " "You're a guy with a good heart — & there aren't many. You've got lots of life and I like to see it. You'll never get ulcers from overwork 'cause you never work!"

I hadn't changed much from high school — I doubt that many people do. I always talked a lot, I suppose, and was a happy, free spirit who didn't like to work too hard, but had a lot of fun when I did — especially as the school's sports editor. But I needed to keep my own cheer-leading counsel. I missed my father's encouragement then as much as I do now. He died at 36 when I was 13. My mother, a secretary with three children and a mortgage on her hands, was having her own difficulties dealing with his death and wasn't capable of being a good substitute.

While sharing some of these thoughts with Debbie, I noticed a twinkle in her eyes. "What's going on in there?" I asked.

"Well, I was just thinking. Why don't you put together a book with your best columns?"

"A book? Are you crazy? And you're the practical one? I can't compete with Dave Barry, Irma Bombeck, Louis Grizzard, Mike Royko, Andy Rooney and who knows who else. Who ever heard of me? No way. Who's going to publish an unknown? You've lost your mind." She looked me straight in the eyes.

"Publish it yourself. You can figure out how."

"Are you serious? Where are we going to get the money?"

"We'll do whatever it takes. But if you're not successful, you'll have to get a job."

Get a job. I had heard it so many times before. I had worked since I was 12. I had been laid off or fired five times in my career, and always came bouncing back. I was strong, just like my father who continued working in spite of his terminal illness. I was a survivor. But now I was older and weary.

Three Choices — Suicide, a Job or a Book

The way I saw it, I had three choices — the gun, the job or the book. The first two weren't really very interesting.

So I called Dr. Noel. "I don't have time to be depressed for awhile. I'm going to write a book and become a famous author."

Then I called my friend Dave Anderson in Los Angeles. We had met in the Army 29 years earlier. I trusted him. "I need to see you. Can you come up?"

We discussed the book during the spectacular six-hour ferry ride through the San Juan Islands to Canada and back. "Yes," he said, "you can do it. I'll be glad to help. But why are you doing it?"

"For my ego. I want to leave something behind before I die. Something I'm proud of. I want to be remembered as somebody who was smart and talented."

"Do you want to make money?"

"No, that's not important."

Two days later I called him at home. "Dave, I want to make money. I hear only two percent of authors make a living with their books. I want to be one of them."

I like challenges. But I didn't suspect at the time, how big this one was.

Several people suggested I get a publisher and let someone else take the risk. But I didn't want the rejection slips or the haunting memory of Ivan Goff.

Ivan was the original creator of the TV show *Charlie's Angels*, producer of *Mannix* and had written many major motion pictures. He was nominated for an Academy Award for *Man of a Thousand Faces*, starring James Cagney.

I had met him while we were waiting to have car stereos installed. I told him I had aspirations of being a screenwriter, not knowing who he was.

"I know a little about screenwriting," he said modestly, "Would you like to have lunch sometime?"

Several weeks later at lunch, (*he treated*) he came up with a title for a movie — *Slowly, But Shirley*, but no story to go with it. Six months later, sitting bored at my desk at just another PR agency job, the story popped into my head. I typed it up in an hour.

I called Ivan. "I've got an idea for *Slowly, But Shirley*." He invited me to his exclusive Malibu Colony beach house and read my outline. He was so excited, I couldn't believe it. "Can I work on this with you?" he asked. "It's brilliant." *Me* work with *Ivan Goff*? Yes!

He said we would write the treatment together — his name had industry clout — and he knew the right people. We were partners. So for the next year and a half, I worked with him to write 35 pages. I was learning from the master. He soon became a father figure, always reminding me to be patient. "It's better to be good,

6

than hasty," he would say when I got impatient. I believed in him. He was the expert and would show me the way.

Finally we finished, and I was relieved from the tedium of writing and rewriting according to Ivan's perfectionism.

It was good to learn, but I soon became totally disillusioned. I found out through other contacts, Ivan was finished in Hollywood. Nobody wanted to work with him anymore. He was old and stubborn, they said, and I hated to hear that — I respected him so much, and he was exciting to work with. So I took the story to a contact at Universal Television and made a presentation by myself.

A week later the studio called.

"We love it. Bring Ivan and your agent in and let's sign a contract!" I couldn't believe it! It was happening! I called Ivan.

"Ivan. Universal wants to sign us up. They just want to make a few changes in characters and the location. And they . . ."

"Forget it," he said. "Nobody is going to change *my* work. Those young lawyers and accountants running Hollywood don't know what they're doing."

I'll never forget that disappointment. I had been thwarted from success twice by following my mother's advice, and then by Ivan's. It wouldn't happen again.

Now, I would publish the book myself, without rejection or interference, and take control of my own destiny.

———————————

We arrived at Whistler Mountain. I had taken a box of books along to pass out as samplers. Debbie and Rain waited in the car while I went inside to register.

"Can I have a discount?" I asked jokingly. "I'm a celebrity. Here's my new book. Just came out yesterday." I was shocked. Not only did I get a discount, but two of the desk clerks *bought* the book — paid cash, too. So I gave them a discount, too and said, "No tax. I don't like it either." Then they asked for an autograph. Autograph? From me? I felt strangely flattered and a little uncomfortable. After all, I was just a regular fella trying to get by and impress himself and his wife. But a celebrity? If I remember correctly, I autographed the books, "May you find some rooms in the vacancies of your mind, to lodge some of this sick humor." The quick response challenged my writing skills. I felt good when they both said "thanks" with big smiles after reading my note.

I received curious glances from others checking in. One of them asked to see a copy of the book — and bought it. I ran out to the car. "I sold three books! I can't believe it. I'm a celebrity."

Debbie shook her head. I thought she'd be excited for me, but she just shook her head. I think she was embarrassed and didn't understand my joy. I wasn't sure I did either, but I needed some admiration and encouragement.

When we checked into the first-class room, the phone rang. "Mr. Schwartz, what kind of champagne do you prefer?"

A bottle of bubbles to match my feelings arrived. So did a fruit basket and tickets for free buffet breakfasts. (*Free meals have always appealed to me. For some reason, they seem to taste better.*) Debbie shook her head again. I liked the celebrity treatment. I think she did, too, but wouldn't admit it — or couldn't.

I was on a roll. I sold a book on the elevator, then walked up confidently to several strangers in the lobby. "Wanna buy a book?" I sold two more, then went to check out the Jacuzzi and sold another one to the fitness instructor. She wanted to trade for a fitness session — no way. I preferred the flexibility of cash.

The next day I stuffed a few copies inside my ski jacket. When I fell down and people asked if I was okay, I said, "Sure. Buy my book and I'll feel even better." Being a lousy skier has some advantages. I traded one copy for free ski rentals, sold a couple of copies to the local bookstore and traded a couple more at the French restaurant to help pay for the expensive celebration meal.

The entire box of books was gone! I was ecstatic. People seemed to like me. I was feeling great. I hoped they'd like the book.

That night I stacked and counted the unfamiliar Canadian money. I had made enough to pay for the first day of skiing with a little left over to buy Debbie some daisies. I was chuckling like a little kid counting his loot from a lemonade sale. I was a successful entrepreneur. When Debbie and Rain looked at me with raised eyebrows, I could only explain.

"After my dad died, I had to pay for most of my own food and clothes. My mom said I had to learn to be self-sufficient. I used to stack up the quarters I collected each month from my paper route customers. Then I'd set enough aside for the necessities. There's not much difference now except the amount. And if you take into account inflation, no difference at all. It's just a lot more fun now."

My ecstasy continued into the following week. When we got home, the *Mukilteo Beacon* ran a front-page story about me and the book. I was flattered and embarrassed. Paul Archipley, the publisher, had been a good friend, but I always did question his editorial judgment. He placed my column *Life in the Slow Lane* right next to the most popular article in the paper — *Police Beat*. It should be a crime to mix such serious events with my brand of humor. I've never doubted his judgment since. I've become somewhat of a local celebrity, probably more infamous than famous, although I get no special treatment other than tolerance.

My first official book-signing was at the Mukilteo Coffee Company on a cold and rainy Friday evening. I was disappointed. Only a few people showed up, mostly friends and acquaintances that I had nearly begged to come.

But the next day at the Food Emporium, owner Mike Olson generously provided long-stem roses to those who bought the book, and I sold several copies in just a couple of hours while standing by the check-out stands. I was flying high, feeling important and special again. I was autographing books with clever little personal anecdotes and people seemed to love it. And I loved putting the cash in my wallet and stacking it up to impress Debbie when I got home.

A couple of days later, I did my first professional book-signing at Walden's in the Alderwood Mall. Inside the confines of a real bookstore, I was legitimate and could be taken seriously by others. I certainly wasn't taking myself seriously. I was having fun joking around with the customers and selling a lot of copies. I wouldn't let anyone pass into the store without first flashing a copy in front of them, laughing. "Buy my book!" I'd follow them around the store if I first missed them. I was aggressively enthusiastic and naive, not yet realizing how innocence can be offensive to some and unprofessional to others.

A week later I went to Sequim for three book-signings and a radio and TV interview. My in-laws, Jean and Darwin, live there. I wanted to impress them because I always felt they were wondering, although I was always afraid to ask, when I was going to contribute more substantially to their daughter's well-being.

It was fun pretending to be a celebrity. For support, I asked Jean to accompany me to the live radio interview. After I offended listeners by saying Rush Limbaugh was a great entertainer not to be taken too seriously, the DJ asked Jean what she thought of having a famous son-in-law. Her reply was an early indication of my future fame. She couldn't muster up a single word — only a succession of uncontrolled giggles. I laughed with her.

I don't remember exactly how my *Humor Me, Buy My Book* T-shirt was conceived, but it has became more recognizable than I or the book. I do remember the practical, but clever Debbie suggesting the tag line on the book cover, *Humor Me. Buy This Book.* And I know she suggested the rock star motif on the back of the shirt with the names of cities where I had and would be visiting and doing book-signings.

I felt completely foolish wearing the shirt at first — like a clown. But I enjoyed the faces it lit up with smiles as I passed by potential customers. It broke the proverbial ice, so I could warm them up to look at the book. "You think the shirt's funny? Take a look at this!" I would say as I placed a copy in their hands.

I wondered if I was perceived as a jester, performer or serious author. I had a long road ahead before I could figure that out.

I had done three book-signings at Barnes and Noble bookstores with nobody showing up. Each store had gone to the trouble of putting up big posters of me and my book and included a note about my appearance in their newsletters. I was beginning to understand there was a lot more to becoming a famous author than book-signings.

I had walked around the superstores, selling more discreetly than at the Walden and independent stores, but determined to let people know I was there. I did sell a few copies. Then I was told at the fourth signing that I couldn't solicit the customers and had to stay seated at the table — that my reputation for soliciting had preceded me — I was hurt and angry.

Starving Artist or Profitable Bookseller?

I had driven a long way in bad weather to be there. While sitting at that lonely table that night, I began doodling some interesting figures on my notepad. I sat there faced with the realization, owing to my frenzy to get the book published and subsequent fun with it, I was making less than 90 cents on each book sold by the bookstores. With all the expenses associated with publishing and marketing the book, including travel to these signings and the taxes, I was barely breaking even — and that didn't even include anything for my time to write it!

There was no way I was going to make a living this way.

I tried to be polite as I was leaving the bookstore. I told the woman who arranged the signing, "I'm trying to make a living. I came here to sell books. I thought you wanted me to sell books, too. If I'm not allowed to walk around, I can't sell books. I'm not famous, so nobody comes to see me. You have a wonderful store, and you've been very kind, but my personality and your company's are incompatible. I won't be signing books at your stores anymore."

I walked out to my car thinking of Debbie's dreaded admonition, ". . . or get a job." Her words made me fearful, but they also gave me strength. I opened the trunk and sold three books in the parking lot — and kept *all* the money! Then I went into the adjoining Starbucks Coffee Shop and sold several more while sipping coffee and sharing my financial discovery with others. I was feeling pretty smug and angry at the same time, but mostly hurt that my enthusiasm for selling and meeting people in the bookstore wasn't met with more support.

I hope Barnes and Noble will change its attitude someday. Maybe I will, too — if people line up to buy my books.

Now confident from the Whistler Mountain and Barnes & Noble experiences, I began lining myself up in people's faces in the streets, coffee shops, parking lots, the ferries and anywhere else I could where I felt safe. I was always a little nervous and embarrassed. I was concerned that people would think I was some kind of nut. But I continued selling lots of books, and my confidence was building day by day.

Two years earlier, I had talked to Debbie about driving around the country to visit some of the places where my column appeared. At the time it was financially impractical. But now I was sure I had to do it. I needed to know if I was strong enough, both physically and emotionally, to overcome my fears of death on the road or a return to depression.

Debbie agreed, but on one condition. "You must sell enough books to pay for the motels, food and gas. I'm not willing to send you money for a vacation." Wives sure are a pain sometimes.

I got busy with the planning — driving times, cost, the condition of my old Honda, the condition of my old heart. Could I really sell enough books on the streets of unfamiliar towns and cities to make the trip worthwhile? Would I be able to get Debbie's respect? Would I be treated like a celebrity or a buffoon? I wasn't quite ready to cross the country.

"Honey, I'm going to Los Angeles before taking the big trip. I want to see how the car and I hold up." She shook her practical head the way she always does when I get brilliant ideas.

It was March, 1996. I left Debbie at 5:30 a.m. with a big hug. "I'll see you in a couple weeks."

"Do you have enough money?" she asked.

"There you go being practical again. Sure. I have a couple hundred bucks and credit cards. Don't worry so much."

I didn't tell her I was worried, too. I had as many doubts about my heart holding up as I did about the money. Survival is nothing to joke about. It wasn't fun when I was a teenager, either. It's just something that needs to be done.

I whistled happy tunes as I raced south on I-5, the same highway I had raced north on with tears of regret and disappointment five years earlier. I was excited to show friends how well I could sell books in the streets. I could get their respect this way. I had arranged a few book-signings as well — to make me appear successful and legitimate if street sales were slow.

My mind was racing, but my eyes were drooping, just an hour and a half after leaving. I needed a jolt of caffeine, so I pulled up to an espresso stand next to an old, abandoned truck stop. I ordered a quad — four shots, hold the milk. I turned around and flashed my shirt, my smile and my book at a couple behind me.

"Wanna buy a book?"

"Yeah, we'll buy one."

I wasn't so lucky with the next fellow. I had seen him climb out of the cab of a big truck. He had a crewcut and steely gray eyes.

"Wanna buy a book?"

He snapped back. "You write it?"

"Yes," I said proudly.

"Only queers write books," he said.

I got shaky and uncertain. I quickly changed the subject to connect with him on a different level.

"Do you play golf? There's a funny golf story in here."

"You play golf?" he growled.

"Yeah . . .?" I sensed I was in trouble.

He ran over to the nearby ditch, quickly relieved himself and then picked up a large tree branch. I froze with fear. He came running back screaming. "Only queers play golf. I hate queers."

My adrenaline kicked in, and I thought those thoughts you get when you think life is over, but I was too slow to react. I just stood there, frozen. I was lucky his driving buddy grabbed him. I quickly got back in my car and left, forgetting my quad. I was awake now, and grateful my life was still intact.

I had always been trusting of people, expecting them to understand my sense of humor. I had seen this kind of guy on TV, and I had been warned about the possibilities of incidents like these, but hadn't given them much thought. Now I was convinced. I worried all the way to Portland, stopping only once for gas where I sold another book.

At a Portland book-signing, I met a charming, intelligent and beautiful lady. We talked a long time. (*As usual, nobody showed up to see me.*) She had a Master's degree in child psychology and yet she couldn't find a job. She had struggled for years and had proven herself not only as a teacher and a woman, but as a black woman. But she still wasn't getting the respect she deserved. I felt an intimate compassion for her, and although she didn't buy the book, she gave me a hug for listening to her story.

The hug meant more than a sale. It made me feel good about myself, not the book. This was a lesson I was to learn more as each day passed.

A few minutes later, I saw a guy who seemed to be dressed inappropriately. I was curious why someone looking like that would be in a bookstore. I think his name was Tim. He told me about his life and struggles after I shared a little of mine. He lived in a cabin near Portland, and was doing odd jobs until he could figure out what he wanted to do. He was very intelligent, well read and likable. He was honest and sincere — not ashamed of his present situation.

I didn't think he would buy the book, but he did, then said he enjoyed talking with me. I liked that.

I promised myself I'd try not to judge people again by their clothes. I wasn't sure I could succeed, but at least I was becoming more aware of my ignorance. I was also beginning to understand my new situation as a traveling author. Now I was an observer, rather than a participant of traditional life. I had never been comfortable as a team player, anyway, preferring instead to lead, or not participate at all. The new role was beginning to fit me well.

As I approached San Francisco, fond memories of the great city slowed me down. I detoured off the freeway just to glimpse the inspiring skyline and I parked at the rest stop on the north end of the Golden Gate. I sat on the same concrete post I had sat on several times before and gazed across the bay. The sun was painting the choppy water a golden yellow, and there was no fog to be seen, just the sharp outlines of those famous skyscrapers and a few quiet ships in port.

I sat alone and free — free of obligations to a job, free to inhale the unique and wonderful ocean aroma, free to think of the fish beneath me, swimming independently with or against the tides at their whim — like me. I could also see the train of cars chugging across the bridge with passengers sadly trapped inside.

A Mini-Adventure to Los Angeles

I left those thoughts in San Francisco and returned to I-5, the lonely highway that cuts down through the heart of California's farmlands. The endless rectangles of greenery stretched like a checkerboard across desolate plains and passed by me in slow motion, as I sat comfortably inside the confines of my car where nothing could interfere with the reflections on my past.

I thought about returning to the Los Angeles cemetery where my parents are buried, but it would be too painful. I remembered in 1991, just before I departed for Washington, lying on their graves. I was crying for my mother to reach out with her arms and hug me like she never had when she was alive. I did feel them, and oh, how good it felt. And I could hear her whisper then, as I had wished for so long she would, "Yes, Gary, you can be a writer now. I was wrong. You can do it."

I had trouble forgiving her then for discouraging me from taking the sportswriter job after high school and blocking another opportunity, during my first year of college, to meet Rod Serling who was interested in my *Twilight Zone* idea. I was still bitter that I had done what she thought was best for me, not what I thought.

15

What was I going to do after studying math and physics? I had no desire to be anything but a writer or an entertainer.

And I had seen then my father's youthful face from below, yelling at me like he always did with passion and love, "You'll get a spanking, son, if you ever say 'can't' in this house again." He meant business, and I had long ago learned he was right to say so.

I'll always be sad that he died of Hodgkin's Disease before he could become the rocket scientist he was studying to be instead of the tool and die maker he was. I was proud of him and loved him for always encouraging me to do whatever I wanted to do, not what he wanted me to do.

And I still cry every time I say goodbye to someone I love — or could love. I never had the opportunity to cry and say goodbye to him. He died alone in the hospital, too proud to let us share his vulnerability. He didn't know he was loved just for himself and not for what he did. I hoped my new adventure would help me find my own way to set aside my pride and learn who I really was.

Although each parent still had influence over me, I was fighting to stay on the side of my father while trying to understand my mother.

I arrived that night at Nancy and Richard's house in Monrovia, a suburb east of downtown Los Angeles. Nancy had once worked for me and was now very successful in her own right as a communications executive at a major bank. Trying to convey my success, I bragged about the exploits of my odyssey so far, but couldn't admit I was a little envious of their means even though I had my freedom.

Richard, an ex-corporate geologist, now content to stay home and invest money, cook and be a good house-husband, referred to their home appropriately as Motel Zero, for what I paid them to stay. I enjoyed talking of old times and re-energizing our friendship, but things didn't seem the same between us anymore. I had a new focus and perspective on life now, so the talk of corporate work and financial gain was no longer appealing, but the good food sure was. Richard had learned to be a fine cook.

While spending time with Nancy and Richard, I realized my somewhat successful PR career was insignificant. I felt good that I might have had a little to do with Nancy's success, but a lot of the business talk didn't seem to matter. And all the propaganda I was so good at spewing out before, now seemed so ridiculous. What had I really accomplished except to make rich people richer?

I had felt empty and without purpose in the corporate world. Except for the creative energy I was able to put into writing well, there was only camaraderie, good pay and survival. Now I no longer felt like a fraud — I was an author. I had substance. I had a book. I knew now I had been trying with great difficulty to hide my true nature under the cover of suits and ties, to be someone I wasn't, in an uncomfortable corporate world.

"Here's *my* book," I could say to those in that world who once questioned my irreverence and perhaps, my intelligence. "Show me *your* book."

I left Nancy and Richard's and crossed town to visit Dave on his birthday, but the family had other plans. On their way out of town, they stopped by to observe my antics at a book-signing.

Diann preferred to watch from a distance in the mall corridor. She, like Debbie, will probably never understand how I can talk to strangers and say outrageous things to get their attention. Sometimes I can't explain it either — maybe I prefer not to know.

I was glad to have the opportunity to say happy birthday to my editor and friend. They left after a short visit, and I again felt sad and alone as I always do when I say goodbye to them. I have known them for three decades. They, along with the Reids in Albuquerque, were the only people, since the death of my father, that I could feel any sense of family with.

The next day I met Arnie Morgan for lunch in upscale Century City. He was an entertainment industry accountant for an international firm and had several movie stars for clients. He took me to an exclusive restaurant as he had when I lived in town. He had been a client of mine when I worked at my last PR job. We always sat at the same table — his table. I was always impressed. But mostly I was thrilled that I could eat anything on the menu with my gigantic appetite, and he paid for it with his gigantic expense account. I had always thought I would like to impress people by having my own table at a restaurant, too. Now, if he came to visit me in Mukilteo, at least I could buy him lunch at *any one of my tables* in the Marco Polo Restaurant. Eddie, the waiter there, makes them all special for me, as long as I can pay.

I felt uneasy this time. Instead of wearing a suit, I was wearing my *Humor Me* T-shirt. I had gotten adjusted to the small-town environment and had now become uncomfortable around the power brokers I had once been accustomed to mingling with.

Arnie seemed to enjoy watching me eat. I probably struck him as a starving artist in a palace, and that could be entertaining for someone who ate so well any day he wanted.

For some reason Arnie had taken a liking to me, but I could never figure out why. He said it was because I was just a regular person, unlike some of those Hollywood movie types who made so much money they forgot they had been just regular folks at one time, too.

Here was this man who got paid handsomely for his honesty and expertise managing money for millionaires. And here I was, handsomely destitute, trusted only by those who gambled $12 on my book. But I was free from peer pressure. Maybe I was much richer than I thought.

He said I was a good person because I wasn't trying to get something from him. He's right about one thing, but not the other. I never told him I coveted all of his money and power and all that of his clients, too. I had, while working for him, thought how wonderful that would be. Sometimes I still do when I think how close I came on that project with Ivan Goff.

The next day I began the trek back north. I stopped in Nevada City, a quaint mountain village between Lake Tahoe and Sacramento, to stay a couple of days with Ruth and Dick Schwartz. They once were coincidentally my neighbors, not relatives, in Los Angeles before my father died.

They had comforted me after his death and were the only witnesses to my mother's erratic behavior. When she was angry, she would tell me I was lazy and worthless, then throw me out of the house along with all my clothes and lock the door. In the morning when she left for work, I would break in through a window to get my school books and quickly brush my teeth. I was always humiliated and ashamed but found warmth and comfort at night in the Schwartz' garage, the back seat of their car or a secret spot I'll never tell anybody.

During our conversations about my past and present, I learned they had known all along that I was hiding on their property but weren't sure what to do. I wish they had done something, because on those lonely nights I felt so scared and unloved that I hated my mother. This happened often when I was a teenager. Talking with Dick and Ruth helped me gain some insight to know my mother might have been transferring her anger and pain onto me for not being mature enough to partially replace the companionship and responsibilities of her husband.

I'm still terrified of getting locked out by Debbie, but she rarely gets angry. And I still get that awful adrenaline rush of terror when I think someone is going to ask me to leave. It reminds me of my mother's rejection.

As we talked into the afternoon, it was obvious to me that I was beginning to accept my role as a walking bookstore, actually enjoying it, so I decided to take it to the limit in Nevada City. Dick, a very reserved man, was quite encouraging. "Go get 'em Schwartz," he said. Ruth, always upbeat and outspoken was encouraging, too. "You're crazy, Gary. But I'll always remember you as that sweet, shy little boy next door."

Who was she talking about? I couldn't remember.

Birth of a Salesman?

I left their house and went to a street corner in town, took a deep breath and tried my new approach. This was risky, I thought.

Oh, well, it's just for fun. Passersby were aghast. "Wanna buy a book?" I chanted over and over as they got within range. The scope of their reactions was from startled and amused to startled and repulsed. After a while it didn't matter. Both reactions led to sales. I even blurted out, "Books, popcorn, peanuts, Coca Cola." It was fun.

In one hour I sold seven books, met several interesting people and came back to the house with a big, satisfied grin. I proudly piled the cash on their kitchen table. "Remember when I used to collect quarters for the newspaper? This is much better."

Then I called Debbie. "Hey. Great news! I sold seven books on a street corner here. It was easy and fun. Aren't you proud of me?" She didn't answer.

"Hello? Deb? Are you there?"

"Yes, I'm here."

"What's the matter? Didn't you hear? I sold seven books on a street corner. That's fantastic, isn't it?"

"Well, I guess I don't want to hear about your selling on the street. You know what I think of salesmen."

I had chosen to forget what she thought. I had heard this before, but I needed her approval now.

"What the hell do you think I am now? I *am* a salesman. You're only proud of me when I'm a columnist and an author? Now you're not? How many people do you know who can do it all? Get another husband." I hung up.

Damn! No matter how great I felt I was doing now, it wasn't good enough for Debbie. I was feeling bad again. I remembered when I made the high school tennis team, my mother said, "What about your math grades?" When I became the sports editor of the newspaper, all she said was, "How is that going to help your career?" And to top it off, on the day when I graduated college and came home proudly wanting her approval and admiration, all I got was, "Don't bother me now. I don't feel well."

I called Debbie back to apologize for hanging up on her. Maybe I had misunderstood. We spoke for another hour, but nothing was resolved. I desperately needed validation that I was doing well.

I became more intense and angry. All I wanted to do now was sell lots of books, get divorced and find somebody who appreciated me.

I thanked Dick and Ruth for their hospitality and left for my scheduled San Francisco book-signings. Along the way I asked several people what they thought of my sales approach.

"Hey, selling is the American way. You gotta do what you gotta do."

"No, I don't mind being solicited as long as when I say no, the person leaves right away."

"It's okay in a public place. And tell your wife you're funny, but no thanks, I don't want to buy your book."

I decided Debbie didn't know what she was talking about.

I drove dangerously fast, just like a salesman, but at least, reassured that I shouldn't be ashamed of myself for being one.

When I pulled into the parking garage in Embarcadero Square, I was surprised by the incredible fee. I was late for the Walden store there, so I had to pay — it was too late to park blocks away and walk, and besides, I was playing celebrity. When I got out of the car, the attendant kept his cool as I complained loudly about the high rates. "I'm a starving artist," I blurted out.

A tall, well-dressed gentleman was waiting for his car. He was wearing expensive Italian shoes and a double-breasted suit. He reminded me of myself just a few years earlier, but he was the real thing. He also was wearing a Rolex. As I walked by he said with a deep British accent, "Excuse me, I'd like to see your book."

I handed it to him. "I'd like to buy it," he said immediately.

It was for his girl friend, a geneticist, so I autographed it, "I hope you find what you're looking for in your boy friend's jeans."

I gave him the book expecting I'd have to sign another after I read the inscription aloud to him. Fortunately the British have a good sense of humor — and some are very generous. He smiled and gave me $15. Sometimes the squeaky wheel really does get the grease, I thought. You just need to know when to be slick.

Then the attendant who was watching the transaction with amusement came over and bought one, too. I signed it, "Park this book where you park your butt." He laughed. I was on a roll. And I was having more fun with my autographs. They seemed to make the customers happy, and that made me happy, too.

On the elevator I sold one to a secretary. I sold one to a stock broker in the plaza and another to a lady sipping coffee at a table. Then a security guard came over and told me it was against policy to solicit in the plaza, so I sold him a copy for half price and promised not to sell anymore.

I had sold six books in 15 minutes and made 70 bucks. The customers were as varied in their professions as they were in their personalities. It didn't seem to matter who they were. They bought books if I just asked them to. I wondered why.

When I arrived at the bookstore I was feeling great and didn't care that I was late. I'd probably only make eight bucks for three hours of work. As I started passing copies out, I told everybody about the tax-cheating stories in it — April 15 was approaching quickly. Bad idea. A man in a suit put his hand gently on my shoulder and said, "I wouldn't advertise that too much." He pulled out his wallet and showed me his identification — IRS.

That was a moment I'll never forget. But the next encounter was even more memorable. This very thin man, about 30, had been looking at the book for a few minutes. He came back over to me and said, "I'll take one."

"Great! What's your name? What do you do?"

"Bill. I'm dying of AIDS." I felt heat in my face and knots in my chest. I scrawled the autograph very quickly, as usual, but this time with fear of offending someone. "I hope this book aids you in your departure." I'll never, ever forget his agonized smile.

"Thanks," he said. "I need some humor."

I couldn't look him in the face. I would cry in a public place and be embarrassed as I had been so many times before. I might have held him tightly as I had wanted to do with my father to say good-bye. Only with the death of Bear, my beloved Golden Retriever a year earlier, was I able to consciously unleash that pain held in for so long. The pain will never go away, I thought, after I watched Bill walk out the door.

I called Debbie that evening. Although still hurting from her salesman remarks, I missed her warm, comforting voice. I kept thinking that maybe after I sold a lot more books, she'd realize I wasn't *really* a salesman — I was just using the book as an excuse to meet lots of people who would give me the attention I needed and pay me for entertaining them. Well, maybe it would be more palatable to her that way.

"I'll be home very late tomorrow," I said. "I met a lot of wonderful people who paid me for making them laugh. Isn't that great? Anyway, I'd like to stop in Napa Valley and visit a couple of my favorite wineries. I promise not to buy any wine." I didn't bring up divorce. I just told her I missed her and hoped she didn't mind taking out the trash while I was gone.

"What trash? You're not here to make any." Her humor always makes me smile; especially when it's about me.

I experienced the Hess and Opus One wineries only briefly, honoring my promise not to buy or drink. I wanted to get home that night to see how far I could go without stopping, so I could better plan the big adventure coming up soon.

My endurance wasn't what it used to be. I had to take two short naps at rest stops and got home inconveniently late to read Debbie's note stuck on the refrigerator. "Sorry I missed you. I left the lawn for you to mow. See you tonight." I had arrived at 6:30 a.m. She had already left for work at Boeing.

Neither of us mentioned the word "salesman" as I began to prepare for the trek across America. I notified my newspaper clients of the day I would be arriving and sent them publicity materials. I shipped boxes of books to friends I would be seeing and got the Honda checked and equipped with extra fan belts and windshield wipers. I went to a meeting of the Mukilteo Business Association. "I'll try to make Mukilteo proud," I said. I got a nice hand from the group. It felt good to feel important again. I had come a long way.

Just before I left, Paul and Kate Archipley, the publishers of *The Mukilteo Beacon*, had us over for dinner to wish me well. Kate, an English teacher, gave me lots of good ideas for preparing to write this piece when I returned. "Take lots of notes, record everything, outline your story," she said. I could do that, but would I be able to write well enough?

"Just have a good time," was Paul's advice. "Don't worry about writing now. Wait until you get back. How many people would ever have the chance to do this? Here, have another glass of wine." I preferred Paul's helping hand.

The Big Adventure: America, Here I come!

It was raining in the early morning of April 22. I held Debbie tightly. "Do you have enough money with you?" she asked.

"Yeah. I got 60 bucks."

"That's all? Gary, I *am* proud of you. Look how confident you are this time."

"Yeah. If I don't sell books, I don't eat, sleep in a bed or go very far in a car without gasoline. I read somewhere it's a good incentive for a salesman to be hungry — and I *am* a very good salesman, Debbie."

I was still angry about her earlier salesman comment, but now I was trying to emphasize, much more gently, how much it had hurt and help her understand why.

"You're crazy," she said.

"Isn't that why you married me? I'm going to be gone for five weeks without seeing you. Thanks for helping make this adventure come true. If anything happens to me, no matter what I ever said, I love you."

I saw the tears in her eyes, but turned my head so she couldn't see mine. I drove up the Mukilteo Speedway to begin the big adventure.

In spite of the cold, dreary day, the anticipation of my journey ignited a fire in my stomach which kept me warm — it was either excitement or fear. But I liked the feeling. My good spirits had returned. The confident adventurer I once knew was back!

I thought of 1973, picking up my VW in Germany and taking off on a three-month road tour of Europe. I was alone then, too. And the mission was nearly the same. Mother had died at the age of 48, six months after heart surgery to repair a bad valve that had kept her out of work for nearly a year. She had been extremely depressed. Her doctor said she wasn't taking one of her vital medications because she didn't like the taste. It was an excuse, he thought, for suicide.

After her death I found the beginning of a book she was writing. It was titled, *Branded: The Life of a Widow*. It was so depressing I only read it once and threw it away. She had always talked of being a writer and going to Europe. But she never did anything but go to work and read books. So after she died in June, 1972 and then I almost got killed in an auto accident in November, I quit my good job as communications manager of the California Credit Union League and took the European trip the following April.

I was in a hurry then, like now, to cram as much life into as short a period of time as I could before I died, too. But I was much younger and stronger and more naive then. Could I do it now?

I stopped at the grocery store to buy some apples and bananas. Debbie and the heart doctor had reminded me to eat properly — but somehow I knew I wasn't going to follow their orders. But at least having the fruit in the front seat relieved some of the guilt.

I ate one of each and turned onto I-5 south once again. It wasn't until I got to Seattle and turned east, that I realized I was really leaving. I had rarely driven on I-90. Anxious to get a head start and make it to Salt Lake City in one day, I became angry when the commuter traffic slowed me down. Rapid transit is a good idea for commuters. It would make it easier for people like me to get out of town.

The rain was heavy as I entered Snoqualmie Pass, but it didn't dampen my spirits. I thought of Debbie and my friend Cory, calling each of them to say good-bye again. When the cell phone cut off, I called Debbie again, just in case she thought something might have happened to me, but it was really just an excuse to fish for more encouragement and reassurance she would miss me. I got both.

She doesn't worry as I do, but I always think of being left alone again as I had been by my parents. I hate those terrifying feelings of insecurity that go along with abandonment. I wondered who cared whether I'd ever come back or not. Lots of people wished me well, mostly out of courtesy, some with jealousy, I supposed.

Contemplating Road Signs

When I reached the countryside I started noticing the silly road signs advertising everything from hamburgers to tractors. I was beginning to be more interested in ads now than when I used to write them. I had never paid much attention before — just saw the billboards pass by as an occasional blur. Now that I was an author, it was time I started observing and learning things about this country and its people so I could impart some wisdom to my readers.

One thing I knew for sure. The billboards were the only means I would have to observe the human condition during those long periods between stops and real people.

It took a couple of hours on the road before I started feeling relaxed. This drive was like no other before it. I had a real mission this time, something more to accomplish than just to get from one place to another. Driving a car through the country has always been my second favorite form of relaxing. Like the bathroom, the car is a place where no one can bother me while I focus on private thoughts. And now those thoughts, ricocheting off the closed windows, came into sharp focus for me, even while my eyes were watching the white lines and the on-coming cars.

As each billboard whizzed behind me I was reminded again and again that there were real people who wrote them, built them and produced the products and services advertised. I chuckled.

Maybe I should put a few up in the Seattle area with *Humor Me-Buy My Book* on them — but T-shirts are a lot less expensive.

In the background of thinking about my mission, I was concerned about bad weather. Maybe I would run into a Texas tornado, a Florida hurricane or an Ohio flood. Then my thoughts would jump to whether I could keep the appointments I had made and if I could sell enough books. The stark reality of my journey, my adventure, struck abruptly. This was no vacation. This was a test. Could I regain my manhood and confidence? Could I survive?

I looked only occasionally at my AAA trip ticket. I was an experienced traveler, having crossed the country twice and 16 countries in Europe. Getting lost was, as life, always an adventure. Somehow, I had always found my way, with or without a map. With a fragile heart, this adventure was just more serious and challenging.

As a camper passed by in the other direction, I thought of Steinbeck's book, *Travels with Charley*. I had read it over and over before I left, and it was still with me. I had believed Steinbeck's motivation for his trip was similar to mine. After all, how can you write about America without seeing it? Although his book was an inspiration, it also became my albatross. How could I possibly write my story as well as he wrote his? Of course, I couldn't. I can only write as myself. And although his book is a classic and a great guide, I understand, only now that I've written this much, that our motivations weren't the same at all.

He was sincere when he left to see the country. He had already established his place in the world and was secure within himself. I hadn't been that honest. Who was I kidding? I wasn't going to see how people lived in the places my column appeared. I was going to get some badly needed attention. I needed to feel important and worthy of my existence. Otherwise, why would I have published the book? And now I wanted to continue living. I was beginning to feel good. I was an author now, not just a traveler.

As I drove into Yakima, the billboard read: *Welcome to Yakima: The Palm Springs of Washington*. There were no date trees, no real sand — just a couple of desolate little golf courses laid out conspicuously green in the prairie brown. Sort of like *Boise, the New York City of Idaho*. Little places trying to be pretentious. Always wanting to be more than they are. Create an illusion of sorts and they will come! Advertising. It's what I used to do. Now I could see clearly the ridiculous and insensitive nature of propaganda. But my book was the real thing, and the people who bought it would agree — I hoped. I knew for sure my T-shirt was honest.

When I crossed into Oregon, I saw the road signs *Deadman's Pass* and *Coffin Road*. I wondered if I was going in the right direction — was I going someplace I shouldn't? I had run out of bananas and apples, so I finally had an excuse to stop for real food. I almost missed an isolated café directly off the highway in Huntington, Idaho. I turned around and parked among the pick-up trucks in the rutted dirt and broken asphalt out front.

I sat at the counter and ordered a bowl of chili — the local version is always the pride of any dive. Then again, maybe the chili at this little place was the reason for those ominous road signs I had seen while driving into Oregon.

The chili was already on the counter when I asked the waitress about the quiet town.

"Well, the mayor pretty much owns the place, and there's lots of drug problems and a cop that rarely does anything because he's a friend of the mayor's. There's only one school for my kids, but I haven't figured a way to get out of here yet. And, in order to get fresh vegetables, you have to drive 30 miles. Other than that, it's a great place to live."

Not for me, not for the chili, certainly, and why would it be for anyone else? I felt bad about her situation and wondered about all the others throughout the country suffering imprisonment in minimum security towns like this. Well, I was very fortunate and had a mission to complete.

As I drove off and passed other road signs, *Farewell Bend* and *Hells Canyon*, I figured it was best that I didn't stay around too long anyway. Like I said earlier, somebody produces the advertised products, and I wasn't interested in meeting them yet.

A little while later I saw another sign: *God Raised Jesus From the Dead.* A real tractor was parked in front of the sign with one of those long arms raised. It appeared to be lifting Jesus into the air. Someone either had a good sense of humor, or there was some truth to the slogan. Either way, I figured John Deere wasn't concerned about the gravity of the implications — I got the message — intended or not.

It was dark when I found a motel near Salt Lake City. I was short a few dollars to pay for the room and have enough left for gas, so I went next door to the coffee shop and sold three books. While hanging around the lobby, I sold three more to tired tourists and then traded one to the manager for a discount on my room.

I slept very well considering thoughts of a Big Mac and fries were still troubling me after eating a bran muffin for dinner.

I stopped quickly at the grocery store for coffee and bananas in the morning, but the two forbidden donuts looked better.

Then I ran into memories of Los Angeles, when I caught the tail end of the morning traffic going into Salt Lake City and Provo. I was frustrated, of course, but took advantage of the delay to drink my coffee without fear of spilling it. I shouldn't have cared — my shirt still had some Huntington chili on it anyway.

After getting out of traffic, I enjoyed a relaxing drive up through the mountains and then down into the wide open spaces where John Wayne may once have ridden into the sunset. I stopped at a Chevron station in Moab where I met Carl.

He was a hunter — bears and mountain lions. He didn't look like one — no large scars or scraggly beard — but then I had never met a hunter before. Was I being judgmental again? He appeared to be in his 60's, about five-foot-seven and his oversized cowboy hat shielded his weather-worn face from the searing desert sun.

In a few minutes, he taught me how mountain lions and bears keep deer from overpopulating and why his job was necessary.

"I wish those bureaucrats who overpopulate our damned government and then come down here to regulate land they don't know nothin' about, would become an endangered species." From

29

his tone of voice, I determined he wouldn't mind doing a little hunting in Washington, D.C.

I asked Carl to take me out to see a bear. But even if he had said okay, I wouldn't have gone, I can assure you. "No way," he said. "If you see one, there are more. It's too dangerous." We both agreed on that.

As the heat began to slow our conversation, I learned that Moab is famous not only for bears but also for watermelons. And "the bears like 'em too," said Carl. I'd remember that at my next mountain picnic.

I was beginning to see a different kind of freedom in the people I met. Carl seemed to be a good example of the root strength that holds this country down. He almost broke my hand when we shook our good-byes.

In minutes I was alone again, looking out at the vast countryside, thinking about Carl and the bears and lions and deer roaming in the distant mountains, as I proceeded to Albuquerque.

Carl reminded me that my new work wasn't the only kind that can be done outside the confines of an office or factory. I liked to wander — to be independent. It's a disease — one I wouldn't want to cure even if I could.

That sensation of feeling really good was back again. The drive through southern Utah into Colorado is one of my favorites. I become spiritual there. My mind can unload the garbage collected from years of survival in Los Angeles and take in the marvels of creation. Where else is freedom more colorful and expansive than here, where pure, blue skies are a background to golden brown sand and mountain peaks and there are no boundaries, other than roads, to keep you from wandering?

Later, off in the distance, I saw Chimney Rock looming slowly larger and larger as I added miles and time to my thoughts about freedom. It's a formation so incredible, it looked as if it had been chiseled by hand before time began. A giant broken rock, now sitting uneasily in the sand, it appears almost ready to fall.

Just two years earlier my stepson Rain was with me here. He had wanted to stop and climb the mountains and go in the caves. He was only 10 then — so innocent, pure, and full of wonder. And as I crossed into New Mexico, I remembered the two of us seeing a giant rainbow, and how I had sped up to catch the end of that mystical arch of light and color for him. "I could buy Mom a new house with the pot of gold," he had said. I missed him very much.

Now I was trying to find my own pot of gold at the end of a journey — a more realistic dream, perhaps, but one of equal rapture.

Sleepless in Albuquerque

I arrived at Chaz and Dina's house about 8 p.m. I was exhausted after two days and 1,700 miles of driving. But the joy of seeing my friends and extended family was enough to provide the energy to stay up and talk long after I should have been sleeping.

Chaz and I had been bunkmates at Fort Hood, Texas almost 30 years ago. When his wife Dina came to live with him, I spent most of my weekends at their rented house outside the base. I had lived for an entire summer with the family a few years later and had visited at least a dozen other times — always welcomed, always well fed.

In the Army, Chaz and I had talked idealistically about our glorious futures. He was going to become a serious writer, and I was to be a famous novelist. Little did we know that dreams can come true, as long as you don't expect them to be totally accurate. He was now writing wills, divorce documents and criminal defense briefs as a lawyer, and I was writing novel humor. We got close.

We caught up on all the usual money woes, medical problems, kids and pets. Frankly, their grown-up children, Chris, Candace and Charlie, wonderful as they are, were non-stop annoyances. They prefer nocturnal activities, so I didn't get much sleep. My bed on the floor was too hard, even with carpet. And when I moved to the sofa, it was too close to the front door. Chris, who lived nearby, liked to come in at 2 a.m. to do his laundry and

31

didn't think much about slamming the door shut. Kids! I thought of Debbie, the quiet, the solitude of home.

Dina still amazed me — she reminded me of Jane Fonda. She had always been an achiever, working hard and dancing for pleasure and fitness at nights. Now 50-something, she was a physical fitness trainer, nutritionist and a registered nurse. And she looks great! She got up at 5:30 every morning and began working out. This, of course, didn't help me get the sleep I lost because of Chris. By nine at night, she would fall asleep while I was talking to her. Nothing unusual — Debbie falls asleep when I'm talking, too — at *any* time of the day.

The next morning, in spite of droopy eyelids, I drove to Santa Fe. It was dawn — early mornings energize me. Mornings are good times to be born, to be in the dark and then to glow with the first light of day. Evenings for me are death, the end of a day, and the time to sleep.

I had been to Santa Fe many times, and it became more enchanting on every visit. It's America's second oldest city with a rich heritage of Indian and Spanish culture. Its art museums and opera are very well known. And well-known to me, there's no place in America where the food is any better. I reassured myself of this later in the day by eating more than my share.

Speaking of good food, the fish were biting that early morning of April 24. I had realized several days earlier that, like fishing, there were key times for selling. I sold my first book of the day to a Swiss businessman and his wife at 8 a.m. Then I sold one to the parking lot attendant at the county courthouse. I went there to visit Lily Gonzales, the judge who had married Debbie and me almost five years ago.

"You still together?" she asked.

"Yep. It's tough, but we're hanging in there."

She probably asks the same of all her old friends like me — and probably gets a few similar answers. She happily bought a book. I gave her a discount for remembering me and for starting me out in marriage as well as anyone could, given what she had to work with.

Then I walked over to the famous town plaza where tourists were starting to gather. I approached a couple on a bench. "Wanna buy a book?"

"No thank you." I started to walk away, but they called me back, as often happens when people get over the initial shock and realize I really am an author, not a clown. Maybe it's the back of my T-shirt.

I began with the shortened version of my life story and how I had spent a one-day honeymoon at the hotel across the street. They listened for awhile, smiling patiently. Judy and Larry Werner were from Cincinnati and were on their honeymoon. I felt happy for them and a little nostalgic. I left the book with them to look over while I trolled the plaza.

When I went back to pick up the book and say good-bye to them, they told me how they had met at an animal shelter. They had read the story about the end of my dog's life and were so moved, they decided to buy the book after all. We had moved each other.

Then I gave them my full-life story, taking advantage of the moment — at least 20 minutes of moments — but the Werners didn't seem to mind. They showed caring and understanding. I had spoken many times into my tape recorder, "Stop talking so much. Sell more books." But ever since that first day at Whistler Mountain, I had talked incessantly to anyone who would listen. I still wasn't sure why, but I was grateful they kept listening. They were either being tolerant or thought I was really interesting. I thought I should probably ask some people why they listened, but I was afraid if they told the truth — that they were just being polite — I would feel bad and not be able to sell.

I've never wanted to force people to listen. I've always felt I have something to say, but maybe they're not interested. I did know, despite the Werners' interest, I would have to confront my problem sooner or later.

A little while later, after enjoying a second breakfast of sopapillas (*a wonderful deep-fried Indian bread*) with honey, I was walking briskly down a side street and passed a young couple in front of me. I had that now-familiar good feeling again, having sold several books before noon. I turned around, facing them.

"Wanna buy a book?" Sean and Patti Barrett said "no, thanks," so I kept walking — I never push a book on anybody. Then, Sean hollered out. "Hey, wait a minute." He had noticed Beavercreek on the back of my T-shirt. "You know Beavercreek?" he asked as they caught up to me.

"Sure. My column appears in the paper there."

"We're from Beavercreek!" They bought the book, and I got their phone number. Their city was one of my scheduled stops. My T-shirt was doing its job. Debbie is brilliant.

Tommy Warren and the Five 'A's

A few minutes later, I hit on Tommy Warren in the plaza. He was casually well-dressed and spoke with that deep southern accent that reminded me of Ted Turner or old movies about the South. He first struck me as one of those southern gentlemen I was hoping to meet when I got to the South. He was very polite; either he was amused by my behavior or admired it — I couldn't be sure. That's how smooth those old southern gentlemen in the movies are, I guess. He told me he knew President Clinton. So I asked what he thought of him.

"We Arkansanians have to stick together," he said like a politician. I had hoped for some good political discussion. Oh, well.

Tommy now lived in Houston. I had once worked in the oil business for the Hydril Company and had traveled there many times, so we had something in common to talk about. Then I learned that he designs and builds correctional facilities. He was in New Mexico consulting and assisting local counties with new jails. Apparently impressed with my entrepreneurial spirit, he gave me a generous helping of advice. I really suspect he might have thought my wandering aimlessly in the streets needed some direction. Advice from strangers is usually better than advice from friends and family anyway, so I listened carefully and taped it.

The "five 'A's" he called them. "They can help you stay organized toward your objectives and deal with the sixth 'A.' First," he said, "you need the right 'Attitude' to become 'Aware' of what your physical, mental and spiritual needs are. Then you can 'Adjust' to make things change and move forward into 'Action,' which then leads to 'Accomplishment.' The sixth 'A,' Adversity," he said, "is something to keep in mind, but with the right 'Attitude' it can be overcome."

That wasn't bad advice. I had the right attitude. "Buy my book," I said. He did. Later, by mail, he bought several more.

As I left, I told him to save a vacant cell for me in one of his new facilities. "Maybe I'll get arrested for soliciting," I said with a smile. I sat on a bench and rewound the tape.

Well, I had the *attitude* that I was having fun; I was *aware* that I was physically and mentally out of shape but spiritually free as a bird. I wasn't going to *adjust* until much later, and I certainly was full of *action,* although it was a little slow. I had sold a few books, so I guess I was *accomplishing* something.

Someday, I thought, I'd steal his advice and use it in a book and seminar on how to sell books across America. Maybe that would be a best-seller and I could get off the streets!

I did get off the streets temporarily to do a signing in the nearby mall. I was late, having talked too much in the plaza. When I finally sat down at the table at the front of the store, I was relieved to be inside where it was air conditioned. I started passing books out to anyone who would take one and began my ritual of talking about anything I could think of. I noticed, out of the corner of my eye, a strange, bearded fellow who had been watching me for awhile. He was my age, I suspected, scholarly looking with an intense stare. When I made eye contact with him, he cautiously came to my table.

We talked for a few minutes. He was a famous author like me! Not many people had heard of him either, I suspected. I was talking to *the* William J. Higginson, a world renowned authority on Haiku (*The Haiku Handbook*); that's why I had never heard of him.

We bought each other's books at the counter, no discount, of course, and autographed them. He was on his way to Japan for a Haiku conference and I wished him well. He wished me well on my journey across America.

That night I tried some of his book. Although it was difficult to understand, I learned a frog is a favored animal in Japan. Many thousands of poems had been written about the animal and its singing. I knew I probably wouldn't read much more of this one — it's not my style, but I knew it would be a treasured piece of literature on my bookshelf and I could always share it with literary friends who might appreciate that I had met him.

Before we left the store, Higginson had confessed to me that my humor wasn't his cup of tea, but he still wanted the book and my autograph. That began my thinking about autographs, authors and fame. I had already signed many books, trying my best to personalize them and make people feel good. I knew I wasn't famous, probably never would be; most of my customers knew it too, I suspected, but everybody insisted I sign the books anyway. If I *were* famous, I probably would only be able to write a squiggle of my name and nothing else because there would be such long lines waiting to meet me and get an autographed book.

I hoped part of the attraction of my autograph now was that people were rooting for me to become famous so they could say they had a copy of my first book. People like to root for the underdog. Like Rocky, I certainly was one, though most of my muscles weren't on my body.

I don't think that's why I kept Higginson's book. I think it's because I appreciate his expertise on the subject and not everyone can be famous. I wasn't sure. I knew I needed to learn more about this phenomenon of fame as my journey continued.

The next day, on my return to Santa Fe to check out a new school of fish, I stopped at a cafe and was on my second bowl of pasole, that wonderful soup made of hominy, pork and Mexican spices, when I met Gene and Jean Stark. When Jean told me she was an Indian from the Potawatomie tribe in Oklahoma, I was surprised.

"You don't look Indian," I blurted out with only half-caught embarrassment. I apologized for my indiscretion and then told her my own story about the two soldiers in the Army who had once touched my nose and said, "You don't *look* Jewish."

Ignorance isn't just for others. I still had a lot to learn.

I left the Reids the next day, looking forward to a good night's sleep, even if it would be at another dive motel. I had made enough money to pay for a queen bed instead of a single slumping one. I was enjoying that familiar, good feeling again.

As I left town down San Pedro Boulevard I saw a sign I hadn't noticed before; *Seattle's Best Coffee.* I couldn't believe it! I stopped in for an espresso, and sure enough, it was the real hometown brew. I told the proprietor how much I appreciated the tie to my home. He looked at me with a curious eye. I was so excited, I walked out without paying, but he was quick to run outside and remind me.

I headed east toward my next overnight stop in Texas. The solitude of the wide-open prairies was a welcome antidote to the chaos I had endured with my Albuquerque family. Traffic was light, so I pushed the pedal to 80 mph. As I stuffed my pipe with one hand and steered with the other, I thought of Debbie. "Pipe!" I would say when she was with me. "Light!" I would say after she stuffed it.

I began thinking of all the other little things she does to make my life richer. Sometimes I forget that she's not like me. When I'm angry and acting out my insecurities, I too often criticize her for not understanding my visions and dreams and cynical attitudes about life. Her simple ways of seeing things had many times completely baffled me but had also saved me from making complicated and serious mistakes.

I smiled when I thought of my favorite bagels, coffee and non-fat pudding snacks that she probably would have bought and put away for me for when I got home in a few weeks.

I regained my focus when I saw a road sign for a 72-ounce steak and then another for Billy the Kid's grave site. Everyone has to make a living somehow — I wasn't any different. Maybe a *Buy*

My Book sign on the side of my car would be an appropriate gesture to signify my new tolerance for unusual, independent lifestyles.

Not long after stopping for a lunch buffet in Tucumcari, New Mexico, I heard this joke from some of the people I met. It went something like; "Welcome to Tucumcari, the only city in America where you can commit a murder and get away with it, but don't forget to wear your seat belt."

Apparently the police are not too effective here.

While eating plenty of tacos and beans, I noticed six of the officers having coffee — probably on their seventh or eighth cup — at the corner table. Daringly, I decided to interview them.

They didn't respond, so to lighten them up I read aloud the first story in my book. It's about cops, but none of them laughed. Finally, one brave trooper admitted, "I don't get it." I'm still looking for a cop with a sense of humor. Anyway, when a slightly sweaty, overweight man came in and sat down with the officers, I knew I was headed for another one of my errors in judgment. I plunged ahead anyway.

He was dressed in a wrinkled suit, wrinkled shirt and a tie with older sweat stains. I thought I would try to shock these numb-skulls into a reaction, as I sometimes do to get genuine emotional responses instead of boring comments.

"This guy should be arrested for walking around without proper medical assistance." There was only silence — and a lot of it. He was the police lieutenant. I took a big chance and went to the next level. "Isn't there a law against bald, out of shape officers serving on the police force?"

I still couldn't get even a hint of a smile from the uniformed fellas, but I did from the lieutenant. Maybe he was just biting his tongue. I wanted to think it was a smile.

"I suggest you leave town," he said. Still no humor. I left.

I was finally on my way back to Texas. This is the place where you can drive for 12 hours from its belly and still not cross back into the United States. I was approaching Amarillo when my mind began wandering again. (*a good place for wandering — I could never figure why anyone would want to live in such a desolate area, unless they were raising rattlesnakes or ground hogs.*)

I began thinking of Hydril, the international oil field equipment company I had worked for in Los Angeles. Most of the company's activities were in Texas and Louisiana, so I thought I had come to know the area pretty well. On the other hand, as I looked south, east, west and north, I realized my memories had faded in the Texas heat just as the vegetation had gone from the land. I remembered now, only the heat, the drawl and the good steaks. Good steaks. I could hardly wait. That's worth coming back for!

Driving south toward Lubbock the next morning after the 16-ounce T-bone, I saw a mesquite tree set about a half mile from the highway. Nothing was near it but a few small desert plants. It was just there, seemingly without purpose and lonely. But was it? Or was I projecting my own feelings upon it?

It was green and alive against a dead, gray-brown background, perhaps a remnant of a once lush forest or, more likely, a strong survivor flourishing where others didn't care to be. I felt a deep, momentary kinship to the flourishing survivor as I drove alone down the highway with nothing in sight but the narrowing curves disappearing over the rolling hills and the broken white lines pointing to my next destination. I was glad to be moving.

But the tree couldn't move. It had to endure its solitude without hope. I wondered if the tree's companions and relatives had died or abandoned it in other ways. Did it even care? I knew I did. I cared and I hurt.

It's wonderful to be different — to stand alone and independent — but oh, how lonely it can be. I kept moving.

Hours later I met an interesting man in the small city of Coleman where I had stopped for the night. I was sitting at the counter sampling the local chili when he came running in, carrying a toothbrush and toothpaste.

"Where can I brush my teeth? I'm in a hurry."

The waiter gave him a glass of water and pointed toward the rest room. When the man came back I asked him what was going on.

"I've got a date with this fantastic woman . . . . haven't seen her for 17 years . . . . She's *real* hot."

This guy was an eyeglass salesman. He traveled a lot. I wondered where his sights were set. He was acting like a little kid, but was at least as old as I. I liked him right away. I gave him a quick hug and understood his resistance. Texans don't do hugs. They're big on handshakes and strong whiskey glasses that clink without breaking.

"I hope you get lucky," I said. He smiled and raised his thumb into the air. I turned back to the counter and wiped the toothpaste off my shoulder as I sat down to finish my cold chili.

Wow! That's how I must come across to a lot of people, I thought. Debbie's friend Lars had said I reminded him of Kramer from the *Seinfeld* TV show.

"You always act like him when you come to our house," he once said. Now, every time I visit, I'm careful to walk really slow and methodically to prove him wrong.

But why? I liked this salesman's child-like behavior. It was refreshing and inspirational. I liked his spunk and enthusiasm. Who wants to talk to some tired, stuffy salesman with nothing to talk about except the weather and sales quotas?

Perhaps I, too, was giving people some kind of inspiration. Maybe when they see me having fun in an innocent sort of way as I had just seen, they, too, put me in their memories as I just did with the toothpaste man. I hoped so. I would like to be remembered with fondness, too.

I left Coleman in the morning after suffering from a restless night with the chili. Bananas are good for that sort of thing, I heard, so I stopped at the grocery instead of the coffee shop for breakfast.

I was anticipating meeting Larry Reynolds, publisher of the Seguin newspaper. I had talked to most of my editor clients by phone before. It provided some security to know somebody before getting into town. Having a network of acquaintances across the country kept me from feeling too lonely, and it gave me a sense of importance to know someone was waiting to see me.

As I drove east, the sight of beautiful wildflowers growing in the highway divider reminded me of Lady Bird Johnson's legacy to Texas, if not the country, and of my own wildflowers at home. Some of them should be blooming about now.

Haunting Military Memories

I zoomed into San Antonio, surprised at how much the memories of my time at Fort Sam Houston were pulling at me to return. It was there, those 30 years ago, that I was trained as an Army medic. I wondered if the bowling alley was still there and what my barracks looked like now. Then again, why in hell would I want to return to a military base? I must've had some good feelings about it.

But what I remembered most, aside from the humidity, was the prank pulled on me after some of the boys decided I needed to learn to drink. They made me gulp down several beers, even after I told them I wasn't thirsty after the first. I never was a drinker — never wanted to be. The night before I left for the Army I threw up a bottle of rum all over my mother's bed and walls. What did I know?

So when they dragged me back to the barracks just before bed-check and I couldn't find my bunk mattress, I turned on the lights to wake everyone up. I found the mattress in the rafters and got it down very slowly while everyone was laughing — just seconds before the sergeant walked in. I quickly faked sleeping.

The next night, after finding out who instigated the prank, I got a couple of *my* allies and we carefully and quietly lifted the sleeping culprit's bunk, with him in it, and put the entire heap outside with the mosquitoes. He never knew what bit him.

Distracted by military memories, I took an off-ramp into San Antonio by mistake and was late for my appointment in Seguin.

Larry Reynolds was a Texas-style man who greeted me with one of those typical hammer-lock handshakes.

41

"Well," he said with a boisterous laugh as I tried to retrieve my hand, "I gotta carry a hammer around here to keep the employees in line."

Well, at least I knew where I was.

I stood around chatting with a few of the newspaper employees until a few subscribers finally showed up to meet me. Then I perked up quite a bit. I had thought lots of people might come because Larry had done a nice story about my visit in the paper. I was beginning to see that becoming famous wasn't easy. Even with publicity, I was just another writer. I had no Pulitzer Prizes to brag about, and I don't write controversial things to get me in trouble, so who cares? Perhaps I should write about religion so I'd have my life threatened. Then I could get on national TV — *Larry King*, the morning shows, Regis and Kathy Lee. Being on TV would be nice later, but I was having fun now.

I left the newspaper office in search of more sales. I drove to the local H-E-B grocery store. I went inside to enjoy the air conditioning but got a cool reception and my first Texas "boot" out.

I had already been asked to leave several coffee shops and grocery stores for soliciting, but each time it became more fun. I usually made a sale or two before being caught anyway, and I always left with a smile. Those who evicted me were just doing their jobs, getting rid of the riffraff.

I've always liked the excitement of breaking rules as long as I didn't hurt anybody. For some reason, it makes me feel good to get away with doing something others won't — or can't do. Sometimes I think it's my father's admonition that haunts me but encourages me at the same time — "Never say 'can't.'" It makes me feel special. It helps me survive. Selling books in the street without a license was almost a legacy from my father. I think he would have approved — and that felt good.

I was exhausted. I drove around looking for the best dive my budget could handle.

I slept okay at the motel I found, in spite of the broken air conditioner. Then I went back to the H-E-B in the late morning hoping to have better luck in the parking lot before I got caught. I saw a creepy-looking fellow leaning up against a peeling gray light post. He had a cast on one arm and lots of tattoos on the other. When he asked for a light, I wordlessly lit his cigarette and quickly started to walk away. But then he asked to see my book. I was pretty sure there was no sale here, but was intrigued by the guy.

"What are you doing here?" I asked cautiously.

"Waiting for a friend. He was gonna take me to the hospital for surgery. I was in a car accident and the arm needs some more repairs." I became less cautious.

"What are you going to do if he doesn't show up?"

"Walk, I guess."

I was tempted to offer him a lift, but life in Los Angeles had reinforced my fears. "Good luck." I walked away feeling guilty. I was still judging people by their appearance.

As I approached my car, I met Lynn Teeter. He's one of those famous-people-you-never-heard-of I occasionally like to write about in my columns. He told me he was a country-western singer who once had his own TV show and had cut a new CD with RCA called *Good Morning Beautiful Lady*.

He was very friendly and without pretension. We talked about writing and music. He was quite knowledgeable about both. But he was in a hurry to get back to work, so he invited me for a free lunch at his 50's style diner in back of a 1940's dime store. For some reason I trusted him — as long as we drove in separate cars. And a free lunch? Not a problem.

I ate a once-forbidden BLT, fries and cherry Coke, then began worrying only a little how I had been loading my struggling arteries with fat. But I was so happy to be alive and able to drive around the country without a doctor by my side, that, at least for these few weeks, I wanted to prove I could also eat without fear. I had felt deprived for too long.

I traded Lynn a book for his free lunch — horse-trading they call it in Texas — I'll get the knack of it someday. Then he played one of his songs for me on the jukebox. I didn't comprehend a word, but I tapped out the rhythm on the counter with my fingers — I like it, too, when somebody says something good about my writing even when they don't understand it.

Lynn turned out to be quite a nice guy. It took me awhile to get comfortable with him, as it does when you meet any stranger. But I knew, as I had learned many times before, without the risk, a stranger can never become a friend. And I needed a friend, at least for an hour or two.

And I think he did, too. I felt a strong kinship with him — another artist, just trying to cut out a living.

Oddly, I saw a couple of tears form in his eyes as we departed. He said he'd like to join me on my journey. I wondered why, but didn't ask. It wasn't good timing. Maybe, like me, he had lost something important in his life and longed to travel outside his unhappy world to find it.

I headed back toward San Antonio before making the journey south to my next stop, Laredo, down at the Mexican border. I remembered hauling Army buddies down this same highway to Nuevo Laredo and into "Boys' Town" where boys became men. I had been much more interested in the fee I charged for the ride than their sex education and diseases. I would drop them off and spend the night at a nice, clean Laredo motel, then pick them up the next morning for the ride home.

I enjoyed their boastful stories, but when they asked me what I had been doing, I just led them to believe I had my own girlfriend in town. That's one of the few times I could remember keeping my mouth shut. I didn't really have anything to say.

It was hot as I continued south to Laredo. I was very thankful I had air-conditioning in the car and I wasn't the insect that had suddenly reminded me to clean my windshield. Dying is random, I thought. If the insects weren't there at the time my car was, they would live longer. If 911 wasn't an easy phone number to punch in and I didn't have a good heart surgeon, I wouldn't be able to say so. Why did my father die so young? Why can murderers live out their lives? Would I be randomly mugged or hit by a drunk driver? Would anybody care? Am I sharing my humor with others for a reason, or is my mission randomly insignificant? I didn't have the answers, but knew I was lucky.

Without answers my journey was more meaningful. With them, I might not have taken the risk to find them in the first place.

The gas warning light came on, suddenly interrupting my dark musings. I hadn't paid much attention to it before. I enjoy excitement, but when you're in the desert with no town in sight or even on the map, your thoughts turn quickly from dark to desperate.

I slowed to 65 for about 10 miles, then to 50 for another 10. I was still a long way from Laredo. Poor planning.

Fortunately, Encinal had one gas pump for its entire population of 620. I pulled into the station that looked like one of those in a period movie. Three Mexicans paused, with pork chops in hand, and stared at me menacingly. I was scared. Who would ever know what they were thinking? I knew what I was thinking. I had my hand on the pepper spray in my pocket as I pumped the gas. I squeezed in $5 worth to get to Laredo, then left quickly. They were laughing at me through my rear view mirror as I sped away. Los Angeles paranoia was still lingering in my mind.

I had planned to stay in Laredo for three days. I was tired of no-budget-motels befitting a budget bookseller, so I stayed at a Best Western Hotel. I figured I had earned the privilege because I had sold enough books to pay for it. Besides, I had worn all of my clean clothes, and the hotel had a convenient laundry room.

Learning in Laredo

Odie Arambula, the *Laredo Morning Times* editor, had promised to publicize my arrival in a big way, but I wasn't expecting much. When I saw the full-page, full-color picture of me on the front page of the newspaper's entertainment section, I was reassured that Texans must do *everything* in a big way and was excited to meet him.

He's one of those characters you might see on a TV sitcom. He talks as much as I do but has something to say. He spews out serious and interesting stories, but tells them so fast he's funny. I learned more about the history of Laredo than I could possibly remember, but I do remember it's important to put salt and lemon in your beer while eating fajitas. (*He took me out for my favorite event, a free dinner.*) When I told him I had just been to Seguin, he informed me the city was named after the lone escapee of the Alamo. I wondered if I'd be the lone survivor of his chatter.

I was having a difficult time listening to all of his interesting stories, and that made me wonder how many people were really interested in mine. I've never been a good listener and as I continued talking incessantly to those I was meeting who would listen, I started to believe I may never stop talking.

But when the topic of illegal immigration came up, I became a listener. Odie spent some time explaining the plight of the Mexicans. Some important topics do stop me from jabbering.

"What would you do if you had a wife and three children looking up at you saying they're hungry and you can't do anything about it?" Odie asked me.

"Well," I said. "Where I live there was a newspaper columnist who wrote in the *Seattle Times* about all the unwanted Californians moving into the area. He was a proponent of a group called 'Lesser Seattle.' Members wanted to keep us out. They claimed we were taking jobs away from the locals, causing housing prices to rise and we were clogging up the roads."

"That's a lot different than people just wanting the necessities," he said. "A loaf of bread and a piece of fruit certainly can't be compared to your situation."

I've been chastised many times for simplifying what I believe — that humans are no different than any other animals, except for higher intelligence. We procreate and protect our offspring and stay or migrate wherever we can find food and shelter. People move from state to state, as other animals roam from pasture to pasture.

I was glad Odie agreed with me, but we couldn't figure out a solution for the problems of our friends from south of the border.

The next morning I crossed the bridge into Mexico for a first-hand look at what we were talking about. I saw the Rio Grande with the barbed wire barriers. This reality of life and its limitations hit me hard. I saw a blind woman squatting at the entrance to an alley. She was holding her filthy baby with one arm and a tin plate with coins in it with the other. Then a young boy in tattered clothes walked by and tried to sell me a pet lizard. This caused me great anguish and despair.

I saw clearly the reality that peddling books was no different than peddling products or sympathy. Survival is a common bond among all animals, and I wondered how people were judging me as I was learning to judge myself.

I left Laredo still grateful my air-conditioning was working, that my windshield was clean and that I had sold a lot of books. It's a good city full of history and culture, and I wished I had had the time to hear more of Odie's stories and eat more on his recommended food list. But I had an appointment the next day, so I had to hurry — it was a long way north to Mexia. Texas is like that. Every place is a very long way.

Throughout this vast tract of a state, I had seen a mess of *Don't Mess With Texas* road signs. Fines of $10 to $1,000 for littering are serious business — I was glad the statute of limitations had run out. I had thrown a few beer cans out the window back in my Army days. It was immature fun then. Now I felt remorse.

I continued north. I was running late because I hadn't realized I had forgotten my cell phone at the hotel until I was an hour out of town; it cost me a couple hours to go back and pick it up. This was probably a waste of time. I didn't know how to use the phone away from home. I just thought it would be good to have if I could find someone who knew how to use it during an emergency.

Fort Hood, my real alma mater, was several miles off my route, but again, I couldn't resist. Mexia would just wait longer. I had to see what my war efforts had done to shape the landscape of the once proud 2nd Armored Division.

Speeding west, I began looking for the roads I had traveled in the wee hours of Monday mornings long ago. It was always a challenge to get back to the barracks before being AWOL. Road signs showed the way, but Nolanville and Harker Heights weren't even on the map when I was stationed there.

When I finally found the entrance to the fort, I was shocked by the tourist-like office instead of the guard shack with the sullen MP's of my memory.

Instead of asking me for a permit, the friendly MP handed me a tour guide. I drove in and saw a Burger King and modern office buildings. This was no real Army base. And there was no 2nd Armored Division anymore. I was hoping to see some familiar landmarks of one of the most memorable times of my life. Instead I thought of my junior high school family home near the Los Angeles International Airport being replaced by parking lot C.

I guess there really is no going back sometimes.

Sleepless in Mexia

My eyelids were heavy again as I drove northeast through Waco and out into the countryside approaching Mexia. All I was thinking about was a bed and a morning shower. I thought about them for a very long time.

It was 1 a.m. when I arrived in Mexia. I noticed several cars parked outside a tavern and many more at a motel. The dreaded *No Vacancy* sign was posted, as it was at the other two motels in town. I drove 15 miles to the next town where the one motel was also full. Then I drove back to the Mexia gas station where I had noticed some activity earlier. Unfortunately, the movement was the scurrying kind made by snakes and cockroaches — or, in this case, unruly teens with no place to go and nothing to wear but leather and graffiti — on their skin and on their clothes.

I stayed close to the cop on duty for safety — I was truly fearful for my life — and asked where I might stay. He suggested the comfort of my car in the police station parking lot. But that wasn't appealing because he couldn't guarantee I wouldn't be arrested for vagrancy and forced to sleep on a cement slab instead of in the leather comfort of my Honda.

I chose Waco. I drove back on the dark, lonely road.

It was now 3 a.m. and I couldn't drive safely anymore; weariness was overcoming fear. I stopped at three hotels and motels — all full — a giant rodeo and college graduation were going on. So I did what any intelligent person would do.

"I need a room badly. It's dangerous for me to drive," I said to the manager at the motel with the biggest parking lot.

"Sorry, sir, we're full. But you're welcome to sleep in your car in the parking lot."

"Is it safe?"

"Yes, sir. But I'd suggest you lock your doors."

I slept fitfully for a couple of hours, dreaming that I was in similarly desolate, flat, Fresno or Sacramento, California. Thunder and lightening woke me up. It was 6 a.m. I brushed my hair and walked into the motel to enjoy its free continental breakfast.

I was tempted to ask one of the customers about to check out to give me his key so I could get some sleep in his room before the maids came, but I thought that might be a little tacky. So I just enjoyed my juice and very tacky sweet rolls and then went to the front desk. "I'm checking out."

"What room, sir?"

"Parking lot A," I smiled. "Thanks for the free breakfast."

Still sleepy, I drove carefully back to Mexia and met Lynnette Copley for another breakfast three hours later at the Oil Rig Restaurant. She's the editor of the *Mexia Daily News* and was sympathetic to my yawns after I told my sad story. We chatted for awhile, but after I was asked to leave for soliciting and having an irate customer yell that I should be *allowed* to stay (*a rare incident*), my enthusiasm for book selling was gone.

Still determined, no matter what the obstacles, I regained my composure and, upon hearing those encouraging words ringing loudly in my mind, ". . . or get a job," I went to the Wal-Mart store nearby and worked the parking lot. Not much luck there, but I was flattered by the drug pusher who tried to trade up with me.

Then I went inside and was asked to leave for not asking permission. On the way out, I thought that maybe I wasn't *really* enjoying getting kicked out of places. It actually hurt when I got rejected. I tried not to take it personally — they just didn't know I was a real nice guy. If they had, maybe they'd let me stay.

But as each day passed, I was learning more about that magical "chemistry" people so often talk about. I had already met hundreds of people — nice people. But only a handful of those would I consider asking home for dinner. It was nothing personal, it was just that "chemistry." And I was sure, even though many bought the book and we had shared moments of a spontaneous connection, they thought the same about me. Sometimes, I thought, I was trying too hard to make people like me, and the harder I tried the harder it was for them to see if they did. Maybe it didn't matter.

Perhaps the "magic" is simply the physical attraction; the tone of voice, that look in the eyes, body aromas, the common interests and background, the energy — I wasn't sure, but I thought longingly of Debbie and the magic when I first saw her.

I wished now, that some kind of magic could've made me disappear from Mexia and reappear instantly in Dallas. Sales weren't important. I wanted to see my friend, Barbara McCune.

An Old Flame Still Glows

I had met her at Hydril. I was the manager of employee communications, and she was secretary to the vice president of operations. We hit it off immediately. I started talking too much and she politely asked me to leave — she had work to do, but said, "I'd like to talk to you again sometime." At least I wasn't rejected outright.

In a few months our friendship had deepened. She had been divorced, lost her second husband to cancer and first son to a motorcycle accident. I told her about my parents dying young, and without the details — she understood — as I understood her.

Our relationship continued growing. We shared passions for the same things, and she had the ability to know what I was *really* feeling rather than what I was *saying*, I felt. I would say, "That woman won't go out with me. I don't make enough money." She would say, "You don't have the confidence to ask her." Barbara was always on the mark. And I was good at returning the favor.

It didn't take much longer before I realized it was Barbara I wanted to go out with, no one else. She told me I was attractive, smart and caring. I didn't believe her. Why would a beautiful, intelligent and sexy woman want to go out with me?

One night we did go out. She had a little too much wine. She had just broken off a long-term relationship and was feeling lonely. I'll always remember what she said to me as we sat very quietly on her sofa, cuddling in the candlelight. "Gary, if only you would let women see how gentle, quiet and sweet you are like right now, you'd get any one you wanted."

"I don't want anyone else to see me like this. Just you."

My mother had once warned me about being too sweet. "I won't let you be a 'momma's boy,'" she had said. "Your father's not here to teach you to be a man."

I was in love with Barbara. She appreciated my gentleness and vulnerability. For awhile I became blinded by the intimacy she allowed, even encouraged — without fear, shame or guilt. I was unable to understand that I was just a good friend to her — not the potential mate I had longed to be.

Now I walked up the stairs to her apartment and knocked on the door. When she opened it, I thought she looked as great as when I had met her years ago. Although the romantic love of the past had gone, I still coveted the honest closeness we shared and enjoyed the strong hug she gave me.

In two evenings, Barbara and I caught up on all our references to past friends, lovers and Hydril experiences. I had sold several books at a couple of book-signings and had partaken of Barbara's good cooking and that of a nearby barbecue — one meal on me, one on her.

During our parting hug, she looked me right in the eyes like only she could. And I turned away, like only I could, afraid of what she always saw inside — the truth.

"Gary, I always told you someday you'd be doing what you want. I always told you that you were very talented and didn't need that job at Hydril to be successful. And be nice to Debbie. Don't be afraid of her love."

Barbara gave me what I had needed from my mother — encouragement, warmth and understanding. But Barbara didn't want a needy child for a husband — but a good friend I could be.

I was anxious to get out of Texas. I had been in the big state too long and was feeling guilty about eating at every steak house and barbecue I could find and saying "y'alls" not very well.

On a lonely road again, I began wondering why I was enjoying myself so much and how good it had felt to have some time with Barbara — I needed to know I had a secure, comfortable place to be. Now, it was clear again, I liked to keep moving — to keep the adrenaline pumping and my mind spinning. I spun warm, good thoughts of Debbie as I continued driving south.

I stopped at a Hastings Bookstore in Lufkin to use the bathroom — I knew bookstores have better things to read than gas stations. My book, for example — and thought I could sell a few here. I didn't, but I did meet Jim Conner, another classic for my story archive.

He was dressed shabbily and seemed out of place in a bookstore. But as I had learned in Portland, it's best not to judge people too soon.

As I was showing the bookstore manager my book and getting rejected, Jim came over and asked to take a look at it.

"Well, sir," I said, "it's twelve dollars," thinking he couldn't afford it because of the way he was dressed.

"Hell, I'll take one, even if the bookstore won't."

I told Jim my hard-luck story, but he wasn't impressed.

"You think you have a messed up chest? Here, take a look at this." He opened his shirt. I was shocked by the scars. "Viet Nam?"

"Hell no. Was shot in the chest at close range with a double-barrel shotgun — *my* shotgun. Caught my wife with another man in bed." I wasn't sure I believed him, but his gritty face painted a picture in my mind of a serious character, not of the cartoon variety.

"Yeah. The docs said if it hadn't been close range, the pellets would have expanded and killed me. Now I just have an aortic problem."

"Geez, aren't you worried about dying? I know I sure am."

"Nope. I used to be a welder on the Alaska pipeline. Even had my own trucking company once. I been run over by a train and flipped a truck down a 460-foot cliff in the mountains near Flagstaff. I've had two neck surgeries, three back surgeries and been paralyzed. I still have atrophy in my right leg and hand so I drag them, but I defied the doctors who said I'd never walk again."

Jim seemed more like a cat than a broken man. "I've had an interesting life," he said, so I asked him what he did now and how he felt about women after his tragic experience.

"Women? They're great. I pay for sex now. It's safer and cheaper. No relationships, no hassles. I'm better off by myself. I have a place in east Texas, another in Tennessee. I buy and sell stuff at flea markets and don't have any credit cards. My funds are limited. Learned about money long ago when I got 250 grand from the oil company settlement. Blew half on a bad investment, the ex got the rest. Filed bankruptcy."

I was beginning to like Jim. He was real —not ashamed of his past or his present. As I was leaving, I asked why he had bought my book.

"Well, it's enjoyment for me, some for you, and if I didn't buy it, I probably wouldn't be talking with you."

I was touched by friendships so quickly found. I shook his good hand and started to leave before the tears began to show, when he asked me to stay for "just a moment, please."

He limped outside to his car and came back in with a folder.

"Thought you might like to see my place in Tennessee."

He pulled out some color photos. All I saw was a river flowing between trees in a beautiful mountain setting that could've been near my own home.

"I have a shack there," he said pointing at one of the photos. "Can't see it behind the trees. It's pretty small. But I own the land. Catch lots of fish, too."

Simplicity expands one's potential, I thought. I drove on feeling inspired that selling books in the streets was simple enough.

I left Texas after two weeks. Each town, each city, each pasture and each bookstore — they were all blurs and insignificant. All I thought about were the people I had met, my talking, selling books to total strangers in the streets, gas stations, coffee shops, grocery stores and almost anywhere else I could. The only recurring thought that was sharp and clear — "or, . . . get a job."

I knew pretty well by now I wouldn't be getting a job. With the freedom and satisfaction I was feeling, the thought of going nine to five would kill me. I'd rather die on the highway, or while playing golf. I was an animal not to be caged or tamed. Poor Debbie.

On the way to Florida I had a difficult decision to make. On highway 10 I saw the sign for the turnoff to New Orleans. I had been there many times on business and found the Cajun food too much to my liking — as most food is — but decided if I went there now, a binge would be more than my conscience could digest. So I stayed on course, but when I was almost out of Baton Rouge, I saw another road sign advertising Cajun food and took the off-ramp.

My taste buds overpowered my will. I pulled into the parking lot of The Factory restaurant. Unfortunately, it was closed at 10 a.m. But I saw a man getting out of a van near the entrance.

"Hey, wanna buy a book?" Ronnie Comeaux took a quick look and humored me. When I asked what he did so I could write an appropriate autograph, he said, "I own this restaurant." I was lucky.

I got a free cup of coffee and sampled the wonderful corn and shrimp soup. Then the chef brought in a new recipe made from lima beans and ham for Ronnie to test.

"Hey," I said. "I'm a customer. Let *me* test it." (*I'd trade writing for eating if I could.*) It was good.

I mispronounced crayfish when we were talking about his specialties. I learned in the north it's pronounced "Kray" and in the south, "Craw." He forced me to try the crayfish nachos for my mistake. Much to my surprise, they were delicious.

I was on the road again after filling up my fuel tanks. (*The Honda gets better mileage than I do.*) Things were looking up. I was getting lots of free food and discounts at motels when I could find owners who liked to read. I was making expenses and had sent Debbie a check with some leftovers — not food, cash. And now, as I was nearing Florida, I was excited about seeing the only state on the continent I hadn't been to yet.

Twisting Around in Florida

My Florida visit reminded me of the movie *Twister*. Although my whirlwind tour hadn't blown too many people off their feet, I did stir up some curiosity among the natives.

When I first arrived, people were swarming around the Florida Tourist Center in droves — the scent of free juice draws all kinds of insects in warm weather. As I asked a few of the unwary flock if they'd be interested in a good book, I tried to figure out which of the little paper cups had the Vodka in them. I was disappointed, of course, but mostly because the clerk gave me a motel list and quickest directions to Gulf Breeze, before sweetly asking me to take my books and leave.

The green trees and warm breezes were just what I expected. So was the oppressive humidity. I passed through

Pensacola and across the bridge into Gulf Breeze. It was early May, but the locals could be spotted by their solid tans; no lines where a watch might be. Time was measured here by the rising and falling of the surf.

After a good night's sleep, I went to the local boardwalk where I was told I'd find most of my possible customers. I got there early, so there weren't many tourists around. I noticed a couple of young fellas, one with a book, sitting in a sailboat tied to the floating dock. A reader — maybe I'd get lucky. I approached cautiously.

"Hey, wanna buy a book?"

I got lucky — then had a wonderfully long conversation as often happened after initial introductions.

Andy and Doug had dropped out. Andy was a marine biologist from Texas and Doug, a sales rep from New Orleans. They were taking a "sabbatical" and invited me to go along on their cruise down to the Florida Keys. Andy, who resembled Sean Penn, put on his best imitation from the movie *Fast Times at Ridgemont High*. "Hey, dude, all I need is a wave and a Bud; that's all I need."

I need more, so I declined the offer. But I did enjoy my memory of the scary adventure in Sesimbra, Portugal during my European adventure. A fisherman I had met on shore, who didn't speak English, but understood my broken Spanish, took me out with him on his boat when I showed an interest in his profession. As the sunset approached, I noticed we weren't going toward shore. I became very worried, pointing toward town. He returned my smile but pointed south. "Africa, Africa."

I was relieved that he wasn't a weirdo. He dropped me off several miles down the coast, and I was able to find several buses and a train back to town by the next morning.

I wished Andy and Doug smooth sailing, then walked slowly down the boardwalk, watching carefully for potential customers and good food. I noticed both at the same restaurant.

It was called Hooters. I won't claim I had never heard of it. I didn't order anything because I felt Debbie wouldn't understand if I told her "but honey, the food was good!" What about, "Okay, I feasted my eyes on the women, but didn't eat bad food."

Why tell her anything?

I met a couple drinking "floaties." (*This is beer with ice in it. Apparently "a cold one" in Florida needs help in the hot season.*) They said their friend, working at the ice cream parlor down the boardwalk, would be interested in a book — she read anything. For a joke, I later walked up to the young lady and said, "I know you're going to buy this book, because your friend said so."

But the joke was on me. Before the girl could respond, a strong hand was on my shoulder. As I turned around to defend myself with my best evil glare, I quickly decided it was in my best interest to apologize for soliciting and take this guy's hint. He was at least six feet and for sure as ugly as one of those masked thugs on a TV wrestling show. And he was so close I could've advised him to get a different mouthwash, but advised myself to remember the encounter on the way to Los Angeles with the interesting fellow at the espresso stand. So when he said sternly, "Get away from my ice cream shop. I pay good money to rent this space. I hate guys like you who try to fleece my customers," I left quickly.

Although it was a beautiful day, my little meeting with the local merchant had poisoned my Gulf Breeze experience. As I crossed back over the bridge, I watched several fishermen, looking down, hoping for the catch of the day. I had caught a few rays of sunshine and headed for my next stop.

I called Debbie from Chipley that night and told her about meeting Doug and Andy and what I had been thinking earlier that day — to hell with the book selling. I could adjust quickly to sailing quietly in the warm, blue water without a care in the world except food and drink.

Oh, but freedom and loneliness are like oil and water.

She asked if I missed her, and I foolishly said, "No. I'm having too much fun." OOPS! Wrong answer. Like her remark about salesmen. I'm pretty good at the TV remote, but I'm still working on improving my skills on how and when to use the right buttons that turn things on and off.

Actually, I was glad to hear her soft voice. I was getting weary from the long drives and was starting to long for her hugs. If she had known me as well as Barbara does, she would've known I was testing her tolerance and patience, hoping she'd beg me not to think about taking off but wanting me to come home. But she didn't.

Mom was different. She wanted me *out* of her home. "You must learn to be a man," she always said. "You must learn to take care of yourself and not hide behind your mother's apron."

I had been proving it since I was 13. How long would it take to prove to Debbie that I was a man just as I was before the heart attack?

In the morning I raced to the Chuck Wagon House, my second stop after asking the gas station attendant where the best place to eat was.

There wasn't much traffic and I didn't see many people walking around, but when I got to the restaurant I could see why. The whole town must've been inside. I filled up my tray with all the good stuff — plenty of scrambled eggs, hash browns and sausage. Then I asked somebody sitting at the table to tell me about the town. "If you want a postcard of Chipley, forget it. Everyone here is too bored to take the picture."

Owner Eddie Davis wasn't bored. His food attracted folks from miles around — about 850 a day herded in while his cash registers absorbed their droppings with ease. Perhaps this is where the term "cash cow" originated. His restaurant was very popular. In fact, I noticed several people were in there almost as long as I was.

I enjoyed watching Eddie practice good, old-fashioned capitalism. He bussed dishes, greeted people, served them food and buttered me up with free chow when I told him I might want to write about his place someday. I was still getting pretty lucky.

I took a short break from eating to try my luck at the local Wal-Mart. This time I got permission, but that didn't help. I only sold one in two hours. I was disappointed. It was hot outside and nobody seemed to care about me or my book. Several people said, "I've heard of you." I knew full well they hadn't, and they just walked by. So I returned to the Chuck Wagon where I could eat more good food and have lots of people to talk to — even if they didn't want to talk to me.

Jan Morris, editor of the local newspaper, had invited me to speak to the Chipley Women's Club, the oldest civic organization in town. It was a beautiful Mothers' Day. The sun was shining, and I arrived at the house where several ladies and Mayor Tommy McDonald had come to hear me talk. (*He's obviously a good politician.*) Jan said the club doesn't want men because "they don't do anything." That made me laugh, but I think she's probably right.

Now, talking is something I really like to do, but when they asked me to talk about humor I wasn't in the mood because I really don't know what to say about it. It was Mother's Day, and I asked why they would rather spend time with me and not their families. I guess they thought that was funny, but I was flattered they were there, nonetheless.

Somehow I got on the topic of religion instead of humor — probably because I was very thankful I was still alive and selling books and hadn't come down with any Texas or Florida diseases after eating okra and grits. But I forgot I was in the Bible Belt!

Well, after presenting my unconventional opinions on God and religion, somehow I was still on speaking terms with the gracious people. When I asked them if they would like me to speak at one of their churches, I wasn't too surprised by their honest blushes and deepest regrets. I did get some good insight about their religions, however, and respected their opinions. I hope they respected mine, because I wanted to go back to the Chuck Wagon and praise the Lord for the good food.

I truly enjoyed Chipley and its good people, even without a postcard to take home. I didn't take a camera on the trip because I knew I'd be taking pictures nobody would want to see, and besides, it was costly and would be deducted from my earnings — and I wanted to show Debbie I could make a profit.

Onward to Chattahoochee, a short drive east.

Stan Ramsey, editor and publisher of the *Twin City News* there, had invited me to stay with him and his family. I was excited about staying in a real home after so many flea-bag motels. We had e-mailed each other many times and I felt I knew him and was flattered by his invitation.

Stan is that 30'ish kind of guy I envy — good looking, intelligent, slender and very talented. He plays great golf and writes wonderful humor. I also was fortunate to hear him sing and play guitar at Ernie's Bait & Tackle Tavern, where there is no Ernie, no bait and no tackle — just the owners, Perry and Janeeta — corporate dropouts like me, having fun, doing what they like. I was able to tell golf lies as well as the locals who told their fish stories, and I sold a few books, too.

I sipped a cold beer in the warm night air, and thought of my college and Army days — the camaraderie, the feeling of family, the fun and the laughter. I missed it.

Getting Permission

It's important to note that Chattahoochee is blessed with both a state penitentiary and the Florida State Mental Hospital. I wasn't interested in the prison, but thought the folks at the mental hospital could use some humor, so I stopped in at the employee cafeteria. It was difficult to tell the patients from the employees. Then, of course, with my T-shirt, I supposed they didn't know if I was a patient either. I was told, however, that I needed to get permission from a lady in the finance department before I could sell books on the grounds.

When I got to the finance department, the lady who gives permission was at lunch, so I sold a few books on the other floor while I was looking for the assistant permission-giver, but she was at an all-day seminar. So I sold a couple of books while I looked for the next-in-line permission-giver, but he was sick that day. So on the way out of the building, after selling several more, I ran into the permission lady who was returning from lunch. I asked her for permission, but she said she couldn't give it to me because she didn't know the official guidelines for giving permission.

No wonder people go nuts around there.

I left the Ramsey's home feeling a little sad. I think Stan was a little disappointed with me — kind of like a blind date. We had good rapport on the phone and e-mail, but I guess I didn't share much in common with him except for the love of golf, and perhaps I tried too much to act his age and failed. He has a wonderful wife and daughter, and staying with them for two days reinforced my disappointment that I never had my own child.

I drove south to Cedar Key, my next appointed stop. It was so small I was able to find it without a map. After getting off the main highway, you take one road west until you reach the most beautiful dead end you'll ever find — the Gulf of Mexico.

I had been looking forward to Cedar Key. Connie Raftis, editor of the *Beacon* had told me earlier on the phone it was a quiet, quaint island paradise, rich with character and characters. I needed a rest in a quiet place and certainly appreciate meeting characters.

I drove up to the front of the small office and was impressed by the quaint setting. I could see the ocean down the street and smell that wonderful salt air. I chatted with Connie for a few minutes and met her father, Mike, the owner/publisher. They made me feel very welcome — southern hospitality, I think they call it. Sitting in a chair in the corner was a slender man in his 60s. When I asked Connie which motel to stay at and some good places to sell books, the man got up.

Naked in the Street

"Hi, I'm Van Proctor. I'd be glad to show you around."

I accepted the gentleman's offer and took his suggestion to check in at the motel at the end of the road. The owner warned me about checking in and out. "We're so slow here, it takes us two hours to watch *60 Minutes*." There were no clocks in the room.

When I asked how old Cedar Key was, he said, "The Dead Sea was still ill when it was founded."

Van picked me up in Mike's golf cart. I chuckled at first, until I realized the entire downtown area was only two small streets. I had always wanted my own limo and chauffeur, and it was nice to be getting the celebrity treatment.

Van is a celebrity himself. He pens the *Naked in the Street* column for the newspaper and is also well-known for the straw hat he wears and his almost unbelievable calm and smooth nature.

It didn't take me long to like him. Every time I started talking too much while selling a book, he would interrupt and say to the prospective customer, "Don't mind Gary. He's just trying to come out from under his shell."

This understatement was a fantastic help. Van had a way with people, and I noticed he was especially smooth with the ladies. I sold a lot of books, thanks to him.

We cruised the entire town. Everyone knew him. And he had a big smile for everybody. He told me he had learned how to be suave during his 14 years as an Arthur Murray dance instructor. He had also been a used car salesman, carpenter, heavy equipment operator and had his own business as an awning installer.

And he had had four wives — nothing like variety in life.

"Four?" I asked.

"I was always nice to them," he said. "But they were always jealous because I like to be nice to *all* women."

I didn't pry, but if he was as nice to women as he was to me, I could see how his charm could get him into trouble. I seem to get into trouble because I *don't* have it. I've always been suspicious of people who are nice to *everybody*. Especially politicians.

Mike invited me and Van to join him at the Rotary Club luncheon in nearby Chiefland. When the waitress asked what I wanted to drink, I said "espresso" and she said she had never heard of it. Then she asked if I would like a glass of "sweet tea," and I told her I had never heard of it, so we both learned something. The iced tea was good, but I still longed for hometown brew.

A man running for the local school board was giving a speech about the educational system. Mike kindly introduced me to the group afterwards so I could plug my book. I gave a short lecture about the ignorance of most businessmen, including myself, working in their familiar office confines, who know little about what the poor really need and want in their schools.

I had seen so much poverty and illiteracy on the road already, I said, that I was feeling guilty about my years of isolation in the corporate world and my unwillingness to mingle with and understand the less fortunate. Although I found it uncomfortable being an outsider in many circumstances, I knew it was only temporary and tried to take the opportunity to learn something new.

When I was finished, nobody in the audience was interested in buying my book. But I enjoyed, once again, feeling special. I was an author now.

I slept well without thinking about a wake-up call. Later in the morning I was back in town when I noticed a big commotion at the state park. A film crew from France was there for the release of a rare tortoise by a marine biology group. I saw my opportunity.

"Hey, look at me. Look at my T-shirt. I'm the turtle man!"

I showed the turtle on my book to one of the cameramen and got interviewed. I even got to touch the turtle before they took it out in a boat to let it go home. I was always good at publicity, but felt a little awkward this time. What was I trying to do? Get attention or become famous? Wasn't I having fun without fame?

When I took Van out to lunch before I left Cedar Key, I began feeling the pangs of loneliness and isolation that I always do when I have to say good-bye to someone I like. I didn't let him know how I was feeling. He had been very good to me — kind, understanding, tolerant and above all he humored me. Mike and Connie had taken me out for drinks the night before, and they, too, made me feel part of a family.

So when I hugged Van good-bye at the office in front of everybody else, I broke down crying and couldn't say anything except, "I love you, Van. Good-bye Connie." I was so embarrassed.

I had to pull off the road until I stopped crying. In spite of all my wonderful feelings of freedom, I still envied those who had family and the closeness it brings.

I was beginning to realize that every time I sold or gave away a book to someone I had rapport with, I talked more than usual. It was my way of preventing intimacy so I wouldn't have feelings when it was time to leave. I knew I was afraid of showing my weakness. I often couldn't hide it.

After my 24-hour respite in Cedar Key, I was off to the races again. I had to drive non-stop to Atlanta for another book-signing. I was looking forward to seeing Tom Kerlin, the managing editor of the *Clayton News-Daily* in Jonesboro, a suburb of the soon-to-be Olympic city. He and his wife Gloria had visited us in Mukilteo a couple of years earlier. It felt good looking forward to seeing someone I knew.

I got into town late at night after surviving the Georgia tail-gaters and the ubiquitous state troopers who were giving out tickets almost every five minutes of driving time. I couldn't find a cheap motel and began having scary memories of Mexia. Everything was booked. The Olympic Village construction crews obviously had priority over authors.

I finally found a place in McDonough, another Atlanta suburb. Ken, the motel manager, had once been Jimmy Swaggert's personnel manager. He tried to sell me some religion that evening, but wouldn't trade it for a book. He did, however, open the swimming pool early the next morning, just so I could relax for awhile before returning to what was now becoming a job.

I let the hot sun soak out the tension. When I sat up on the lounge chair, I noticed the enlarged area where my stomach used to be, but fortunately there was no one around to share my ugly discovery.

I was exhausted. I had almost reached my limit for new adventures. I was looking forward to sharing New York City and the trip home with Debbie. Soloing was getting lonely.

While I was relaxing in the sun, Lem showed up to clean the pool. I said hello to start a conversation, but I became a little concerned when I found out he was an ex-convict. He had sold drugs and had been a thief.

He went on to tell me how his mother had to raise four kids alone in Harlem. Lem was inevitably involved with gangs and had been beaten with a baseball bat, knifed, left hanging over a bridge by one leg, had a crushed skull and broken knee caps.

His sister had gotten her throat slit, and her boyfriend had also once stabbed Lem. At other times, he had been stabbed in the hand, chest, head and shoulders and had been in several car wrecks trying to evade the police. He had been in prison several times and had a child he hadn't seen for years. When he found his mother again after several years, she died just two years later. Other than all that, Lem was just like anyone else — just trying to survive.

Although my background wasn't tragic like his, we shared deep feelings of kinship. He thanked me for understanding his desire to go straight without judging him, and I thanked him for sharing his life with me without making me feel guilty I have it so much better.

I regret that I forgot to give him one of my T-shirts before I left town. I hope when he reads the book I gave him, he still thinks well of me.

Gone With the Wind

After a book-signing in Atlanta later in the afternoon, I drove to a nearby restaurant where I met Tom and Gloria to share the good dinner they bought for me.

Tom is a real cowboy. He wears the right hat and boots and "cuts" his own horses. He talks like one, too, (*a cowboy, not a horse*), but he's no redneck. He's as sharp as a tack when it comes to writing stinging commentary and has been known to get into hot water at times through what he has to say. He's my kind of guy.

Just like a cowboy on his horse, he steered his 4-wheel drive through the city, cutting like a steak knife through the traffic at the conclusion of a Braves' baseball game. I was trying to glimpse the Olympic Village activities but was getting bored — thankfully not gored — looking at all the parked cars in front and in back of us trying to move somewhere — anywhere. But I got excited again when we stopped at the famous Varsity Restaurant.

We slurped down a few greasy chili-cheese dogs and fries — his treat, of course. I saw the pictures of U.S. presidents and other famous people on the walls, so I figured either the food must be good or famous people have bad taste. Either way, I couldn't resist. If I hadn't died by now, I figured I could make it through a couple more weeks of bingeing. Why do famous people stop at these little dives all across the country? I knew why I was there, but nobody asked to put my picture on the hallowed wall. I would just have to keep working at this fame thing.

As we drove through Jonesboro on Tara Boulevard, Tom explained that it was the main road to Scarlett O'Hara's place in *Gone With the Wind*. I wasn't too impressed, I guess, because I never cared much for Scarlett and was still thinking about the good food we had. But I knew Debbie liked Scarlett — she likes history — and had liked Tom and Gloria, too. They were real people; they were fun to be with. I wished Debbie had been there to share the fun — but not my chili-cheese dogs. One pig in the family is enough.

I was now gone with the wind — heading north. As I had been checking out of the motel, I had noticed three junky cars packed with household items and clothes. People were either moving, running away from spouses or looking for work. How forlorn they must be; or was I judging again based on my own experience? I remembered how I felt moving up to Washington and living in a motel for a month with no place to call home. I was feeling that way again and began yearning for home — and the comfort only Debbie could provide.

I began driving faster now. I arrived in Dunn, North Carolina to meet Lisa Farmer, editor of the *Daily Record*. She was very kind and charming — laughed at all my stories. She and members of her staff took me to lunch, free, of course, at Ernie's

Buffet. Barbecue pork, yams, potatoes, crab cakes, beef and seafood casserole, pork skins and fat back. Chicken, baked and fried, salads, peaches, ice cream and yuk — turnip greens.

While I was in the streets hustling books, Cathy Wood had called the newspaper office looking for me. Apparently she was a fanatic fan. I had seen her type in the movies, and the celebrity thing continued to be a phenomenon stimulating my curiosity.

She found me at Sherry's Bakery. She arrived on crutches and was excited to meet me. She said she reads my column all the time, and she relates to it. Poor Cathy. But she was quite a woman in other ways. She had been going to college for nine years and finally had decided to get a degree in criminal justice so she could fight crime. I joked with her that I hoped she wouldn't arrest me for some of the things I write.

As far as I can remember, she and maybe 10 others who read my column, had been interested in meeting me. I was flattered. She made me feel important and special.

I was almost certain by now that I wasn't going to become a famous author. However, when I left Cathy, I realized that out of the thousands of people who might read my column, there are at least several hundred who enjoyed it. But why would it be such a big deal to meet me? After all, I wasn't a Colin Powell running for president nor an O.J. Simpson lawyer. I wasn't a beloved Irma Bombeck or Lewis Grizzard, nor a Hemmingway or Steinbeck.

I was just a regular guy trying to scratch out a living like everyone else I had met. True, I had an unusual method of selling. At the time, that was good enough. But was it good enough for Debbie? I would soon have to find out.

On the way through Virginia, I saw lots of cemeteries and signs directing me to historical Civil War monuments. So far, Ernie's and Junior's were my favorite monuments. I saw lots of patrol cars hiding behind trees waiting to catch me, but fortunately, they were napping or eating donuts when I zoomed past at 80.

I wondered how to tell where the South ends and the North begins. How can a Yankee know when it's time to go home if a southerner doesn't know where to tell him to go? I didn't know, but I did drive far enough north not to care.

I stopped in Williamsport, Pennsylvania, home of the Little League World Series. It was cool and raining — a great relief from the southern heat. I had never really been here before and hoped Debbie would forget I had told her when we first met, that I had participated as a player in the big event. It could be embarrassing when we got to Cooperstown. I slept extremely well that night, knowing my fib was still intact, at least for a few more days.

I got up in the morning with more energy than I had had for many days. I would need it. There was a long drive ahead and then the dreaded big-city drivers. But it would be worth it to see Debbie and my cousin Barbara.

Barbara is the only blood relative I can relate to. I haven't spoken with my brother and sister for years — we're a model dysfunctional family. Maybe someday we'll all be too old to care, too weak to fight, and then we'll laugh and cry about the sad things that happen, or don't happen, among family members. It's a dream that may come true, but it probably won't be too accurate.

Anyway, Barbara is all woman — all six feet of her. She's passionate, intelligent, occasionally obnoxious (*she is a New Yorker, after all*) and always wanting more out of life than what's within her reach. She's outspoken, opinionated, argumentative — but a marshmallow inside the iron shell. She's a lot like me.

Debbie Nibbles on the Big Apple

I was really excited when her husband Marty and I went to pick up Debbie at the Newark airport. Barbara was out hustling houses like good agents are supposed to do. Just to impress upon Debbie when she arrived that I was sincere about no jobs for me, I worked the airport, selling books while waiting for her flight.

Debbie was beautiful. She was wearing my favorite tight jeans and blue blouse. Sometimes she thinks more of pleasing me than of her own comfort — so I gave her my best imitation of a

Robert Redford kiss, her favorite dream, to show my appreciation. Dreams can come true, if . . . .

We all talked long into the night, but I talked too long. Debbie fell asleep, and the only luck I got that night was the left-over smoked salmon in the refrigerator.

In the morning, Debbie and I took the bus into the Big Apple. I had warned her to remove her jewelry and to leave her purse behind. The crime, the crime. I sold two books on the bus and when we arrived at the Port Authority, I approached a cop for a reality check.

"Sir," I asked with my greatest respect and patronizing attitude. "Is it okay to sell books here?" "No."

"Is it safe around here?" "Yes."

"What about outside?" "Yes."

Michael Robles was a nice cop. Intelligent, too. Said he was thinking about teaching in the near future. He made my paranoia seem foolish. Then he asked to see my book. "How much?"

"Twelve dollars, no tax." Debbie left, embarrassed as usual, to buy an espresso for me nearby.

Michael looked inside his wallet. "I don't have enough. Wait here a minute." He walked over to a man wearing a suit. They obviously knew each other. I saw Michael take a bill from him.

"Here," he said, handing me the $20. "I'll take one. Do you have change?"

I reached into my front pocket and removed my wallet from the metal case. "Yes." As I began to put his $20 into the wallet, Michael pulled his walkie-talkie from his belt and said, "Okay, men, come on in!" He reached for the cuffs.

Oh my God! A sting! I had been set up for soliciting.

But Michael was a good cop. Smart, too. He really bought the book. He didn't know about my heart condition; his joke really scared me. But as we were leaving the Port Authority three days later, I asked another cop to pretend like he was arresting me for soliciting and to call Michael in for help. He smiled, I smiled. The prank worked. Michael came rushing out and smiled, too.

New York's Finest has its soft spots.

I found another soft spot at the famous Carnegie Deli in Manhattan. I had told Debbie that the Seattle area is missing one important thing — a real deli. They are found only in New York, Chicago and Los Angeles. The oversized corned beef and pastrami sandwich she had seen at home at the Schwartz Deli in Bellevue, although formidable, looked like a mole hill against the mountainous Woody Allen Sandwich at the Carnegie.

Imagine getting a separate plate of rye to go with the sandwich. It was provided to make several small ones out of the big one. I had never seen such a large monument built in homage to a cow. It was about six inches thick and even with my big mouth, I couldn't make a dent. The $15.95 price tag was worth the admission, but no amount of money could help me walk better when it was time to leave. My desire for corned beef and pastrami has diminished considerably.

I sold a lot of books in the streets of New York. "If I can make it in New York, I can make it anywhere." We met lots of strange and interesting people like me. Among them were comedian Jackie Mason and the doorman at Trump Tower who told us juicy gossip about the rich and famous.

Debbie wanted to go shopping. Under ordinary circumstances with ordinary women, this idea would cause me a panic attack and worry of bankruptcy. But Debbie is the best shopper in the world. She looks at everything, buys nothing. So we went our separate ways for a couple of hours.

In the prestigious Sardi's Restaurant in the Broadway district, I was impressed with all the celebrity pictures and thought how wonderful it would be to have mine there, too. But after I was asked to leave the premises for soliciting, I thought my picture might be posted where I wouldn't want it, so I left without a whimper to meet Debbie.

While walking slowly down a busy street, we noticed a long line of people. They were waiting to get into the *David Letterman Show*. I thought that would be fun, so we got in line, and I began trying to sell books. Then I thought, why be in the audience when I could be on the show?

Debbie gave me the special stare she gives me when I have great ideas. I got out of line and went around to the other side of the building to the entrance of the show. There was a guard at a podium inside the glass door. I knew from my public relations experience, somewhere inside was a producer.

I took a deep breath. Debbie shook her head and gave me lots of space. "Watch this," I said boldly. Then I ran into the hallway. "Sir, I'm late! I'm late! Please help me. Which floor is the Letterman show? Here's a free copy of my book."

He looked at me incredulously, then pointed at the elevator. My heart was pounding. I got off the elevator, walked boldly into an office and dropped a copy of the book on the producer's desk. "I'm available. Call me. My number is inside the book."

I left quickly before I got caught. (*When I returned home, Andie, my barber, told me she saw Letterman telling a story extremely similar to the first one in my book. I didn't look into suing because, well, who cares?*)

Before we left New York I wanted to show Debbie that I was a class act when I wasn't selling books, so I took her to the Plaza Hotel for dining and dancing. She got more excited than usual. "That sounds wonderful."

Some things always sound better than they really are.

I bought her a couple of those expensive, heart-shaped chocolates in the hotel candy store, then sang in her ear my most romantic version of *Send in the Clowns* as we danced in the empty ballroom at 10 a.m. Debbie is a trooper. She thought it was fun.

I was sad to say goodbye to Barbara and Marty. After four days, Debbie, who had never met any other members of my family, had a better understanding of the loose links family members have to bear in the heredity chain. Barbara's erratic personality and mine are quite similar. Poor Debbie. Poor Marty.

I was excited about heading west, homeward after six weeks on the road. And a new adventure was brewing, driving with Debbie. It began immediately.

On the New Jersey turnpikes, you have to pay money and it's easy for a tourist to get lost. So when I took the wrong turnoff, I blamed her for not telling me which one I was supposed to take because I was busy avoiding New York and New Jersey drivers.

Then when I asked her for the correct change to put in the basket at the toll booth, she didn't have it. So we waited while I searched for change, which I didn't have either, then waited for the attendant to cash a $20 — all the while, cars were honking behind us. This was good. It got my adrenaline going, so I was able to drive faster to Cooperstown, home of the baseball Hall of Fame, in time for lunch. We didn't say a lot to each other on the way.

If you drive in beautiful upstate New York and Pennsylvania, someone told me, car insurance is more expensive if your policy includes "road kill." We saw several deer laying dead in the highway. It's sad, but deer should know better where to cross the roads. Drivers sure don't pay attention to those *Caution. Deer Crossing Next 10 miles* road signs.

Besides my playing in the Little League World Series, I had also told Debbie when I first met her, that my Little League glove was in a glass cabinet in Cooperstown. She wasn't big on sports at the time. I told her I had broken a Little League record by not making any errors throughout an entire season. So, of course, the first thing she wanted to see was my glove. I gulped and got another one of her glares.

Incident at the Gates Motel

We arrived in Rochester, New York late at night. We were going to visit Gates-Chili, a suburb, so instead of paying higher prices in the bigger city, I said we should go to our destination "and save some bucks." We were both extremely tired, having left New

Jersey very early in the morning. It was about 11 p.m., and I was getting that Mexia feeling again — couldn't find a thing.

I stopped at a gas station. "Where's the closest motel?"

"The Gates-Chili Motel is about three miles that way," said the attendant with a curious grin.

We pulled up and noticed several beat-up cars and unusual people who appeared to match them well. Being the take-charge kind of guy I am, I walked into the office just as some kind of lady was leaving loudly, arguing about being charged for two hours instead of one. "You gave him my room number, you (expletive, expletive.) I'm going to kick your ass."

She left. The clerk then looked at me. "We get all kinds — by the hour or day?"

"Overnight," I said naively. "That'll be $35."

"Let me take a look at the room." He gave me a key. There were no dead bodies to be found, so I took it. It wasn't safe to drive any further. Debbie will never forgive me.

The first thing we noticed was the toilet paper stuffed in the holes in the front room's drape. The bed was sagging in the middle and there were several dark red stains on the carpet where it hadn't worn away to the wood. The area where the door lock goes was chipped away and the shower had no curtain or spray nozzle. The water level in the toilet was as low as my pride.

I reassured her. "It'll be fine. I'll go out and find some food." I felt my manhood coming back. Now I was a hunter.

"Okay, but leave the pepper spray." Debbie had been totally opposed to my defensive arsenal. Perhaps now she'd understand.

When I returned, I saw another rotation of interesting people talking to each other through car windows and going in and out of the rooms. After I knocked our secret code on the door, I went in and Debbie immediately sat back down in the same position in the chair, pepper spray in hand. She refused to use the shower or the sink. "I'm afraid what will come out," she said.

When I woke up in the morning she was sitting in the plastic-covered chair — pepper spray in hand. And our car was the only one in the lot.

After the Bates, I mean Gates, motel experience, we didn't stay in town at all. We didn't care to sell any books. Nobody else seemed to care either.

We did stop to have "Breakfast at Denny's," with Bob and Bobbi Heinkel. I had sold them a book at the Hess Winery in California. They had told me to call when we came to town, and sure enough, I had good taste. They were as generous as I thought and paid for my Grand Slam breakfast with extra bacon. For a tip, I got Debbie's special stare.

On the road again, I sprung my big surprise on her.

"Honey, you've been so wonderful I thought you might like a little romance." "Okay," she said with her usual exuberance.

But when I told her we were going to Niagara Falls, she got *really* excited. "Oh, that's very nice. I'm sure we'll have a good time." She must have thought, how could Gary ruin a natural wonder? She put her hand on my shoulder and gave it that tender rub I like so much when I deserve it. I felt guilty already. Something would go wrong, I must have thought.

I found a very nice hotel just walking distance from the falls. I tried to trade a book for a discount, but the clerk didn't think much of my gesture. I asked where I could rent a barrel, but Debbie whispered politely in my ear she didn't think I could fit. The hotel had a large bed, swimming pool and hot tub. I turned on my Redford charm to soften Debbie up for the evening ahead.

First, we had a romantic walk to the falls while I stopped only a minimum number of tourists to look at my book. I even held Debbie's hand. Then I complimented her several times on how great she looked — every five minutes by my watch — and then we had a wonderful dinner while she watched me eat lots of food.

This was a special occasion, so against her warning, I drank a whole bottle of good wine. Now it was time to go to the hotel to cap off the romantic interlude I had promised.

My headache started at 9 p.m. and didn't subside until we arrived in Bowling Green, Ohio, 24 hours later. Debbie drove all the way — no complaints from me. It's bad policy to criticize a saint.

I was scheduled to give a talk to a group of library people. I didn't know what kind of an audience to expect.

The city is the home of Olympic ice-skating champion Scott Hamilton and the national tractor-pulling championships. The people would either be real slick or real rugged.

The Truth Sets Me Free

I was given the celebrity treatment there, complete with a free dinner and a big poster in the library lobby announcing my presentation. That was good, but I didn't have a presentation.

I had spoken to groups many times before without a presentation, just getting by with my incessant need to talk — about anything. When I walked into the room there were about 15 people, more than I expected. I was properly introduced and began telling everybody about being a celebrity author.

"And folks, being an author is fun. It gives you lots of great ideas for tax deductions and gets you free meals and makes you respected. I don't know what you want me to speak about, but I can tell you I'll stay as long as you can listen."

I did get in about 10 minutes before I noticed a lady with piercing eyes. Nobody was laughing or even smiling at my impromptu presentation. I sensed a problem and stopped jabbering for a moment. "Ma'am," I asked. "Am I offending you?"

She said without hesitation. "I wish you'd stop telling stories and tell us who you are." I was stunned. I felt that heat in the face I get when someone pushes that certain button. I stopped performing.

"Okay. I was suicidal several months ago. This book has given me some sense of substance, and I'm feeling a lot better because people like you come to meet me. Quite honestly, I don't know what you want me to talk about."

I was scared again — like I always am when my protective shield is removed. I had always felt like a fraud — a big talker with no substance. And I was feeling that way again.

I could feel the rush of those dreaded tears. I looked and saw, through my own, Debbie was crying, too. "If it wasn't for that woman there, I probably wouldn't be here today."

At that moment, I realized the book had opened the door for me to feel okay about being vulnerable. No matter what anybody thought of me as a person, I could still be respected for my accomplishment. There was no shame in being vulnerable — just a lot of risk and with it, fear.

"You know, Gary," said the woman. "You should consider going on Oprah." Quickly back into my controlled manner, I said, "No way. She'd make me be real like you just did. I can't see crying in front of millions." I then talked about my life instead of sales. The audience seemed to appreciate my candor.

I found out later the lady who had pressed me to be honest, was a retired dean of English at Bowling Green University. She could understand real characters created by authors, I figured, but had difficulty with the phony character I had created right before her eyes. I hoped she liked the real character she made of me.

We left in the morning headed for Beavercreek. We were very tired. I had talked into the wee hours about my difficulty being vulnerable and safe at the same time. The talking kept Debbie at a distance, too, but at least she listened as usual — without saying much. She's a very good audience. Sometimes when I'm talking a lot, I think it's because I had never gotten to finish discussing things with my parents before they died, so I have to say *everything* very quickly with people because I won't get another chance.

As we headed south, Debbie commented that there were an awful lot of cows, cemeteries and cornfields on both sides of America's highways. She was right. After nearly 11,000 miles, America had become a gigantic game board for me. Just roll the dice, I thought, and you could be in a big city, in a quiet little town or in the country. Best of all, you could be roaming free with your fleeting thoughts of past and future, while only the changing landscape brings your attention back to the present.

Once in awhile I broke the spell. "Pipe. Light."

I had told Debbie about meeting Sean and Patti Barrett in the streets of Santa Fe. She was a nurse and he was in the computer business. That's about all I knew. When we got to Beavercreek that evening, I called them, and we met for bagels in the morning.

Sean was logical and reserved, Patti was emotional and outspoken. We had a good time, and once again I demonstrated my eating prowess. The bagels were just okay, because I had to pay.

Patti said she really enjoyed the book — had read it all, in fact. I didn't really believe her. But later that afternoon, they came to visit me at the grocery store where I was selling and bought another copy for a relative.

I was surprised they had shown up, after all the other promises that so many people had broken when I was more naive than I had become. I sure liked them. I think they liked me.

As I was leaving, I gave Patti a hug and shook Sean's hand. My eyes were filling up again. I think I could see some extra moisture in Sean's, too, but I could have been wrong. I hope I was right. Even reserved people might have something going on inside that I don't know about — maybe the same feelings and fears I have.

Debbie and I began talking more about going home now, than about the next three stops. I was glad. My adventure was winding down, and I was beginning to worry about my health. I hadn't once used my workout clothes, and I was losing my courage to challenge my heart with forbidden food. But there only were a few days left, so what the hell.

Racing along the highway into Illinois late that day, we suddenly came upon The Park Inn, silhouetted against the plain. I had promised Debbie another nice place to stay after the last dive in Bowling Green, so we stopped. When I found out the dining room was having its grand opening the next morning, I signed up for the room quickly — on the condition that I could be the first breakfast customer and give my ratings to management.

The service was great, so was the breakfast. The entire staff of five served us efficiently, and I got extra large portions of prohibited eggs and sausage. We were the only customers in the place, so that probably had something to do with it. But I'm *sure* telling them that I might do a review for this new book had a *lot* to do with it.

The big breakfast had curbed my appetite for selling, so I was late for my appointment with Dick Westerfield, the publisher of the Pontiac newspaper. My previous experience that nobody much cared to meet me wasn't a good excuse to slack off on my obsessive on-time policy. I paid the price.

Dick had arranged a couple of celebrity appearances for me at the coffee shop and grocery store — even publicized them in the newspaper — and I had clearly disappointed him. I felt very bad. But Dick was a nice guy and still took me out to try Pontiac's famous rhubarb pie. I really didn't want any, but he was treating — well, it was very, very good.

I had a dinner appointment with Anita Bird, publisher of the nearby Kewanee newspaper, so Dick understood when I said we had to leave before seeing the rest of his city. I thanked him for reminding me how important it is to be on time — to think of others and not just yourself.

We were only a little late because I hadn't listened to Debbie when she told me I had taken the wrong turnoff on the highway. I called Anita to let her know. Fortunately, she had extra work to do in the office, so she didn't mind.

Anita was much like Debbie. She didn't say much but always made eye contact. She made me nervous — I was waiting for a sign from her to stop talking about myself. She suggested the Reuben sandwich and fries and, for dessert, the peanut butter pie. Debbie looked at me with her stare, but I couldn't resist. I had never had such a dessert, and although peanut butter is one of the best artery-cloggers known to science, I felt invincible, at least for a few more days, so I dug in — and was content to let the two ladies have a quiet conversation.

But even I have limitations. The pie was *too* rich for my blood, even though Anita paid.

That night, in the first-class motel room I had traded up for with my book, the private Jacuzzi overflowed. I blamed it on bad plumbing; Debbie said it had more to do with the tub's oversized contents. I got out quickly.

Anita had made arrangements at the local Wal-Mart store for me to sell books. So in the morning I was hoping for a big day — but sales were weak. I had a bigger day in another way.

My Most Memorable Moment

A young girl, 13 or 14 perhaps, asked to look at my book while I was working the check-out lines. She looked at it while sitting on a bench, for about half an hour. Debbie was out looking for cemeteries — she likes old things, for which I'm grateful. She was scheduled to pick me up at 2. By 2:15, when Debbie arrived, I was jumping around frustrated, afraid we would be late for a scheduled dinner in Monmouth. I walked back to the young girl with her thick glasses and mussed hair. I reached down for the book.

"Sorry, but I have to leave now. I hope you liked it."

She looked back at me like a lost puppy.

"Gee, sir," she said. "I wish I had the money. I'd really like to buy it. I've never met a real author before. I write all the time and someday I want to be a writer just like you."

I took the book, patted her on the shoulder and said "thank you, good luck."

Debbie and I hit the mat in front of the automatic door but before I walked out I caught myself. "What the hell am I doing?" I ran back to the girl. Fortunately, she was still there.

"Hi again, what's your name?" She told me and I wrote in her new book, "You will be an author someday. And when you are, remember it's important to encourage others to follow."

For the rest of my life I'll never forget the tears in her eyes that came with her "thank you." Before I got out the door I had lost it — again. Fortunately, this time, only Debbie saw. She approved, putting her arm on my shoulder.

The incident reminded me again of my father's admonition that was still driving me. "Don't ever say you can't. If you do, you won't." I hope she does.

Debbie and I talked a lot on the way to Monmouth. We were both getting very excited about our last stop — not because we were excited to see the city, but because it was our last commitment. Then we would have a couple of days left to enjoy the cows, cemeteries, corn and an occasional golf course, without requiring me to jump around selling books and worrying about what people thought of me.

We arrived in Monmouth and parked in front of John Stiles' house. He was editor of the local newspaper. He had invited us to stay with him. John had struck me as quite a character when I had occasionally spoken with him on the phone. He had a strong personality, which I found interesting and stimulating. He was especially entertaining when he told me about a lady who had been accused of being a witch and how he had written some editorials defending her that had aroused the ire of several folks in town, including the management of his newspaper.

We were greeted by his wife, Bobbi. She was very sweet, low-key and beautiful. I was curious to see if my imagined picture of him was at all accurate. I wasn't disappointed. When he arrived a little later he was wearing his hair in a ponytail beneath a baseball cap — and yes, he *always* wore that baseball cap, even at work — and according to Bobbi, in other unusual places, too. He was "cool."

We all went to dinner that night. Since Monmouth, Illinois claims to be the "Prime Beef Capital" of the country, I just naturally had to find out how good it was. My theory that dreams come true if you don't expect them to be accurate, was all but washed away. This dream was accurate. I ate almost two pounds of prime rib and watched Debbie squirm as I demonstrated, once again, my will to challenge my heart. Sales had gone well, and since I had a free room that night, I didn't mind paying for a change. John and Bobbi didn't seem to mind, either.

Back at the house John and I got entangled in a heated political discussion. He's a Viet Nam veteran and has strong beliefs that corporations are evil and the poor suffer as a result. He seemed very angry. Since I had worked several years in corporations, I tried to assure him that not all people working in them are selfish, profit-only capitalists.

We never did agree on anything, but I felt we both respected each other's opinions. I felt a lot of the same anger John felt. All he seemed to want was to be "cool," and to this day I haven't figured out what that meant to him. I thought he was cool. Debbie thought he was cool. But I don't think *he* really thought he was cool yet. He obviously needed to prove something to someone, or to himself. I could relate.

I did see, by his actions in the newsroom with his staff, that he was very kind and would go out of his way to help anyone who needed it. His anger, I believed, was based on the loss of friends in the war and of his dad that he talked so much about.

I gave him an awkward hug when I left. He seemed to like the gesture even though he was as uncomfortable as I was.

I hope he finds his "cool." I'll always remember him fondly.

Before we left town, we stopped off to meet the witch John had defended. Karen Vance, owner of the wonderful novelty shop, By the Book, certainly didn't brew up any controversy with us, as she had in town. She said that someone had seen her unusual gifts, including the tarot cards, and other religious hand-carved and painted items, and complained to local school officials that Karen was practicing witchcraft and Satanism.

This former nurse sent us on our way with a care package of mustard pretzels, coffee beans and peanuts. We didn't feel any spells being cast upon us after eating her offerings, only the uncertain gift of knowledge that there still exists such ignorance in the midst of modern civilization.

Going Home

On the way out of Monmouth, I felt a great sense of relief. I had been on the road for a fast-paced six weeks and now had no more obligations other than letting Debbie drive while I lay back, slept and watched the cows, cornfields and cemeteries flash by.

By now we had invented a silly little game.

She would see cows and say, "cows." I would spot a cemetery for her and say, "cemetery." The same for cornfields. And since we both liked playing golf, once in awhile we would both see a course and say simultaneously, "golf course." But, mostly, it was just "cows, "corn" and "cemeteries."

We stopped to see where General Custer had his last stand, but there were no scalps or lemonade to be found. Later, we stopped at Mount Rushmore. As I stood proudly, having sold enough books to pay for the trip and meet Debbie's requirements, I looked at those handsome faces carved into the mountainside. Then I looked at Debbie's beautiful and distinguished face and said, "I feel so good. I sold books, ate like a pig, didn't get a speeding ticket and didn't die. Do you think someday my face will be carved into a mountain so people can remember *me*?"

She smiled with another of her special looks. Was it the one of patronizing admiration that I had taught her to use when I needed attention for my inner child?

"Gary," she said. "You always make mountains out of molehills. But this is one time you really did have a mountain to climb. And you did it all by yourself. I'm very proud of you."

I turned away, still not comfortable receiving what I had always craved from my mother. Intimacy, I learned, will always be difficult for me.

She hadn't exactly answered the question, but at home a couple of days later, I noticed two of my four Barnes & Noble book-signing posters on the kitchen wall where everyone could see them.

I just *knew* those posters would have better use for me than those discouraging book-signings!

After 13,000 miles and six and a half weeks, I was home. *My* home. I wouldn't get thrown out with my books or my clothes. I had met Debbie's requirements, and more importantly, exceeded my own. I wouldn't have to get a job to prove my worthiness and manhood anymore — to anyone. I had survived with character, determination and a lot of good food. No heart attack, no tickets, no illness and no car trouble. It was fun!

I was okay now. I was a success. There were many times when I had felt the ghostly presence of my parents in the car with me. I heard my dad yelling at me to sell more books when I was discouraged, then felt his gentle pats on the back instead of swats on the butt, when I did.

Success had also given me the courage to forgive my mother. I gave her spiritual presence lots of the hugs she never knew how to give me and probably needed herself. And she even agreed to take the advice of a successful writer; to change the title of her book she had started to *Branded: The Success and Glory of a Surviving Widow*.

I didn't need her approval now. Debbie wouldn't have to play that role again, except occasionally when I forgot my lesson.

I had created my own career — my own path — one that matched my personality, talents and limitations. My mother's fears that I couldn't be strong, secure and happy as a writer, influenced me no longer. I *was* a writer. She had only wanted me to be strong so I could survive. I wish she had known that being vulnerable, affectionate and encouraging would have made me stronger than her trying to be "tough." I hope I have learned that, too.

So — What Was It All About?

I was exhausted for several weeks. We went back to our routines — Debbie is good with the structure of a regular job, reading books and being my designated audience when nobody else

83

will listen — and I went back to healthy cooking and messing up the kitchen while I contemplated where I would sell books for the next several months, and what I had seen, experienced and learned that I could share here with others.

I feel satisfied, not exuberantly happy, as I'm finishing this story. I realize I've grown up. I gave birth to a book — symbolic of the child I never had. I've taken the responsibility to create it, nurture it and watch it grow. I'm a father. And I'm about to become one again next month. My success and new responsibilities have also made *me* feel reborn. So now there's more growing still to do.

After meeting thousands of interesting people across America, I realize that being an author is just an opportunity to introduce myself in a unique way. Fame isn't important. What I saw were people just trying to survive — to raise their children the best they could — and leave something of value behind. Just like a book.

As I watched my symbolic child circulate among the people I had met, I said, "That's my book. Isn't it beautiful? Isn't it smart? Isn't it a miracle?" I left something of value behind and shared the joy of its creation and its substance with others and now it has its own life on bookshelves and wherever else it may be resting. But still my emptiness lingers. It's not a child, it's only a symbol. I must help real children whenever I can. Perhaps coaching T-ball again.

Now that I've grown up, I must protect that frightened and lonely little boy still inside who was tragically abandoned by his parents. I won't let him feel as insecure and lonely anymore as he had been before my journey of discovery. I'll always reassure him he was my favorite companion and that he grew up quite well — in two years, just like me. I'll do my best to relieve Debbie and others of the burden to nurture him.

I've also learned to appreciate my wife for the anchor she is to my free spirits. Without her support I might just drift away.

This certainly wasn't what I had expected to learn on my journey, but just because my dream wasn't totally accurate, doesn't make it any less of a dream come true.

It's November, 1997. Soon the UPS driver will bring this, my second child, to my garage, and he'll become more exhausted than before. I'll let him do all the labor again with this even bigger bundle of joy. And Debbie, Rain and I have another ski trip planned to Whistler where I will prove that I can go down mountains without stumbling too much, as well as I have just climbed the others.

I hope those I have met in grocery stores, gas stations, boats, planes, restaurants, bookstores, coffee shops, bars and all the other places I tried to sell a book, were inspired, or at least entertained, by my performance. They certainly inspired me by paying the price of admission — listening and/or buying my book.

I can now stand in public in a humorous T-shirt, proud that I am one of the two percent of American authors who make a living solely on the sale of their books. I won't feel like a clown, just a regular fellow, trying like everyone else to survive with satisfaction.

All across America, wherever I could find someone to humor me, I sold to those who could afford it and gave away to those who couldn't, all of my books.

Now that Debbie thinks I'm the greatest salesman she's ever been married to, she's encouraging me to become an even better one. If I can bring smiles to more people than before — in person and through my writing — then our new dream will be accurate.

And I *won't* have to get a job!

13,000 MILES LATER....

JDM

OUT-TAKES

These are a few more incidents, anecdotes and people that made my journey interesting and rewarding, and sometimes gave me strength to continue. There were hundreds more. I selected these randomly as they came to mind after I had finished writing about my journey.

While selling books on the airplane to Las Vegas, the passengers gave me an ovation when I finally sat down. The pilot was waiting for me to finish before he could take off.

In Las Vegas I traded a book for an upgraded room at the Hilton to impress Debbie. The room had a mirrored ceiling. She wasn't impressed. I interviewed Cynthia Pensiero, a Mrs. America contestant I had met at the hotel's buffet. I gave her an autographed book. She later won the contest and sent me an autographed black and white glossy photo. Debbie wasn't impressed.

Out-Takes From the Author's Diary

In Albuquerque, 12-year-old Jason Divenere approached me at a book-signing. "Are you as good as DeGeneres or Tim Allen?" he asked. "Probably not," I said. "Are you interested in my book for your parents?" He replied. "After I'm done with it I'll give it to my mother, but only if it's any good."

At the Hess Winery in Napa Valley, California, I sold a book outside to a man who looked like a field worker. When I went to autograph it, he said, "My name? Hess, Donald Hess. I own the place." I was later kicked out for soliciting.

On a highway in Utah, a sheriff's patrol car was crawling along at the 55 mph speed limit, just a few hundred yards in front of me. There were no other cars I could see on the stretch of open desert. I wondered how much he was being paid for escort services, just to make sure I didn't speed past him during the next 100 miles.

On the Kingston ferry, I sold a book to man dressed in a white uniform. I thought he was a deck hand. He smiled as he handed me his card: *Rear Admiral Bill Center, Commander, Naval Surface Group Pacific Northwest.* I saluted with an Army instinct I had learned 30 years ago. As we were walking off the ferry, someone in a car offered him a ride. He got in the back seat. "What about me?" I asked. He smiled. "Rank has its privileges."

In a Texas rest room at a truck stop, I slid a book under the stall where a man was doing his business. "Here's a great bathroom book." He screamed expletives. I waited outside 10 minutes. He bought the book, and I felt lucky he didn't deck me.

Joe Cardinale had a great line. He introduced me to Shannon, his pregnant wife. "I'd like you to meet my first wife." They later sent me a note. Their child is Alexandria Rose.

Adventures of the Unknown Humorist

Gerald Gordon, an actor, director, acting teacher and friend now living in Las Vegas, sent a note: "Funny book, but I could feel the sadness underneath. Moved me! You're a good writer." We both once lived in Los Angeles where I struggled to be a screenwriter.

At Niagara Falls, I sold a book to Tom Morgan, then took his expensive camera to take his picture for him. He later sent the pictures he took of me along with a letter saying he had kept one eye on me and the other on the falls. He thought I'd vanish into the crowd with his camera. I would be suspicious, too.

At the Reptile Gardens in South Dakota, I sat atop a gigantic, 100-year-old land tortoise. I didn't sell any books to the curious onlookers, but the employee who asked me to get off, bought one.

Maureen Vis said that the fact that I trusted her to look at the book while I was selling to others, gave her more reason to buy.

Rick Kaminski, "The Peanut Man" for the Seattle Mariners, was playing golf with me. I didn't know who he was until after the round, but I was glad he bought the book with cash instead of nuts.

At a Christian bookstore in Canton, Pennsylvania, the owner was considering buying some books for her shelves. I suggested there might be one or two stories that might offend customers. She took the book home at lunch to review it. When I returned the clerk gave me an envelope with money the owner had left. She wasn't going to buy any for the store, but she wanted two copies for herself.

At Friday Harbor, San Juan Islands, I met Linda Lawrence who had the exact same address as the first house I lived in as a child in Manhattan Beach, California. That same day I met Scott and Jeannie Wood, who live there now, only six blocks from where I did, and had moved there in 1947, the same year my family did.

Out-Takes From the Author's Diary

In Cannon Beach, Oregon, I was sitting in a deli drinking coffee and relaxing. I saw a poster on the wall. "Salesman who cover chair rather than territory find self on bottom most of time." I couldn't enjoy the coffee and didn't finish it.

On the San Juan ferry a man tapped me on the shoulder. "I know you," he said. "I met you at a coffee shop in Monmouth, Illinois. You tried to sell me a book." I remembered the coffee shop. "Did you buy it?" "Nope." "Do you want to buy one now?" "Nope."

Bob Brennen finally encouraged me to get going before the traffic got out of hand. I had stopped at the Maryland visitors' center to get a map so I could skirt Baltimore and avoid the traffic. I talked to him for half an hour. The traffic was horrible.

I met Jamie Pratt on the Bremerton ferry. His last name and British accent sounded familiar. Adrian, his brother, is a Georgia newspaper editor I had spoken to several times trying to sell him my column. Jamie took the book to Georgia for Christmas. Everyone liked it. Adrian still hasn't bought the column.

John Smith, a man I met at an Atlanta book-signing, said he was coming to Seattle to visit and would call me to have coffee. I didn't believe he would, so I offered to buy. He called, I bought.

I promised **Roger Twitchell**, who I met in a Bellevue, Washington shopping mall, that I would call him for golf when I got to Florida where he lives. I didn't. I apologize, Roger.

Skip and Lisa, owners of Harbor Bookstore, Friday Harbor, tolerated my talking about book-selling woes on several occasions, and gave me extraordinary support to continue my journey.

Cheri Lerma, owner of the Cannon Beach Cookie Co., must have special ingredients in her cookies. At 46-years-old and 123 pounds, she broke the world power-lifting record in her class in Durbin, South Africa, when she squat-lifted 275 pounds.

Elizabeth Morris, a fantastic, upbeat lady, cheered me up during a bad sales day, then wrote a letter saying "we need all the humor we can get."

John Conner Vogan, a 5-year-old, ran up to me with money to buy the book after his parents had earlier passed on the idea.

Brooks Monroe, part owner of Friday's Crab House, Friday Harbor, tossed me out for hollering, "Buy my book." Later, he bought one. Now we're good buddies, but last time I saw him he told me "Save your oxygen and sell on the Internet." Thanks, buddy.

Sandi Rockne opened her wallet to show me pictures to prove she was really related to the famous football coach. Her husband is a grandson. She later sent me a note saying "I'm speechless that you really wrote." She didn't expect to ever see the Christmas promotion I had promised.

Kathleen Cockrell, a secretary at the only high school in Groveton, Texas, cheered me up when I was feeling low. She taught me a lot about small-town life, including, "If you haven't heard a rumor by 8 p.m., it's time to start one."

Postmaster **Martha Merricle,** also in Groveton, on a very hot day when she saw I wasn't selling well in the lobby, said with a chuckle, "Some people draw business, some draw flies."

Cristy Caracane, in Little Falls, New York, didn't have enough money to buy the book, so we traded for her $10 lotto "scratcher."

Out-Takes From the Author's Diary

Tommy Csatari approached me at a coffee shop in Little Falls with cash to buy the book, but didn't say anything. He was only seven, but could read my autograph. I was impressed.

Judith Cooper, owner of Black Bart's Barbecue in Cooperstown, New York, seemed out of place with her stylish manner. She was a former Revlon executive and Johnny Carson personal attendant. She was also a distant relative of the family the city was named after.

Ted Conde, a young man at a book-signing, sent a note regarding the new book: "I can't wait . . . tell me the date . . . I'll be there. It'll be a good birthday present, considering my birthday is in April." Sorry, Ted, for being a little late.

Jaci Oseguera, who bought three extra books for Christmas wrote, "Thanks for remembering me." Thank *you*, Jaci!

Don Hubert, while I was trying to sell him a book in the street, said "Don't over-sell. I've already decided to buy it. Stop selling after it's sold." A salesman himself, he bought four more at Christmas.

Virginia Corcoran, when I asked her why she bought the book said, "Because it would be a lost opportunity not to. Nobody has ever walked up to me and said, "Humor me, buy my book."

Gari Lillis bought the book because she wanted her name printed in this one. I had never met a female with my name, so I did.

At the Front Street Ale House on Friday Harbor, I sold a book to a man who said modestly with a smile, "I'm just a farmer." He was Philip Oberti, of the olive company bearing his name. He said he would send some olives to me, but I told him that in all my travels nobody ever did what they said they were going to do, unless there was something in it for them. He said he'd be the first. I said if he was, I'd mention it in my new book. I waited and waited, finally sending him a fax to remind him. His wife, Klina, sent me a nice note reminding me "never to say never." I got the olives. Here's their reward!

Fred Friedel, a history teacher, wrote in my address book, "History doesn't repeat itself. The French general staff didn't know this in 1940." I had just autographed his book, "If anyone knew your past, history wouldn't repeat itself."

Dolores Robbins didn't want to carry the book with her, so she gave me the money and trusted me to mail it to her. It was the first thing I did when I got home.

Gary Finkelstein, a real estate salesman and former comedian, told me that "humor is self-inflicted."

Dennis Carpenter manages the Boeing 777 flight line. Several weeks after I sold him a book in the streets, my wife, who also works there, heard from one of her colleagues that he had told her about meeting me and that I had a lot of guts walking up to him.

Monica Vessell gave me a very encouraging lecture when I first started out, then bought five copies for her friends. I'll never forget.

Mary Genske, a wonderfully feisty senior citizen who could out-talk me, sent a note, "Your book is very funny, crazy like you." Ditto, Mary!

MORE ADVENTURES
OF THE UNKNOWN HUMORIST

PART ONE
In Pursuit of Trivia

Is Horoscoping in My Future?

I never believe what's written in horoscopes or fortune cookies, unless it's truthful and in good taste.

They were this week. My fortune read: "You've lost your mind. Corniness is your last recourse."

The horoscope said: "There's a cancer in your imagination. Do something quickly before it rots."

I didn't hesitate. Instead of taking time to reason, I created this horoscope based on Zodiac mascots and strange thoughts I vaguely remember while star-gazing on the lawn after last New Year's Eve party.

Eat a corn dog before reading further.

Aquarius: Jan. 20-Feb.18: You are adept at water sports and can withstand the tides of change. Drink bottled water now to improve your chances of survival after carbonated drinks are banned by the FDA. Your natural ballast assists you in staying afloat during crises involving floods, drought or dry humor. Aquarius people are all wet.

Pisces: Feb.19-Mar.20: You live an aimless life, searching endlessly for porpoise. Your natural abilities enable you to dart in and out of trouble in your quest for new adventures. Your slippery character can be scaled back by avoiding getting hooked up with the wrong crowd. Find your own direction. Don't swim with sharks or octopi. Befriend Cancers and Aquariuses.

Aries: Mar. 21-Apr.19: Your tendency to butt heads with your friends and adversaries might win you a lucrative Advil commercial, but you should consider minimizing confrontation to save your skin. Rejoice in being horny. Read Dr. Ruth. Learn pro football in St. Louis.

Taurus: Apr.20-May 20: You were born during the anniversary of the Great Bullfight of the Spanish Inquisition. Therefore, you have strong political inclinations. Your ferocious appetite for power serves you well in galloping for office. The ability to sling the bull and your massive strength to over-run your opposition, bodes well for victory. You instill both confidence and fear in your followers. Beware of men in colorful, tight pants who wave red flags and bear sharp weapons.

Gemini: May 21-June 20: Your body double gives you great advantage in taking off from work without being noticed. Don't be greedy. Give your significant other equal opportunity. Be distrustful of mirrors after drinking, and your shadow that moves without you. You communicate well with talented, double-talking Cancers. A move to Minneapolis/St. Paul is in your future.

Cancer: June 21-July 22: Your crabby nature provides an opportunity to claw out a successful career as a talk-show guest. Your protective shell wards off criticism from friends and family about your profession, but stay in touch with your soft inner-self. Avoid tasteful seafood restaurants and don't name your child Louie.

Leo: July 23-Aug.22: You rule your jungle with unquestioned authority. But beware of flies carrying the sleeping sickness. Stay alert, watch your tail. Buy screen doors for your den and flea-dip regularly. Beware of intruding flocks of migrating Democrats threatening your kingdom. Get a haircut, get a job. Protect your future.

Virgo: Aug. 23-Sept.22: Your virtue is admirable. Seek guidance somewhere.

In Pursuit of Trivia

Libra: *Sept. 23-Oct.22:* Your scale is unbalanced. Weigh your opportunities now. Put your money on one side, your conscience on the other. If the loot is heavier, give some to charity. If your conscience outweighs the money, you have a mental deficit. Rob a bank, then go on an intellectual diet or get your head shrunk.

Scorpio: *Oct. 23-Nov. 21:* Your future is in music. Take a bite of the opportunity. Endorse Sting's next album. Beware of buzzards, snakes and talent agents. Hide your fortune under a rock and pray for continued scorching weather.

Sagittarius: *Nov.22-Dec.21:* Target practice is in your future. Shoot your arrows accurately and abundantly. Cupid is your salvation. Love is blind, but don't ask your targets to put apples on top of their celestial bodies. You're no William Tell. Use caution when shooting for the stars. A tainted arrow will fall from the sky and hit you where the moon don't shine. Batman and Robin Hood will soon pay you for their lessons.

Capricorn: *Dec.22-Jan.19:* You continue being blamed for acts you didn't commit. Change your ugly ways. Be more selective in what you eat. Leave leftovers for others. Escape goat syndrome. Climb mountains instead of junk piles. Your trashy reputation is unfairly ordained. Eat with gusto the Leos, Pisces, Scorpios, Cancers and Tauruses. Share the feast with your brethren, the Aries. Share the blame, don't take it.

Have I lived up to the prophecies of my fortune? Is horoscoping in my future? Sometimes the truth is tasteless.

But fortunately, the cookie wasn't.

When the Cat's Away...

"When the cat's away, the mice will play," is an old adage referring to children and employees who enjoy their freedom when the boss is gone. In most cases there's little difference between the two except for the games they play.

I chose to be a lonely writer just to avoid the restraining environment of a real job where you have to get dressed every day and look busy when the boss walks by even when you really have nothing to do. But my wife reminded me yesterday that I might soon be living lonely if I continue belly-aching about the difficulty I have playing games on my computer instead of doing the household chores that make her happy and the writing that makes us money.

I believe strongly in the work ethic — for others, but not for me. Sometimes I miss the regular work environment where it's more fun playing mousy games because there are more people playing and it's not so lonely. I remember one time many years ago when I worked in a small office with five employees.

The boss had just left town for a two-week trip to Italy with his wife. They went first class, leaving us to wonder where he got all the money because he didn't have any for bonuses or raises. We ran the business successfully, in spite of him calling every day to check up on us. We told him how busy we were because we were.

We democratically agreed on some new rules. Two-hour lunches, tardiness up to an hour, writing messages on scratch paper instead of ugly pink forms, personal business anytime as long as we said where we were, one-hour educational rest periods for reading, twice-a-week movie matinees for stress reduction and 4 o'clock champagne staff meetings.

One particular day I recall vividly.

I was second in command, so Charlotte, Sylvia and Gwen asked me to watch the phones while they attended to important personal business.

"Charlotte stepped out for a few minutes. May I take a message? Hold please." I pushed the red button. "No, Gwen is at an appointment. Any message? Oh, hi Al. Yeah, she was running a little late. She'll be there in a few minutes, I'm sure. Hey, I hear you guys are getting married. OOPS! I wasn't supposed to know? Sorry. Gotta run."

I pushed the other button. "Sorry to keep you waiting. Oh, sure, no problem. I'll tell her you called." It was Charlotte's sister reminding her of their shopping date in the morning.

My lunch was getting cold and my drink was getting warm, so I went in the back to get another cold beer and microwave the pizza. Then two lines rang at once.

"No, he's out of the country. Please hold." I took the other call. "Hey, Linda. How are you? Hang on a minute. I'm alone on the phones." I got back to the other call. It was the boss' tennis instructor. "He missed his lesson? Oh, he's playing in the Italian Open," I joked. "He probably doesn't need your lessons anymore." The instructor didn't laugh, but left a message that he wanted his $45 fee anyway.

"So what's going on with that new boyfriend of yours?" I asked Linda. Then the other line rang. "Sorry I'm late," said Charlotte, "but I'm doing my laundry. I forgot to put soap in the washer, so I have to recycle." Another call. It was Sylvia. "I won't be back in today. My dog had an accident so I have to rush to the store and get carpet cleaner."

"Linda. I'm working too hard to talk now. I'll call you tonight." Then I got a call from Gwen. "If Al calls please tell him I apologize for missing our lunch date, but I got hung up at the mall buying his wedding gift." "Yeah," I said. What a mess *they* were in.

I got in a few rounds of golf during the two weeks, and did a lot of work at home studying TV talk shows. And it was nice getting a tan at the pool without the stress of office work.

When the boss returned, I remember feeling that tension you get when you think you're going to get caught after doing something wrong. But he was relaxed and smiling, just like us. He called a staff meeting to discuss what happened during his absence. He told us some good stories about Italy and we told him some *great* ones about work, but we sure missed the champagne.

We were actually very glad our boss was back.

He was the only one who could sign our paychecks.

Gadgets Can Be a Sticky Subject

The good folks at the 3M Company sent me a promotional package for a new, revolutionary, indispensable tape dispenser. The company, of course, wants me to write good things so you'll run out and buy it, but I can't do that — I'll just stick to my regular, old fashion dispenser, thank you, and save more money by not even buying presents that need wrapping — if any at all.

Touted to assist those who wrap lots of presents, the plastic device attached to an elastic wrist band, dispenses pre-cut, 2-inch pieces of Scotch tape to make it more convenient for adorning your gifts. You can also purchase a weighted dispenser if you can't get the one-size-fits-all elastic band to fit on your wrist.

Once I got the elastic wrist band on and fumbled around getting the tape refill into the plastic holder, I started popping out strips of tape. Since I had nothing to wrap I just stuck them on my desk, table, computer, pants and fingers. They popped out as advertised, but then my wife came home and saw me with all this tape stuck all over, and got hysterical.

I'm all for making a buck here and there, don't get me wrong. But sometimes these gadgets make me wonder about admittance to the human race. Does qualification include the ability to find more ways to be lazy?

I bounced this thought around for awhile and decided I could compete with anyone who thinks I'm a fool to buy their products when I could make a mint inventing my own. Like chocolate mint glue for the personalized vanity stamps with my picture on them that I've been working on with the Postal Service.

Here are some others I'm developing:

Magic Clothes Hangers: These special, velvet-coated magnets seek out the nails in stud posts behind walls. They insert into the collars of shirts and blouses and the waistlines of pants and dresses, so you can throw your clothes conveniently on the wall. No more bending down to pick them up off the floor, or looking for space in your crowded closet. Delicate magnets available for delicate fabrics.

Scent of Descent: This pill-sized chemical breakthrough completely destroys offensive odors once dissolved in liquid. Drop one tablet in the toilet before sitting down, or two, depending upon your eating habits, and avoid any embarrassment you may cause yourself, family or friends. Put a tablet in your left-over seafood casseroles and unwashed scrambled egg pans, and leave your worries behind when you go out to eat. Can also be used under armpits if squeezed properly before exercise.

Exercise Vanity Mirror: This computerized, lightweight, full-body length reflection panel allows you to see yourself in many fashionable shapes and sizes. Programmed with the body of Crawford, Fonda, Arnold, Simmons and others, you first scan your face into the computer. The attachable mini-camera makes your celebrity body mimic precisely what you do, but *your* smiling face is on it instead. Watch the pounds melt off as you observe your ultimate fantasy.

Budget Buster: This device grabs your $1, $5, $10 and $20 bills like those change and vending machines, and attaches a bright red strip across the bills making it impossible to use them to purchase anything. The stripes are chemically treated to disappear in 5, 10, or 20 days, depending on your budget, so you can spend them only after they return to normal. Cash your paycheck. Treat yourself to debt-free living while your cash enjoys a longer life span.

Bug-Be-Gone: Tired of removing those generous insects who gave their lives to remind you to keep your windshield clean?

Now enjoy your summer driving vacation with this new product guaranteed to serve both as a safety precaution and proper burial container for your beloved insect friends. The pre-cut, see-through plastic wrap, similar to what you use in the kitchen, will be dispensed in a handy, portable wrist band. Just pull out the material and stick it on the windshield before you get bugged. Remove and replace as needed. Tinted versions available. (*A special thanks to the 3M Company for the idea.*)

We all wish we had invented the paper clip, clothes pin, pop-top, match, disposable diaper or TV remote control. If we had, we could be so lazy we wouldn't need a wrist band to help us wrap gifts — we'd pay someone else to do it, probably our new personal assistant. Or, more likely, our gifts wouldn't need wrapping. New cars, houses and vacation trips look silly wrapped in paper anyway.

I wonder if 3M could invent a sticky device to filter out junk mail from the mailbox.

Trading Places — Let Students Run the Country

Exhausted parents are relieved. Summer vacation is over. Their children are now being disciplined, educated and lectured to by teachers who should get paid like corporate executives for their tolerance and troubles.

School is, after all, a training playground for real life. Children learn to get along with jerks and authority figures, wear fashionable clothes, struggle for status, learn how to break rules without being caught, and develop romantic interests frowned upon by hypocritical bureaucrats. Learning the 3R's — reading, righting, rithmatic and spelling — is equally important for the impending challenge of earning a living. The stakes for success and failure in the workplace are higher, but the routine is about the same.

In Pursuit of Trivia

Politicians, like children, also get long recesses from their political playgrounds. They bicker within their own system to strengthen our educational system, but quibble like youngsters about the changes required. They didn't ask me, but here's my idea.

Adults should get summers off while students run the country — on-the-job training. The economy would suffer, but the monetary loss would be offset by the elimination of payrolls. Students would be gaining critical experience money can't buy.

What would the students and grown-ups learn during their summer vacations?

I got Tyrod Tickleman, president of Tinsel Steel Company, and Cory Peasley, an accomplished ninth-grade skate-boarder together. Here's what they said.

Tyrod: "Great idea. The kids will enjoy playing with fire in the furnaces. They can even wear their dirty, baggy clothes, but long hair, well, there are safety rules, you know."

Cory: "Yeah. It would be cool. But I'm not going to work for a tyrant like Mr. Tickleman. We'll choose our jobs and bosses like in school. I'm going to get a job that lets me skate to the Coke machines in the office and a boss who lets me watch *MTV* when we get those coffee breaks every fifteen minutes."

Tyrod: "The kids will learn about finance and taxes, too. I'll give them the books so they can make the numbers simple — just lop off a couple zeros and make believe it's allowance money. The IRS will be baffled. I won't be responsible for the audits."

Cory: "The coolest thing is I can boss other kids around instead of having someone else always be the boss of *me*. And I'll get a big desk with a leather chair that I can slop pizza on and nobody will yell at me. Three or four phones, too, so I can talk to my friends at other companies to make deals and decide where we'll hang out when we tell our parents we're working late at the office."

Tyrod: "They'll get educated about the law, too. When they learn rules about discrimination, sexual harassment, unfair labor practices, unlawful terminations and industrial espionage, they'll realize how lenient their parents really are."

Cory: "No way. We'll have company parties every morning, at lunch and before going home. We'll put the costs on our company expense accounts, just like grown ups. While we're partying we'll use democracy to vote for what music will be played on the intercom and who will be responsible for chores like writing reports and putting toilet paper on the spools. We'll have so much fun we won't have time for rules."

Tyrod: "Hmmm. How can you think about having fun at work? It's a jungle out there. Business is tough. Discipline is critical. You must always look over your shoulder to cover your butt. You gotta make a profit."

Cory: "What are you going to do at home while we're working this summer?"

Tyrod: "Haven't thought about it much. Probably make plans for what I'm going to do when I get back to work — if there's a job to go back to."

Cory: "Grown ups worry too much. They don't know how to have fun."

I saw Mr. Tickleman at the candy store yesterday. He was arguing with the 12-year-old manager that he was charged too much for two-and-a-half ounces of gummy bears. The manager told him with a big smile, "I haven't learned fractions yet. Sorry."

"What I did on my summer vacation" essays will certainly be interesting and educational.

A Fish(y) Story

Fishing season is near. It's a time to tell big lies, but mostly it's an opportunity to relax for hours watching my colorful bobbers floating quietly on the water's surface. The fish must like watching my plastic buoys, too. They seem to prefer processed aesthetics to actually tasting the ugly little offerings on a hook. Can't blame them. I too, prefer buying beautiful fish fillets at the market rather than killing and cleaning the real thing myself.

But with costs at the market going up and an unexpected jolt of testosterone kicking in, I've caught the bug to do it right this year. I asked around for a good instructor. I found another one of those famous-people-you-never-heard-of living in town. Tom Kane has fished all over the world. He's an expert. So talented, in fact, he practices summer fly fishing in Death Valley with a beer in one hand and a swatter in the other. (*Lie*) His claim to fame? He won an Alaskan halibut derby by hauling in a 198-pounder — not including the bait, and once made $63,000 in nine weeks working 18-hour days on an Alaskan fishing boat. (*No lie*) He survives on nothing but salt water taffy, McFish Sandwiches and Ocean Spray Cranberry Juice. (*Lie*)

With a degree in marine biology, years of experience as a commercial fisherman and once an owner of his own fish market, Tom is uniquely qualified to provide a platter of good, fishy information. (*No lie*)

First I learned it's important that if you trawl for bottom fish, it's important to report to the police any snagged human bodies, as he once did, even if it's your biggest catch of the day. (*No lie*) You probably wouldn't be able to keep it anyway, he says, because the licensing authorities haven't made a final determination of limits. (*Lie*) When I asked him how to catch my favorites, shrimp and lobster, he said most of it is raised on private farms. "So if you must, do it at night when no one's looking."

I've always been curious about the difference between a prawn and a shrimp. I wasn't too surprised to find out they're both about the same except in Texas. There, anything with a shell and claws is a shrimp if it's not a lobster, tortoise or armadillo.

I usually buy fish at the market on the way home from my unsuccessful fishing trips. I've always bought trout, of course, because they look pretty good and they're easier to find and to lie about how the big ones got away than say, a 60-pound black sea bass in a Minnesota lake. I've always wondered why cod fish is never offered in stores as a trout substitute for these frequent occasions. Tom says "They have a face only a mother would love." (*No lie*) Enough said.

One of my favorite fish is salmon. I like it prepared several ways, but mostly smoked. Tom said he likes it, too, but prefers halibut rather than smoked salmon. "It's difficult eating someone's fish after they've already smoked it," he said. "It's difficult keeping it lit." (*Lie*) I understood why Tom said his humor is salty. "When I throw out a line, it usually goes down like a sinker." (*No lie*)

He began talking about the different methods of catching fish. I learned halibut are caught on lines as long as a mile on the ocean's bottom with hooks attached every six feet. "They like to roam along the bottom eating rotten fish, so after laying the line you have to wait a day for the bait to spoil." I was hoping he was lying again. (*No lie*)

For years I was turned off by the smell of fish. Tom said that fresh fish don't stink and asked where I got mine from. I told him by the time I was usually done fishing, the ice had melted in my cooler, so when I picked up the trout at the grocery store before it closed and before the long drive home, well . . . .(*No lie*)

I was curious about when fish might some day be depleted. But Tom said not to worry because, like cattle, sheep and chickens, more and more fish farms are being started by private citizens. "Most restaurants and grocery stores," he explained, "prefer buying farm fish because they know exactly what to expect in texture and color. Consistency is important." I asked him what he would raise on a fish farm.

"That's easy," he quipped. "Gold fish. They go for $350 an ounce!" (*Lie*)

Tom gave me a sample of smoked chub. "Here," he said, "the lure of eating these delicious morsels is twisting and pulling the heads off." (*Lie*)

I'm glad fish don't like my bait. After watching Tom work behind the fish counter at a local grocery store, I know I prefer watching my bobbers. But when I get that urge to go out and catch a fish, I'll give him a call anyway and see what he's got on his scales.

The price might be high, but an ounce of good fish goes well with a pound of lies.

An Animal Act for My Wife

Wives are always telling husbands to clean up their acts. No surprise — most women claim we're just wild animals that should be caged.

Since I prefer the freedom to roam my house without fear of captivity and would rather have my wife's affection than her scorn, I decided to surprise her. Since my act as chef and house-bound writer requires performing miracles in the kitchen and office, I did what any intelligent husband would do. I called for help.

Jennifer is the local manager of Merry Maids. I had met her at the grocery store last week when she suggested I would look better without food stains on my shirt. She really had lots of suggestions, but when I explained that I wrote better if I was comfortable, she just smiled and gave me her card.

Jennifer wouldn't quote a price on the phone. "I'll have to take a look," she said, but I suspect she was concerned the house was *comfortable* like my shirt, and she wouldn't be able to clean up my kind of miracles.

She arrived promptly and was alert, very professional and, not surprisingly, her clothes were very clean. She wrote down all the details as I began the tour.

First, my office. Her sweet smile quickly turned sour.

"Don't worry about those brownish cobwebs up there," I reassured her. "It's just from the pipe and cigar smoke. Nothing to worry about. Your people can scrape the nicotine off the grill by loosening those four screws. That vent is always getting clogged."

"We don't do mechanical work. That's $50 extra."

"OK," I said. "When your people get to my pipe rack, I want each pipe scoured completely, inside and out. Some of the charred tobacco in them is at least 10 years old, so tell them to be very careful."

"We don't do pipes," she said. "But for $10 each we'll try."

No problem. But as Jennifer watched me lifting the trash can from under the desk, I saw she suddenly needed some help — some of my favorite spiders were working on their web sites under my computer desk. "Here, take it easy, sit down."

Jennifer quickly jumped back up from the sofa.

"Whoa! What's that noise?"

"Oh, it's probably just Mickey. He likes to come in when strangers stop by. He's a lonely mouse. You *will* clean out the old cheese from under the sofa, won't you?"

"That'll be $75 extra."

"No problem."

"Mr. Schwartz, when is the last time you dusted or cleaned out the cobwebs?" she asked.

"A couple years ago, I think. I kinda like the spiders — they eat the mosquitoes and flies that bother me all the time. The dust? Well, I do get angry sometimes when I'm trying to read last month's bills. After I wipe them with Windex, I have to call up the people to see how much I owe."

Jennifer obviously wasn't as cheerful as when she arrived.

We went into the house. "It's pretty clean in here," I told her. "I usually do it myself, but the vacuum broke about a year ago and then I hurt my arm playing basketball. We did just have this no-clean linoleum put in a couple years ago, so you shouldn't have too much trouble getting all the colors off my floor canvas. I like artistic things, but my wife seems to prefer the boring, original black and white checkerboard."

"I believe you mean no-wax linoleum," she said. "And what *are* those color spots?"

"Well, I've got several catsup classics, those yellow and red ones are egg yolk and strawberry jam icons and the green ones are still aging — they're from my homemade bread, I think. Or oatmeal, I'm not really sure."

Jennifer stopped taking notes.

"Want to see the bathroom?" I asked.

"No. But do you have some Alka-Seltzer?"

"Sure." I plopped a couple tablets into a glass I took from the shelf. She looked at the glass carefully, then put the brew into the sink without drinking it. "I feel better now. Thank you anyway." I was delighted she didn't want to see the bathroom. Bathrooms are so personal. I didn't want her to think I was a pig.

She sat down with a calculator and started tallying up the bill. "That'll be $2,500, not including the bathroom."

I was just a little surprised. That's not really too much to keep a good woman. I signed right away. Then I called my wife at her folks where she had been living for six months.

"Honey, you can come home now. I've cleaned up my act."

Watch It! Time Is Money

I'm rarely late for anything except the dentist, and since I usually don't care what time it is unless it's for eating or sleeping, I wasn't ticked off too much when I lost my Timex. But when I missed our cheap flight to Los Angeles and had to pay a bundle for the next flight I knew it was time to get a new watch.

We talked about it on the plane. How much to spend, what brand, digital or wind-up, pocket or wrist, color, Swiss, Japanese or American, one that has numbers you can read or the fancy kind that makes you guess, metal or plastic watchband, with or without alarm, with or without dates . . . the food arrived just in time. I was spared further confusion.

My friends didn't wait at the airport to pick us up, of course, so we had to spend another bundle on a taxi. After eating, my friends dropped us at our hotel to freshen up for an evening celebration of dancing and champagne. We agreed to meet in the lobby at 8, so I walked a few blocks to a mall to buy my new watch while my wife took a nap. I got back late because I couldn't find one I liked, so we lost our reservations and had to take another taxi to another club and wait for two more hours to get in.

I could tell it was time to leave when, after the first glass of champagne, I stepped on my wife's new shoes while dancing and then fell asleep at the table.

After breakfast at the hotel with my friends, (*the wake-up call worked*), we were startled to find an entire room off the lobby where two gentlemen were selling watches. There they were, displayed in all their glory on six long tables. We guessed 500, but were told there were 850 of them. Awesome.

We walked around, amazed by the dazzling opulence of the jeweled timepieces. Only two salesmen, and no watchmen!

There were some that talked. "Today is October twenty second and the time is seven fifty and ten seconds." You couldn't be late with that! I picked up this incredible watch with 28 diamonds and 14 of those red emeralds or green rubies or whatever.

"Honey, look at this. What a great gift for your mom!

"And look at this other one." It had a skull and crossbones, studded with diamonds, mounted on a big motorcycle seat that would fit nicely around the wrist of a gorilla. "Great for your brother." (*He rides a Harley.*) I got really excited when I found one attached to a belt-buckle. It had red jewels in the eyes of a bull and diamonds on the toes of a boot. "This would be great for Charlie." (*He's a friend who rodeos in Texas at night after a full day of tending bar.*)

I found some with pearls and feathers and beads. Those in the glass cases were especially interesting.

"Honey, look at these Rolexes." I picked one up so she could see how light it was. "They're usually too heavy for me."

In Pursuit of Trivia

The selection was overwhelming. I asked one of the salesmen, "Do you have anything I can afford?" He showed me the Casio in the fancy black box.

"It's quartz. Keeps excellent time. Has a built in stop-watch, alarm, calendar and a five-year battery."

"How much?"

"It's on special. Only 10 bucks."

My wife was getting anxious. "We'd better hurry, we'll be late for the plane."

"Okay, I'll take it. By the way, how much is that one with the built-in computer and modem?"

"Ten bucks. It's on special too."

"And that bracelet that talks and the one with all the diamonds?"

"Ten bucks."

"The Rolex?"

"Ten bucks."

I grabbed the Casio.

"Say, do you know what time it is?" He pointed at the hotel clock on the wall. "Nine fifteen."

"How come all the watches are an hour behind?"

"There's an 11-hour time difference in Somalia."

So, we were late for the plane again. It was okay, though. I had saved a bunch on my new watch.

But I almost puked when I opened the black box and saw this ugly Army-green watch and matching rubber wristband.

Maybe I can sell it at our next garage sale with all of my other watches that don't work.

A Good Loser Isn't Hard to Find

I lost my shorts.

No investment or sports bet was involved, but I was angry just the same.

They weren't in the dryer, they weren't in the pile of clean clothes on the bed. They weren't in my workout bag, nor were they clinging to the shirts I hung up. The dryer didn't eat them, because all my socks were accounted for in the same load. I last remember seeing my new shorts at the gym when I took them off and rolled them into the wet towel that was now dry and on the bed.

The mystery made Fathers' Day a memorable event. As I stormed out the door, late for the trip to my father-in-law's house, I continued ranting about losing the workout shorts. I was so frustrated, I forgot my keys on the way out, but fortunately my wife had hers. I was able to get back in to look for them without success, so I had more to complain about as we left.

I wasn't at any loss for words on the trip. I repeatedly traced every moment of the previous day — taking the shorts off, showering, putting them in the bag, washing them, drying them — putting them somewhere. Now it was the keys. Were they in the brown pants, the green pants or on the end table? Maybe they were buried in the sofa cushion? I continued hopelessly searching my memory for answers.

My wife's patience with irritable behavior was exhausted, so I lost my tongue when she suddenly admitted she forgot her father's gift. She asked why I didn't put it in the trunk, but all I could do was shrug and whisper, "I forgot where it was."

When I told my in-laws about losing my shorts, they laughed, but by then I had calmed down and could laugh with them. It was a ridiculous yarn. But it was a good tie-in to discussing how Hillary Clinton could conveniently lose documents and then find them when it was necessary to cover up. We shared several lost and found tales before I went into town to pick up groceries for dinner.

In Pursuit of Trivia

I've never been good at driving on country roads, so I got lost and had to call from a gas station for directions home. When I finally got back, my mother-in-law asked where the strawberries were for the shortcake. I had lost the list she gave me — I was sure it was in my wallet, but it must have fallen out with the map they had drawn when I was looking for the $20 bill I thought I had.

Everything went well at dinner — at least I hadn't lost my appetite. But when we started talking about the virtues and faults of Bill Clinton and Bob Dole, I supported the independent ideals of the Freemen. My father-in-law, recognizing I was losing control, suggested reading a good book, but I had forgotten my reading glasses, so I surrendered the day as a lost cause.

We got home just as the last quarter of the Seattle Supersonics and Chicago Bulls basketball game was starting. I sat down in the recliner and reached for the remote, but it wasn't there. I was too exhausted from being a loser to look for it or to even get up and turn on the TV. I sat frustrated in silence until my wife returned from the grocery store and found the remote under the newspaper on the floor. It didn't matter. The Sonics were losers, too.

Not missing the opportunity to take advantage of my situation, my wife challenged me to a game of gin rummy. This time I lost my shirt to the tune of $75 but couldn't find the checkbook.

I went to bed early, putting my head gently onto the pillow where I wouldn't lose my mind worrying about my losses. But I woke up with a headache and found my shorts inside the washed T-shirt in the gym bag and the keys safely in the door lock where I had left them.

If you know where to look, a good loser is easy to find.

Who Wants to Hug a Diamond?

Most people will agree that a dog is *man's* best friend and a diamond is a *girl's* best friend. Probably true — although unfortunate for the dog.

Dogs provide companionship and unconditional love for a low initial investment — but if you add food, medical care and an occasional bone, the animal costs more than a diamond. The stone, on the other finger, with its costly initial investment, becomes more valuable as time goes by, but requires no maintenance.

But who wants to hug a rock? Reluctantly, I had to do some research on this illuminating gem last week before I purchased diamond earrings for my wife's Christmas present — I felt she wouldn't accept the usual pair of slippers or fruit cake because I hadn't earned enough good-behavior credits this year.

I began at our local jewelry store, where Toni and Jim convinced me, after an hour of my interrogation, that I was doing the right thing. Toni pulled back her hair and let me get a twinkle at her two sparklers. "So what's the big deal?" I asked.

"They make me feel special," she said. "I like looking at them. They're beautiful."

So I asked the obvious question. "Do you stand in front of a mirror all day?"

Her husband Jim smiled, obviously enjoying my dilemma, and handed me a brochure, *How to Buy Diamonds You'll Be Proud to Give.* I looked it over quickly, stopping where it said, "How Much to Spend. Two months' salary . . . spend less and the relatives will talk, spend more and they'll rave." That's for an engagement diamond, but a diamond *is* a diamond!

That made sense, so I asked Jim, "What do you have for 99 bucks?" I was surprised he *did* have a diamond fitting my budget. After I put down the magnifying glass, I figured it really was too small for practical purposes. "It's not necessarily the size," he said, "that makes it valuable. It's the carats, clarity, cut and color."

In Pursuit of Trivia

Since I'm not Bugs Bunny, wasn't clear what I was doing, had already decided round wasn't going to cut it and that the color Jim referred to probably was the green he was going to collect, I left the store and went to my new bank to take out a loan where Nicole, the loan officer, was very helpful.

"You should borrow more money," she said. "Your wife will appreciate how much you love her and it's a good investment."

She smiled broadly as I signed the document whereby, if I died, the bank would repossess the earrings but ". . . donate our profits to your wife for a down payment on another pair."

No dummies, those bankers.

Just then a Marilyn Monroe look-alike stepped briskly out of her office. I asked her to show me all her diamonds. "Not bad," I said. She fluttered about, giggling, and sang "Diamonds are a girl's best friend." She explained she'd been married six times and ". . . their diamonds lasted much longer than they did and they're much more dependable." Same relationships with my dogs and women.

I understood her clearly.

So, I picked up my loan check and drove back to the jewelers. The brochure said, "Diamonds are the oldest gemstone in creation, some born in the fiery depths of the earth more than three billion years ago." It explained diamonds are 2,000 times harder than rubies or sapphires, and no two are alike. It described the way diamonds reflect light to produce the desired affect, (*Which, to my way of thinking, is to blind your judgment and make you buy one*) and that they're very difficult to get out of the earth. So what? It was more difficult getting money out of my pocket.

Jim smiled. I looked forlornly at Toni. She smiled. I looked at the two stones and shook my head. I had always thought *gold* was the standard of wealth. It's the standard on which national economies and dental fillings are built. "Everything that glitters, isn't gold," and "There's gold in them thar hills," are familiar adages. *Goldfinger* and *Golden Eye* were better Bond movies than *Diamonds Are Forever*.

I enjoyed the glitter in my wife's eyes when she opened the package. But I still don't understand. I sat back and sipped a glass of fine Cognac which she doesn't understand either.

I did appreciate the extra doses of romance I got for three days. I guess my friend Kate was right when she suggested the gift. Kate says diamonds are an excellent way of expressing love.

But I still prefer hugging my wife or a dog — not a rock.

Truckers: True American Heroes

I met the famous Dana Moore at a Seattle Mariners baseball game recently.

Like you, I never heard of him either. He was sitting next to me chomping on a burrito the size of a blown-out truck tire. I noticed the embroidery on his jacket; *National Truck Driving Champion, 1993*. This explained why he could swallow the entire meal in six bites — eating quickly at truck stops must surely be a requirement of any great American trucker.

I'm always excited when I meet famous people I've never heard of, so I had to get his attention.

"I think truck drivers are the most dangerous and obnoxious people on the roads. They're slightly more intelligent than road kill." He gave me an intelligent smile.

Dana told me he had won three state championships and placed second twice. State champions qualify for entry in the national contest. He had to pass a written exam, an interview, then pre-trip and driving tests.

"The written exam requires knowing how many feet it takes to stop an 80,000-pound truck going 60 miles per hour, how to put out a tire fire, what to do if a hazardous substance gets in your eyes while loading or unloading and how far to stop before getting to a railroad crossing."

In Pursuit of Trivia

Those were the easy questions, he said, so I guessed the answers. "About 600 feet if you're going 60 and 300 feet if the patrol car alongside has flashing lights. To douse a fire use the extinguisher, but only if you have time to stop without being late for your delivery, or drive faster so the wind will put it out. If something gets in your eyes use your sleeve or Murine. At railroad crossings, stop if you see a train, slow down if you see cattle and speed up if the lights are flashing and it's too late to stop at all."

Dana shook his head. He explained the interview. "It's mostly about a positive attitude and courtesy on the road. He always respects his employer, customers and other drivers. He lets faster vehicles pass and always stops to help drivers in distress, even if they are men."

I wanted him to know I knew about courtesy, too.

"When leering at females with short skirts in passing cars, always be polite — wear sunglasses and don't honk. Always hog the highway by driving next to another truck to keep expensive cars from disobeying speed limits, but let cheap cars with small engines get a head start when going up hills. When stopped by the cops, always offer to share your cold French fries and warm soda. When throwing litter out the window, use the rear-view mirror to make sure no one is watching, and have your phone number emblazoned on the trailer so expert drivers can call you with driving tips."

Dana lowered his head. He described the skills test. "It's precision driving with time limits. Things like parallel parking within four feet of barricades placed in front and back of the trailer, backing up to a dock within 18 inches and not touching it, turning corners as close as possible without touching the curb and . . ." I couldn't let him finish.

"I'd be good at that. I drove a truck in the Army once. The regular driver was sick. I broke an axle driving into a ditch, but I got a license anyway because I was skilled at leaving the scene and blaming a buddy who was asleep in the passenger seat."

"The pre-trip test is the most fun," Dana said. "They mess things up and you have to figure out what's wrong. A loose cotter pin in the brake push rod, a loose fuel cap, the fifth wheel might be unlocked, the load unsecured and the landing gear disabled."

"You're right. That would be fun. First I'd light a match so I could see if there was any sugar in the fuel tank, listen to make sure the stereo speakers were balanced and look for illegal, out-of-state fruit, rodents and insects in the trailer."

Dana bowed his head lower. "Do you drive a car?" he asked.

"Sure. What kind of question is that?"

"What's your license number? If I see you driving, I'm going to do one thing that made me the national champion."

"What's that?"

"I always get off the road when the hazards are serious."

Dana is definitely a true American hero.

The Simpson Case: Definitely a Race Issue

It was definitely a race issue. Consider this.

O.J. Simpson *raced* from opponents while playing football, he *raced* to airports advertising rental cars and he *raced* from the law in a Ford Bronco. The only thing he hasn't run for is public office. Not a bad idea. He proved his ability to lie with unflinching composure during his testimony at the civil trial.

Now that the social, economic and legal drama has finally lost its juice, it's time to move on. American life isn't just black and white. There's a lot of gray in between.

If you were watching President Clinton's State of the Union address, you know what I mean. The O.J. verdict came in just as Clinton was winding down to his final, explosive rendition of the "Bridge to the 21st Century." The jury on that classic theme will be out for a long time. But it was quickly determined that most people chose the real-life mystery of a good, celebrity "whodunit" on their

In Pursuit of Trivia

TV sets instead of the predictable, boring rhetoric of someone's fantasy. It may be sad, but it's the truth.

After Clinton was finished, Republican congressman J.C. Watts began his intelligent and eloquent rebuttal. It was certainly more honest and uplifting than Simpson's. Unfortunately, his contribution to American life was downgraded from important to J.C. Watts who? — O.J. stole the show — and the ratings. The timing made TV executives sweat. They had to decide between politics and drama. What was more important? The issue is still being talked about. (*I admit switching channels to the verdict, but did read Watts' rebuttal on the Internet.*)

So what would happen if O.J. ran for public office? Let's say, just for discussion, as mayor of Death Valley, California. (*Clint Eastwood made his day as mayor of Carmel, California, and Sunny (sic) Bono was hot as the mayor of Palm Springs*.) As a celebrity Republican politician, Simpson could be an excellent prospect for raising TV ratings.

"He would certainly draw huge ad revenue on the talk shows," a recently unemployed network executive told me. "As a sponsor, Bruno Magli would do well selling its brand of bad-ass desert moccasins, 'where the only tracks they leave are those to your city's most prominent parties.'"

Of course, if Simpson was the mayor of Death Valley, he'd have to take political junkets where it's cooler during the summer — like to Idaho to play golf in the Mark Furhman Celebrity Invitational. Simpson could plant his golf gloves in Furhman's bag. Then if O.J. loses big side bets to some of the other celebrities like Lance, Marcia, Johnnie Cochran, Larry King, and Kato, he could claim he couldn't play well without the gloves, pointing to Mark Furhman as a thief.

"I think," said the TV executive, "that once O.J. has paid off his civil case debts on his credit cards, his image will improve. Okay, it's possible he committed a major crime against humanity, but so do many politicians and businessmen. Just look at the Nixon clan and that Keating fella. When they're hot they sell, when not, they rot. Ratings. It's all about ratings. It's capitalism, it's the American way."

America needs its heroes. It's the lawyers, the media, publishers, agents, accountants, photographers and painters who keep them healthy for our pleasure and immortalize them for future trivia games. This case wasn't just a black and white issue. It was a green issue — envy of those who could race to the bank with the most money. What's fame without cash?

Paul Newman was a charismatic and well-liked convict in the movie *Cool Hand Luke*. He escaped from prison several times while his comrades cheered. He was finally caught and killed, but the inmates refused to believe their hero had fallen. He was just too cool. Just like O.J.

If the real life Paul Newman killed his wife, there's no doubt his trial would draw the public's scrutiny and curiosity as well as Simpson did. Would it be a race issue? Someone would probably bring up his car racing exploits. And after all, anyone who can do that certainly could be called a racer.

I admire O.J. as much as anyone for his accomplishments. Most of us aspire to attain more success than we already have. But the higher up you go, the longer the plunge down. Sometimes the race to success isn't worth that risk.

It's just that simple.

Tooting Ferry Horn More Fun Than My Own

I met George Terek, a famous-person-you-never-heard-of. He blows loud horns on some of the 22 big ferry boats that haul cars, trucks and people all over Puget Sound, the inland waters from Seattle north to Canada. He's an interesting man, but not like Popeye. He slurps split-pea soup instead of spinach, smokes good cigars instead of make-believe pipes, speaks fluent Russian instead of Cartoonese and is built more like Bluto than the sailor man. We had lunch to discuss a possible new career opportunity should my writing days be numbered.

I asked how he got started.

"I was a college hippie," he said. "What was I going to do with a degree in Russian? So I hitch-hiked across the country from New York to the west coast several times, doing odd jobs. Then, when I 'grew up,' I graduated from a two-year Deck Officer program. I always liked the water."

He worked several years on tugs and fishing vessels as a liaison between Russian seamen and American businesses, then joined the Washington State Ferry System.

"My first job was Ordinary Seaman. I got to clean the latrines, wash the decks and maintain the officers' quarters. I had to put in sea time, you know." I had lost interest in *this* career already.

"When I got promoted to Able-Bodied Seaman, I didn't have to clean the toilets anymore, but had to do windows — just the outside ones, and load the vehicles and clean the stairs. The inside windows were cleaned by the Ordinary Seamen." This was good news, I thought — more prestige.

"After a few years, I passed the officers' test and got my penguin suit." Now my interest was really whet.

George explained his duties as Chief Mate — supervise the deck crew, navigation, and sometimes steering the 150 to 10,000-ton vessels that vary in capacity from 1,115 people to 2,600 and have diesel engines that generate 20-32 thousand horsepower. "Some have 100,000-gallon fuel capacities," he said, "enough to go to China." Good. I like travel.

George had showed me the interesting computer graphics on the big, round radar screen used for navigation. "But before you can become an officer you must be able to draw charts from memory. This is called 'pilotage.' You watch carefully, many, many times, as the ship passes certain landmarks, then draw the navigation charts."

He thinks he has a better idea — he calls it "swimmage."

"This is where you swim the ferry route to get a *real* feel for the territory. I've swum the 3-mile, 5-mile and 15-mile routes to learn them. Maybe I'll get a role on *Baywatch*," he said grinning. I grinned back, thinking he has about as much chance as I do.

"I'm planning to swim the longer routes, but I'm still looking for someone who has a boat to assist me." He looked at me intensely. I quickly changed the subject.

"What interesting questions do tourists ask when traveling on a ferry?"

"They want to know if the islands are still there in the winter. We tell them they're hauled in by tugboats, just for their viewing pleasure. They ask if the ferry is on underwater tracks and we tell them, sure, just like at Disneyland. And when they ask which end of the ferry to get off when we dock, we tell them it depends on if they want to get wet or not."

I laughed, but he was serious. That was even funnier.

When he told me about the dangers of fog and playing an occasional game of "chicken" with crazed boat owners who aren't required to get licenses, I decided this career path idea was all wet.

I did accept George's offer to toot the ferry horn during my next ride. It should be more exciting that tooting my own. After learning about his exciting life at sea, I decided stories about honking my car horn on driving trips weren't much to hoot about.

Watch Yourself When Watching People

People watching should be an excellent hobby. It's as much fun as watching squirrels collecting nuts for the winter, birds chasing each other's tails, ants carrying parcels hundreds of times their own weight and dogs and cats demonstrating happiness all the time wagging tails and cluttering up litter boxes. People are just plain fascinating, and you can even watch them without going outside in lousy weather.

People watching is also free! It's a hobby you can do well anywhere, any time. And, unlike stamp collecting, model airplanes or photography, you can't mess up or make mistakes — there's not much risk, unless you get caught.

Most people like to people watch, but I've never taken the hobby seriously enough to investigate why. I enjoy watching people until they catch me doing it. When they do, I usually lift my head quickly, trying to find that imaginary UFO or mosquito flying by. I know I'm not fooling anybody, especially indoors, but I've always wanted to ask them what they saw *me* doing that was so entertaining. Then I could share with them what *they* were doing that got my attention.

I decided to do some serious research. I went to a mall, a football game, a park and a grocery store. At each place, I took notes. I figured if I got caught staring at someone they would be curious enough to ask me what I was doing and then I could learn something. I did.

At the Mall: I found a vacant bench, cleaned it up, and sat down to watch a lady in the nearby shoe store. Her face was tinged with anger. Her two small kids were having a tantrum as she tried to get them interested in a pair of white shoes rather than the wild colors they preferred. I wondered why this lady was so frustrated. The kids were just doing what they've seen their mom do at shoe stores — being picky and indecisive. Poor sales clerk! The lady came over to me. "Hey, mister. What are you taking notes on? What's so interesting about me?"

I was polite. "Just admiring your self-righteous behavior with your children." Wrong answer.

"Well, I watched you wipe mustard on the bench, stuff a hot-dog wrapper in the planter and then stick your chewing gum under the bench. Put *that* in your notebook!"

Football Game: While eating a box of Cracker Jacks, an ice cream bar and regular hot dog, I watched a huge fellow sitting next to me consume six large beers, three foot-long hot dogs and two orders of Nachos. He was especially interesting because of his "National Champion, 1996" jacket. I waited until he returned from half-time with his main course, then started taking notes.

"Hey," he said shortly. "What are you writing about?"

"Just curious about the eating habits of an overweight national champion." Wrong again.

"Well, if ya gotta know, I'm a Sumo wrestler in training. Wanna wrestle?"

"No," I said quickly.

"Well, it would be as much fun for me as it was watching you wrestle with that Cracker Jacks box to get the prize out. Don't you think you're a little too old for a little toy?"

The Park: A man coaching some kids on the softball field had a rather disturbing habit of scratching his butt real quick after every pitch. Then after the kids hit the balls, he scratched his. When a foul ball came my way, so did he to collect it.

"You a scout or something?" he asked.

"Nope. Just people watching."

"Seen anything interesting?"

"Well, it's a bit unusual to see the coach, rather than the players, do the baseball scratch."

"Believe it or not, mister, the kid on second base called time out. When I went to see him he wanted to know why you were picking your nose and leaving all the treasure under the seat."

OOPS!

The Grocery Store: A man grabbed a handful of candy from the bin and ate it. I followed him, taking careful notes. Then he took an apple and ate it. Next he took a small bottle of orange juice and drank it. Then he tore out the free software diskette from a computer magazine and put it in his back pocket, leaving the magazine in the rack. Then he went to the check-out stand and paid for what little was in his cart. I followed him outside.

"Excuse me," I said. "I'm doing a story on people watching and you were very interesting to watch. Don't you feel guilty stealing all that stuff from the store?" He looked at me sternly.

"Steal? Hey, the manager knows me. I paid for everything, even the magazine. See this receipt? I saw you taking notes and taking the same things I was taking. Did you plan to turn me in? Where's your receipt?" Uh, oh!

I learned that the odd things we see other people do are really just the same things they find interesting about us. It's like looking in a mirror. The secret to successful people watching, is to not get caught!

I think I'll get another hobby.

The Aliens Among Us: Beware of Strange Neighbors

Aliens, politicians, teenagers, neighbors and other strange life forms have a special historical place in the human imagination.

Crude cave dwellers, loose-tongued orators and deranged writers have always instilled fear of unusual behavior and appearances through creative images and words. *We've found the enemy — it is us!*

My observations of strange, Earth-bound life forms, suggest that we're mostly afraid of each other, not creatures from outer space. But I'm not surprised that the movie *Independence Day* stimulates in us a collective fear of aliens from other places, even Texas, California or Washington, D.C. The "New kid on the block" is a phrase that means a new neighbor is being closely watched for behavior unlike ours. I recall being frightened by the classic movie *Invasion of the Body Snatchers*. Aliens inhabited the bodies of normal humans and neighbors became suspicious of each other's unusual behavior. We don't need movies to teach us this.

During one month I visited Gulf Breeze, Florida, where UFO sightings are serious business, saw *Independence Day*, read a story in *Newsweek* titled *Out There* and watched the *X-Files* on TV. Suddenly I became fearful of my neighbors and watched everyone while walking around town. Who was from outer space? Who was out to get me and who might be a friend? Was the naked guy playing tunes on a wash basin at the lake a *real* space cadet? What about the guy at the bus stop twirling drum sticks to who knows what kind of weird music on his portable CD?

I'm no expert on what explicitly depicts alien behavior, but even I get that occasional glance from someone who thinks that *I'm* an alien. Could be. I'm not sure. I do think I have a pretty good idea how most people determine alien behavior. Generally, it's simply acknowledging their suspect is just plain different than they are.

If you see a teenager wearing sagging, baggy pants, and an extra large shirt, be cautious. The alien is either hiding invisibly inside the clothing, or the teenager is possessed with other-world fashion fantasies. If you see a man wearing a baseball cap backwards, he's an alien walking the wrong way just so you can't see the extra eyes in the back of his head.

If you witness someone at a restaurant turning over a fresh bottle of catsup to pour over French fries and puts it down without getting it to flow, you should become suspicious immediately. If it looks around to make sure nobody is looking and sticks a straw in the bottle, get out of the restaurant quickly. If you're at a country-western tavern and see someone who drove up in a Bronco, dances the *Moon Walk* and wears only one glove, leave quickly. If you speed away in a Mercury, Saturn, Probe, Voyager or Galaxy, don't be shocked if you're followed. Aliens need new friends, too.

Beware of a TV "talking head" that wears a smile on its face while describing terrorist bombings or train wrecks and wears a hat to conceal another strange part of its body. If your kid reports a teacher who silently passes out homework or tests and then observes classroom behavior, he or she is a suspect. If your child is silent, polite and doesn't complain about chores, you know the teacher is equipped with alien powers.

A cop who smiles politely while giving you a ticket, is most likely safe. But if he accepts your bribe and gives you a receipt, speed away and take your chances. When a disheveled panhandler asks for $30, you give him two twenties and he gives you change, he's obviously an under-cover alien.

If your spouse becomes unusually passionate after seeing movies like *Natural Born Killers* or *Friday the 13th Part XXIV*, or laughs at *Star Trek* plots, leave quickly. If your boss gives you a raise without discussing your performance and future and doesn't make you fill out an evaluation form, get a new job.

Of course, you don't have to be from outer space to be an alien. You can be alienated just by keeping to yourself and living, working or playing where someone doesn't understand or want you.

Like the movie *Space Balls* so eloquently stated the obvious; "May the Schwartz be with you!"

Serious Headlines for Serious Readers

Time Magazine's recent cover exposed that highly dramatic (*and already old*) news that comedian Ellen DeGeneres is enjoying being gay. "Yep, I'm Gay" blared the headline. Who cares?

I try to be a serious reader, so this check-out counter sensationalism, this farcical comedy of promotion, made for serious headlines on my brow as I scowled at *Time's* latest ridiculous effort to sell more copies. I canceled my subscription to the once prestigious magazine.

Being gay isn't important enough to get excited about — it's not news. Various sexual preferences for insects and humans are historically commonplace. I guess some moron decided that people who enjoyed sex with their own were having more fun than regular folks, so he playfully coined the word "gay" to describe such behavior.

I considered writing about other celebrities who might soon come out of the closet, but I think we've all heard enough about politicians' skeletons. Then I started to write about how to determine if you're gay, but after reading my line " . . . if you're a man buying lingerie for your woman and try it on first to see if you like it," my wife suggested I refrain from exposing my ignorance and concentrate instead on just the topic of what makes a good headline. Good advice!

Headline writing is an art form which has as much importance as the story itself. If a story doesn't catch our attention quickly, we would certainly pass it by unless our name was in the obituaries and an alert friend let us know. These days, the headlines are usually more interesting than the stories. Maybe that's why serious readership among the masses is declining.

Look at the circulation numbers of the tabloids compared to real newspapers and you'll get the idea. "Five Babies Live to Tell of Their Ordeal" would be a good headline if I were to write about quintuplets. A more proper headline might be "Mother Survives Ordeal of Bearing Quintuplets," but it wouldn't sell as many copies.

Here are a few headlines that made news more entertaining than it was. My own version of the story behind the amusingly misleading headline, follows.

"*Something Wrong in Jet Crash, Expert Says.*" The dead pilot's last words weren't acceptable because he had never crashed before. "*Police Begin Campaign to Run Down Jaywalkers.*" The city's mayor was inundated with complaints from citizens cited for crossing the street where an old crosswalk hadn't been re-painted for years, so he ordered the police to practice high-speed chase techniques to scare pedestrians back onto the sidewalk.

"*Iraqi Head Seeks Arms.*" An assassination attempt on Saddam Hussein went awry and several suspected citizens were tortured in his attempt to locate the arms of a new lover he could trust. "*Shot Off Woman's Leg Helps Tiger Woods to 66.*" During the 1996 Master's Golf Tournament, Tiger lost his putter, so a compassionate woman with a wooden leg offered it up to help him stick some birdies. "*Stud Tires Out.*" Sex in the back seats of cars was found to be unsafe by an out-of-commission local Romeo whose car slid down an icy street and smashed into a tree. He blamed the accident on the town's ban on studded tires.

"*Is There a Ring of Debris Around Uranus?*" Astronomers discover bathroom humor on another planet. "*Stolen Painting Found by Tree.*" A miraculous new plant-growth hormone enables a tree to branch out over a foreboding river, lifting some kids out on its limbs to discover a painting hidden in an undiscovered cave. "*Include Our Children When Baking Cookies.*" A new, macabre recipe for lining the frosting bowl with soap to punish children caught with their hand in the cookie jar.

"*Typhoon Rips Through Cemetery: Hundreds Dead.*" A distraught reporter under pressure from a cynical editor, is sent out to get a good story but finds nobody was injured during the storm. He goes to the local cemetery to uncover some names to print that nobody would recognize. "*Red Tape Holds Up New Bridge.*" An excerpt from President Clinton's program for the 21st century.

I'm sure *Time Magazine* is just struggling to keep up with all the other simple-minded stories that are more entertaining than some of the real news of the day. I understand — it's more profitable. A serious gay issue like an Aids cure *would* deserve a *Time* cover.

But if it were *my* story it would be buried on the third page with the headline; "*Man Discovers Aid for Bad Headlines.*"

And nobody would care.

Being a Nuisance Can Be Deadly

Protecting territory is common to all animals — from earthworms to humans. In the best of circumstances, peaceful coexistence is possible, but fleeing an invasion or destroying the intruder is usually more likely. Since selling my house wasn't an option, I recently stood my ground against an insidious opponent.

In Pursuit of Trivia

My new lawn was truly beautiful. I had worked hard last summer to spread the seeds and fertilizer and had tenderly nurtured the seedlings with water three times a day. Now that the grass is lush and green, I'm allowed to show off my work to friends and neighbors, and I'm accustomed to defending myself and my new lawn against stray dogs and large birds. But recently an unusually large bulge in the ground suddenly triggered my fiercest territorial instincts — I called the good folks at Animal Control.

"Get someone out here quick. There's a giant snake in the grass. It's crawling under my backyard."

"What kind is it sir?"

"How am I supposed to know? It's hiding underground and moving closer to the basement. Hurry!"

"Sir, most snakes don't crawl underground. And the only snakes in this area are too small to make bulges in your grass. Are you sure it's not a mole?"

"Sure I'm sure. I've never seen a mole, but I know a snake when I see one."

"But sir, you said you haven't seen it. It's probably a mole. We'll come by in two days to see how you're doing. Put some Juicy Fruit gum or hair in the tunnel for now. That should do it. If not, get some mole traps."

"Juicy Fruit? Hair? Are you guys nuts or what?" I hung up.

I looked out the window. It was late afternoon and still very warm. I went outside. I sat and waited with my two axes and old bowling balls by my side. I was ready for the slithering thing to show its ugly head. When it started getting dark, I put the flood lamps on and waited some more. Another hour or so went by before I heard some strange noises. I looked in the front yard and saw the small crowd that had gathered. I guess I looked pretty silly sitting on a chair in the middle of the lawn at night with all that gear. I walked very lightly over to the neighbors. "Shhhh. There's a giant snake in the ground. You'll scare it and make it angry."

The crowd dispersed quickly — probably afraid of me. Most of my neighbors have seen me doing strange things in the past.

In Pursuit of Trivia

Some of them were even fortunate to see me get arrested for sunning myself nude on the roof last summer. Anyway, I got back to my chair and noticed the bulge had moved a couple feet closer to the house. I jumped up again and jammed the hose in the back part of the burrow with the water on full blast. I'll drown the varmint!

I waited a few minutes. Then I heard a loud shriek from the back door. "Turn off the water! The porch is flooding!" I wasn't aware of the crafty varmint's secret passages.

After my wife finished dumping the wet towels into the washer, she came out with a cup of coffee. "You're crazy. There's no snake in there. It's a mole."

I finally tossed my finely tuned territorial instincts into the wind and followed the advice of others. Earlier, just in case, I had run out and bought some gum and traps and Mickey the barber had a couple handfuls of hair he could spare. (*My wife had already cleaned hers out of the shower.*) So now I punched a small hole in the burrow and stuffed it with hair and put some Juicy Fruit in other spots. Then, trying to relax with the last of my coffee, I suddenly saw a small head poke up. With an awful squeal it upchucked on the grass. I rushed over with my ax, but was too late. The creature was back in its hole. The slimy little ball of hair smelled like Juicy Fruit.

"Honey, it's a mole!"

I stayed up another two hours with my axes and bowling balls, but the mosquitoes were winning the battle. I retreated into the house, waiting for early morning for another attempt to catch my worthy opponent.

When I went out just before dawn, hoping he was gone from my yard, I was shocked to find six new burrows stretching all across the front yard, and a gaping hole in the side of my drainage ditch. Now I was angry! The yard looked like a malformed waffle. This fella obviously didn't have the stomach for gum or hair, so I finally planted the traps and went to the library to see what moles look like. They aren't pretty, but I figured they don't find us attractive either — probably why they prefer working underground.

The next day I was excited to see one of the traps had been sprung. I couldn't bring myself to pull it up, so my stepson Cory did it for me. When I saw the poor critter all mangled and lifeless, I felt sad, not victorious.

Now I wonder how many humans kill or despise other humans just for doing what we do naturally — or just for being in the wrong place at the wrong time.

Being a nuisance to others can be deadly to you.

Cleaning Up —the Rite of Spring

This important information is brought to you by the good folks at Servicemaster, a company that cleans your house, picks up the trash and takes *out* the cash. The cleaning company grosses $4 billion a year!

According to its survey *Spring Cleaning Report*, most of us prefer visiting the dentist, paying bills, filling out tax forms and doing almost anything except spring cleaning. This is an astounding discovery, I'm sure you'll agree. We need more insightful surveys like this to keep our minds as tidy as our living quarters should be.

"Cleaning takes too much time" or "takes away from other activities" were the most common excuses made by the 1,000 pollees. Other cop-outs were that "within a month of a big cleaning, the house needed it again" and "everyone doesn't pitch in." (*We're not told if the pollees had ever been evicted from their apartments for scandalous slobbery, or were just plain lazy like me.*)

Chemist Dr. Bond, the company's vice president of technical development, urges us to think of cleaning as a sporting event. He challenges us to "play hard ball," rounding the bases and "hitting home runs" in the cleaning field. I challenge him to *my* game of spring cleaning.

In Pursuit of Trivia

First Base: The Kitchen: Dr. Bond says to use a mild dish-washing liquid for counter tops and rinse well afterwards to prevent residue from getting on food. For vinyl floors, mop with a mild detergent and wait a while to allow it to penetrate the ground-in dirt, which reduces the physical work required for cleaning. Finally, the walls should be wiped with an all-purpose cleaner because cooking oils in the kitchen area accumulate dust and dirt.

The Challenge: Brush debris from the counter tops onto the floor. Leave jelly and honey smudges to catch flies. Wait a week or two for the junk to decompose on the floor, then just vacuum it up. When cooking with oil, be patient. Keep the heat on extra low to prevent splattering. If you must cook quickly, cover the walls with Handi Wrap. Remove and replace weekly.

Second Base: The Bathroom: Dr. Bond says for the bathtub and shower, don't mix cleaning products like ammonia and bleach together because they can be toxic. Use an acid-type cleaner to remove hard-water deposits and soap scum. For porcelain/ceramic tiles, use bleach and water to remove mildew. The good doctor must be very clean-minded, indeed — he doesn't provide solutions for the problems related to porcelain toilets.

The Challenge: To prevent scum from accumulating in the bathroom, keep scumbags from using it. Hook up your garden hose outside for pre-cleanings like they do at public swimming pools and Jacuzzis. To minimize toilet-bowl cleaning, a low-cost Porta-Potty for the backyard is recommended.

Third Base: Bedrooms: Dr. Bond recommends store-bought glass cleaner instead of homemade brands. Wipe one side in a vertical motion and the other horizontally, so you know which side to re-wash. Use newspaper or lint-free cloth for best results. Vacuum draperies or have them dry cleaned.

The Challenge: Who does windows anymore? Grow large plants outside every window, so you can't see the dirt. This eliminates the need for cleaning the glass and the drapes. Plants also are good weather insulators and protect privacy. For those who require knowledge of their neighbors' activities, creative pruning will allow just the right views.

Home Plate: The Living Room: Deep-clean fabrics which contain dirt left by "couch potatoes." Use shampoo or dry clean, depending on fabric. Deep-clean carpets that endured heavy traffic during the winter. For wood floors, use solvents such as non-toxic dry-cleaning fluids. Use waxes after cleaning to rid the wood of the harsh effects of winter snow, mud and salt.

The Challenge: Keep a sofa, chair and table covered all year except for those important occasions when the boss, in-laws or household insurance person visit. Buy previously-owned furniture at annual garage sales and re-sell each year. No cleaning required. During the winter months, cover floors with large, plastic trash bags, tape them down and remove when heavily soiled. Your original floors will maintain their luster — no cleaning required.

Nobody hates spring cleaning more than I do. If you follow my helpful hints you'll be clean-free and have plenty of time to spend doing something important.

One drawback. Unless you go out a lot, you'll probably be starring in your own version of the movie, *Home Alone*.

Computers for Dummies

Steve Gregg is a computer scientist. He graduated from High Tech with a Master of Bytes degree and now he fixes computers for a living because installing phone lines for the phone company was too easy.

Now he has something even more challenging — me. I'm just a computer dummy with a high degree in computer frustration, but I can sure mess things up quickly for Steve.

He readily admits to the mistake of being my friend *and* selling me a new computer. (*I didn't really need one. The old one worked just fine, but I thought I should keep up with my friends who had better stuff.*) Steve had always lived by the golden rule, "Never mix business with pleasure." But because he needs a couple shots of Wild Turkey to calm his nerves while I project my frustration on him until my computer works again, he's running the risk of becoming an alcoholic at my expense. His new motto: "Always mix a drink for pleasure; never fix a friend's computer for business." Most of his clients don't have his home number, so he's thinking seriously of busting me to client status and changing his number.

"Hello, Steve, I've got a problem. When I boot up the computer nothing comes up on the screen."

"Did you do anything unusual?"

"When I kicked it, I think my boot hit the start button."

"Well, it's two in the morning. Can you wait until noon?"

"Sure," I said. "Your usual?"

"Okay."

Since I couldn't do my work, I had plenty of time to buy the oysters, shrimp and crab legs for Steve's fishy appetite — the usual payment for his services. I still had some Wild Turkey in the cabinet. Then, I waited, and waited and waited. Steve finally showed up at 6 p.m., just in time for dinner.

"Sorry," he said. "One of my paying clients had a network problem. Somebody had hacked into the Solitaire Security Code and all the lawyers were trying to win money instead of earn it. Well, let's take a look at your problem."

He turned the computer around and plugged the power cable back in. "It's fixed. Let's eat."

"Wait a minute, Steve. How come every time you get it to start back up that icon appears in a different place? Sometimes when I click on it with the mouse it disappears."

"Are you dragging it before you click, or clicking before you drag?"

"I don't know. I just know it's a drag when I can't get the games to work. Do you think I should exchange the mouse for an elephant? Maybe it can remember what to do better than I."

In Pursuit of Trivia

"Very funny. Look, I told you this new computer is top-of-the-line. It has the best hardware available and it's very fast. You need to follow the directions because I can't keep coming over to fix your mistakes. That wasn't part of our deal when you bought it."

"Yeah, but there aren't any directions except that stupid 'help' icon. And even when I understand *what* to do, it takes forever to find out *how* to do it. Then when I figure out how to do it, I'm so mentally exhausted I don't want to do it at all. What's the point in having this machine, anyway? It's more headaches than pleasure."

"Are you using the Internet a lot?"

"Sure thing. I log on to weather reports every day to see if I can play golf the next day."

"That's good. I told you you'd find lots of important things to do when you had the new computer. That information helps a lot, doesn't it?"

"Yeah, but I rarely get e-mail because most of the people I send it to don't have time to respond because they're too busy doing important things. I don't have time to go to the movies, make any money or even play golf because the weather reports are never accurate. And I don't have any money to invest and I don't really care that much about baseball anymore because I lost all my money to an on-line bookie."

"How do you like playing Doom and Quake? You couldn't play them on that old dinosaur you had before."

"Sure. They're great. They keep me from thinking too much about how much money I wasted buying this thing. Now I spend more time on useless things than on my work. Then when finally I get to my work, something goes wrong because I clicked on something I shouldn't and then have to call you to fix it."

Steve left. He's a good guy — never charges me anything except the gourmet meal for fixing my mistakes. He just charged me a lot for the new computer — a mistake that's taken a big byte out of my bank account and time to do what I'm supposed to be doing.

But I have the most modern computer to be a dummy with.

PART TWO

Dollars & Nonsense

Getting Booked for Tax Evasion

It's that time again.

I went to see Dianna, my tax accountant, to brag about my tax-deduction plan for this year. Last year, I wriggled out of some substantial tax payments with my backyard worm-farm business, but a slimy IRS auditor couldn't take a joke — I had to pay up.

Dianna gave me that curious smile and raised eyebrow greeting I get every year.

"Hi. Good to see you," I said. "Thanks for taking care of the audit problem. I got rid of the worms — planted some trees, plants and shrubs to fill those awful holes. Home improvement deductions, right?"

"No."

"Okay. I have a better new business going this year — more deductions, free travel, fame, easy money and . . ."

"Sit down." Her professional glare is worth her fees. "What is it this time?"

"A book. Lots of deductions, I'm sure."

Dianna leaned back as I arrogantly tossed the paperback on her desk. "There it is. *Adventures in the Slow Lane.*" I emptied a folder of receipts. "I'm a publisher now. *Hardshell Publishing.* Look at all these deductions."

She looked. "Where's the income? You can't have deductions without it."

"Sold quite a few already. Test marketed in San Francisco, Los Angeles, Portland and Seattle. Getting ready for my national tour — places like Mexia and Seguin, Texas. Then I'm off to

Dollars and Nonsense

Florida to visit Chattahoochee, Gulf Breeze and Chipley. Then Dunn, North Carolina, and Salamanca, New York, and places like Beavercreek and Fostoria in Ohio, and Jonesboro, Georgia and Kewanee and Monmouth, Illinois, Shawano, Wisconsin and . . ."

"Where are these places? I've never heard of them."

"Doesn't matter. I got maps — figured 13,000 miles in old Betsy — tax deductible, including the good food. I'll meet interesting people, too. Listen to these other deductions.

"The illustrator charged a bundle to draw that cover of me riding the tortoise out of the big city. Printing preparation and production. Now I've got huge, tax-deductible debts for employees who have worked diligently and for long hours without pay — shipping clerk, bookkeeper, salesman, production supervisor, marketing director, editor, writer and insurance coordinator. That's about $100 grand in salary deductions already. Of course, I'm saving a lot . . . I'm deferring payments for doing all those jobs myself."

"Insurance coordinator?"

"Yup. Insurance is killing me. I got picked up several times by the cops for soliciting — malls, restaurants, bars, rest rooms and doctors' offices — legal fees. I got lots of tickets for illegal parking in those big cities — couldn't afford those high-rise rates. Car got impounded three times. I need fame insurance, too, in case fans start ripping off my clothes and humility insurance for when I get rejected and need psychiatric care to help me figure out why I'm doing all this work without making any money."

"Tell me about the other deductions," said Dianna.

"I'm deducting big bucks for the special *Humor Me, Buy My Book* T-shirts I wear. Billboard advertising, you know. Then there's the trip to Hawaii. I bought a tent and air conditioner, lounge chairs, balloons, banners and a surfboard. I figure $10 grand, including air fare, drinks, catering and surfing lessons."

"You can't do that. That's not all deductible."

"Sure it is. You said anything involved in selling is deductible. How can I attract buyers on Waikiki Beach without some sales gimmicks? Gotta go to China, Europe and Australia, too. Just think of all *those* deductions. And there's that trip to Los Angeles to have lunch with Arnie for that movie deal I didn't get."

Dianna wasn't impressed. So I told her how I would promote her on TV.

"I figure when people read how to get big tax deductions by publishing and selling their own books, I'll become a celebrity and be on national TV. I'll tell the world how you helped me account for my success. You'll be swamped with new business."

Dianna lowered her head with fear and sympathy. "You're dreaming, aren't you?"

I asked her to figure how much money I was going to make.

"Nothing. You'll have a $50,000 loss."

"Great! No taxes!"

Publishing your own book brings fame, travel and exciting adventures at tax time. If all goes well, I'll still probably have to get a job to pay off the bank loans. Unless, of course, I sell all the books or can think of a better tax scam for next year.

April 15th: The Deductible Holiday

"You're the best tax accountant I've ever had," I told Dianna. "You've taught me to understand those forms and reduce my taxes so well, I've decided to do my own this year. I'll finally be able to save by not paying your fee — of course I would feel guilty if I get audited and have to drag you to tax court with me."

Dianna was disappointed. She once said she enjoyed fixing up my taxes because I make her laugh with my annual schemes. They give her moments of relief from tax-time stress.

"Why did you come in if I'm not doing your work this year?" she asked.

"I just wanted to show you how much I've learned," I answered, pointing at my worksheet.

Dollars and Nonsense

"Look! I'm going to get back $9,358!"

"How did you come up with this?" she asked. "You only made $15,439."

"Deductions. Lots of deductions. When you did my taxes last year I saw all your figures for using my home as a place of business. You left out lots of things. I also realized I get to deduct medical expenses if they're a certain percentage of my income. Then there's travel and entertainment. So I started adding everything up and . . . well, I had a huge loss last year — more than $30,000.

"There's $3,100 for a new roof, $2,200 for new computer gear, $600 for fixing it, $12,254 in mortgage payments, $1,600 for plumbing and yard clean up. I had to pay a $500 deductible for medical payments when a carpenter I hired cut off his finger sawing wood to repair my office, obviously without much success. Then there was . . ."

"You can't get away with this," said Dianna. "The IRS won't allow deductions unless they're related *directly* to the cost of doing business. These aren't direct and you can't deduct mortgage payments, only the interest."

"Yeah. Well let *me* be direct. The IRS just spent a couple billion dollars on a new computer system that doesn't work, and it's just blowing it off as a loss. There's a direct example of incompetence; and part of that money was taken directly out of my pocket as well as yours and we don't get to deduct it. I'll bet those boys at the IRS certainly deduct all their office expenses, don't they? Even when they work out of the offices of their victims!"

Dianna wasn't laughing. Instead I got that familiar stare. "You're being unreasonable again."

"I don't think so. Look, I've got $18,000 in medical expenses for haircuts, bar tabs, weekend getaways, sex therapy, golf, exercise equipment and videos, psychiatric care and . . ."

"Wait a minute. Those aren't medical expenses directly related to work!"

Dollars and Nonsense

"Sure they are. Keeping hair out of my eyes is directly related to seeing where I'm driving when I go to sell books and seeing the computer screen when I'm writing. Some of my best writing material comes from listening to sad stories at the bar and I always pick up the tab for my informants. I do my best writing when I rent a cabin at the lake for long weekends. Sex therapy helps me understand I'm not expected to perform like I used to, so I don't get too depressed and golf relaxes me so I don't get stressed and revert back to unhealthy habits like smoking."

"This isn't funny," she said. "You'll get audited this time."

"I'm not worried at all, Dianna. My psychiatrist recommended all these things to keep my sanity. He said 'a healthy mind and body are the keys to success.' Since success is directly related to my business, I pay him a lot for weekly check-ups."

Finally, Dianna started laughing uncontrollably.

"This is the worst scheme you've ever come up with. It won't work. No way is the IRS going to send you a refund check for $9,358. But you will get an invitation for an audit. How are you going to explain this?"

"Dianna, I owe you an apology. I was just having fun. I'm not even going to file this year. I've concluded April 15th should be a deductible holiday, so I'm taking the day off and ignoring taxes all together. When the IRS catches up with me, you can do my taxes again. Then I might have enough to pay you with the money I'll save by not paying them."

Dianna is a great tax accountant. She laughs at my jokes when others don't.

Pennies Make No Sense

Pennies make no sense at all. If you want my two-cents worth, they should be eliminated. The penny was long ago raped of its copper content, making its inherent value obscure except to rare-coin collectors and naïve little kids.

Every time we buy something with cash (*a rarity in this obscene credit-card era*), we rely on that little tray of the worthless coins to support the tax demands of our state and local governments.

I try to be optimistic that the government will soon realize the cost of making pennies is more than they're worth. I suppose the economists can't figure that out, as with so many other areas of government waste. Perhaps it's time for us regular, down-home citizens to begin making a stink by rolling all the little fellas into rolls and mailing them to our congressmen for campaign contributions. Maybe all those useless coins will impress upon their penny-weight minds the need to reassess our currency.

Let's send the little things around the world for foreign aid so they can be melted down for making fishing weights or used in "penny loafer" dress shoes for third world military personnel.

The real value of the little orphan coin has all but vanished from our lives. No more penny arcades — a shame. Penny bubble-gum machines are gone. Now, it even takes much more to expose one's ignorance — I'd be hard pressed to come up with something intelligent when someone offers "a penny for your thoughts." A couple of bucks might be more encouraging.

We're cheating our children whose piggy banks are loaded with these worthless, lightweight coins which once were the foundation of good saving habits. Parents must now dole out dimes and quarters to instill in their kids any sense of real cents.

With the penny's demise will come an entire new coining of our culture. The song *Pennies From Heaven* must be changed to *Quarters From Hell*, and the Beatles' song *Penny Lane* will be re-named *Quarter Street*.

Dollars and Nonsense

The J.C. Penney company seems almost obscene and irrelevant. The government will probably require it to become a dime store. "Two bits" still carries some weight, but probably not enough to prevent those once-revered silver pieces from joining aluminum cans in our recycle bins.

The penny was once enough to crank up a Las Vegas slot machine or pay for a treat at the candy store. It inspired large donations to worthy wishing wells, but now even the fish ignore them, attracted only to the glimmer of silver. Where once a penny was worth a wish, it's now a whisper — only a quarter can be heard.

"A penny saved is a penny earned" used to be a worthy phrase. Say that today and you're giving away your age and sustaining the same kind of falsehood that makes children believe Santa Claus will give them what they dream for if they're good.

If you don't believe pennies are worthless and should be eliminated, try this. When you buy something and get a few pennies in change, drop them on the ground and see who picks them up. Nickels work better, but drop a quarter and witness the primitive nature of mankind.

Give a few pennies to a homeless person and learn what it's like to feel real shame. Financial generosity isn't determined anymore by sharing pennies. I gave a handful of pennies to a young kid last week for bringing the newspaper to my door during a rainstorm and he asked politely if I had a quarter instead. Another kid challenged me to "lag" for a quarter, but I wouldn't take the chance. I lagged a penny and lost — and the kid walked away laughing without picking up his winnings.

More recently, I didn't have the three cents for a $1.33 purchase. The generosity of the clerk overwhelmed me when she let me have the bag of jelly beans for $1.30.

The government ought to change the tax laws to a allow a flat rate tax system to eliminate the need for pennies. Manufacturers would surely like to price their products appropriately, too. The dime has become the true, lowest common denominator in determining the simple values of our monetary system — it looks better, too.

"A dime saved is a dime earned," might not sound familiar, but it could soon be integrated into our nation's new economic order of things.

If the government stops manufacturing the worthless penny, it can reduce wasteful spending. I just don't want the pennies buried in my pocket, piggy banks and recovery bowls in stores.

Then I could say the government is still pound foolish, but at least it got penny wise.

Banking on Customer Service

It's obvious why there are so many banks willing to store our money until we need it for Christmas shopping, bookies, IRS back taxes or alimony.

They all need our money but most banks have similar rates. So what sets them apart now is customer service. That's important to me. I've always loved the free samples of crisp, new $100 bills they ask me to test for "spendability," and the birthday card with a blank check to buy myself a present. Nice touch. It's definitely better than the old toasters, coffee-makers and sets of cheap crystal I remember from years past when opening a new account. (*I changed banks pretty frequently then, of course.*)

Things are a little different today. If you don't like the service at your bank, there are lots of choices. Customers demand free checking, car washes at the drive-through, free espresso or beer, (*even lunch depending on where you live*) and $500 at the ATMs when their accounts have only $5. (*It's called over-draft protection, a new service perfected by the U.S. government.*) Customers wearing ski masks are even demanding musical videos of their banking activities for home or prison entertainment.

Dollars and Nonsense

One day last week I walked into my bank, the one I've been using for four years, to get into my safe-deposit box for some cash I've always hidden from my wife. I was in a hurry and the *only* customer in the place. I stopped at the customer service desk, signed my easy-to-forge (*it's illegible*) signature and stood and waited and waited and waited. I felt invisible; nobody in the bank even acknowledged my presence.

After waiting about 10 minutes, another customer came in and she was helped immediately. If nobody had seen me, they certainly began to *hear* me! This wasn't the first time this bank had neglected me. Needless to say, I did what any customer with dignity would do. I closed all my accounts immediately to help the bank realize it had a problem. I was hurt when I wasn't begged to stay, but I suppose if I had more than $89 in the accounts, it might've made a difference.

When I opened my new account at another bank, I informed Kim, the new accounts executive, that I expected to be treated with respect and be recognized when I came in. And if they were busy, at least to smile and wave while I was waiting. And I wanted a free checking account and coupons for free dinners and a few fill-ups at the gas station next door and a personalized parking space.

After I got my new safe-deposit box, I was excited to show Kim the diskette with my new book on it. She said it was against the bank's policy for her to look inside the box. So I took the disk out and put it in her face and said, "Humor me, buy my book, or I'll find another bank." She agreed, of course, and the other employees tried to smile a little.

I was relieved to be assured that my new bank provided "first and foremost, good customer service." I watched as a young mother came in with her two-year-old. A teller came out, picked up the kid and gave him a big hug. I was impressed. Now, that was *excellent* customer service. But when she didn't offer *me* a hug, I warned her about age discrimination — and she warned *me* about harassment! Sometimes no interest is good interest.

Dollars and Nonsense

I offered the kid a handful of change for his piggy bank — a quarter, a couple nickels and four or five pennies. His mother said he knew the value of money. Then he snatched the quarter and scrambled around the bank with a big smile. The teller and the kid's mother were in hot pursuit. As he approached the open vault where the Brinks boys were unloading the loot, he was stopped. He handed one of them the quarter. His mother was right. He was just investing in his budding banking career.

As I left, all of the bank personnel smiled and wished me well. I was impressed with their efficiency. It took just six minutes to open my accounts and two hours talking to the employees to make sure I would get the attention a good customer deserves.

When I returned the next day to get in my safe box to secure some more quarters, everybody was busy and I had to wait and wait. While I was debating about going to *another* bank down the street, each of the nice ladies smiled and waved at me, and the free coffee and cookies were at the table right next to me . . . so I waited.

I'm banking on good customer service once again. I have too much change to put in my piggy bank, but not enough to keep changing banks.

You're in Good Hands with Your own Insurance

Insurance is a risky business — I can insure you.

I once tried to insure my hands for a million dollars. I wanted to protect myself against loss of income if I couldn't write. I was shocked that the Good Hands company writes pretty well, too. It wrote its own policy against losses from characters like me who have wild imaginations. Even the Good Neighbor company put up a fence and wouldn't let me in.

I also failed to get insurance for my autographed World Series baseball and my bronzed baby booties. There's probably a law against this kind of discrimination — but it's probably a good policy for insurance companies.

Why pay large premiums to insure all your valuables if thieves trash your house and leave with little more than a TV and stereo and leave behind the priceless paint-by-number art that Aunt Millie left you in her will?

Insuring our special interests should be easier and less expensive. I got all of my intelligent and influential friends together to solve the problem. After the two of us decided to start our own insurance company, my partner took a vacation to insure himself against embarrassment while I hustled up some business.

During his morning jog, I convinced a weary President Clinton to buy insurance against a "Big Mac Attack" and later sang a persuasive song to convince Dolly Parton to insure her massive assets — her wigs, of course. I sold Mickey Rooney a "wife-insurance" policy and O.J. was happy to pay for our term-life policy.

During the campaign and after lots of small talk, I insured Bob Dole against political defeat once he signed a contract agreeing to say something important. Pat Buchanan was easy prey. He bought a life insurance policy should his followers finally learn he can neither part nor walk on the Red Sea. (*I made him agree to make me the beneficiary.*) Lamar Alexander got insurance to pay for his music lessons to join a real rag-time band if he didn't win at politics.

I insured Mayor Sullivan against impeachment if unhappy citizens sue him for making bad political decisions after sampling too many of his own micro-brews at his pizza parlor. Even my favorite neighbor, Art, bought a policy. He covered himself for fraud in case we found out he re-wired our house without a contractor's license, dog-sat without the proper vaccinations, fixed our plumbing without the proper toiletries or didn't pay taxes on his son Sean's hefty income from washing our cars.

And now our new company is offering embarrassment insurance. This is available for those who want to leave the country after barfing at the table when the boss invites you for dinner and the food is lousy. It also covers situations like ripping your pants or skirt at bowling championships or paying the plumber to dislodge the large meal you had eaten the night before.

Special occasion insurance is also available. If spouses forget birthdays or anniversaries you collect a specified sum to buy yourself a gift for someone who has everything except a spouse who cares. If you throw a party and nobody shows, you get reimbursed for the food and have enough left over to hire some new friends.

With the small fortune I collected in premiums, it was easy to pay the famous Lloyds of London insurance company to insure my hands. Now I'm able to use my writing skills to assist other insurance companies to write policies that more closely relate to the needs of common folks.

Car insurance will soon be announced that ties premiums to the value of the driver, not the vehicle. Life insurance will soon be available that pays the policy holder cash incentives to stay alive rather than die, and new policies that will reimburse wary parents for household damages inflicted by teenagers and toddlers.

Insurance is a risky business. I can insure you. I finally found a company that wrote a policy for my hands. It was expensive, but didn't include coverage for writing bad checks — or bad columns!

Wasting Time and Money

I've always been pretty lucky when it comes to wasting time and money. I seem to have the time to spend money when I don't have any, and the money when I don't have the time to spend it.

The other day I forgot to take a bottle of shampoo with me to the gym. I was late getting home, and I had to rush my shower so my wife would think I had worked out. I also forgot to wet down my gym shirt. Before I could throw it in the washer, she picked up the dry garment and gave me her famous frown.

Dollars and Nonsense

The next day I really did work out, but forgot to buy a new bottle of shampoo. Fortunately, it was raining, so my sweaty hair wasn't an issue when I picked up a bottle at the 7-11 rather than driving the extra mile to the grocery store. I reluctantly paid the $5.14 for the $3 bottle and went home to watch TV while eating lunch. I realized later that I had wasted two hours and 14 cents.

A few days earlier at the mall, I had bought a name-brand work-out bag for my daily gym routine, only to have the bonus pocket rip out when I filled the bag with books for a sales trip. My wife gave me the frown again when she handed me the half-cost replacement from the discount store located only a couple miles further than the mall. My guilty puppy look got me nothing. I think she was still upset about the shampoo, too.

Now I'm working to become more efficient so I can stop wasting so much time and money. Here's how my new, efficient lifestyle has gone so far.

First, I've used the same coffee cup all week without wasting time or water to wash it. Instead of trashing the paper plates and plastic forks, I use them two or three times, and sometimes just eat simple finger foods like pancakes and sausage, cake, barbecue ribs and M&Ms. I haven't wasted time driving to the fast food places, either. I just use my speed dial to call for home-delivered pizza or Chinese food.

Instead of going to the grocery store several times for fruit and vegetables, I've planted trees and a garden. Instead of going several times for paper towels and toilet paper, I've emptied the pantry and filled it with toilet paper and paper towels. I began reading my neighbor's morning newspaper each night instead of watching TV news and wasting time speculating with my wife about what really happened. I saved even more time and money by not buying any more self-help books, but helped myself instead by doing all the constructive little things that my wife tells me to do.

Instead of wasting time thinking about investing in the future, I've been taking healthy walks in the present and spending the pennies I had invested in the past. Now I don't waste money buying shampoo; I wear a baseball hat so my hair won't get dirty. I replaced the wasted time arguing with my wife, by agreeing with whatever she says and doing what I want when she's not looking. I didn't waste money on new clothes, because I worked out at the gym and ate only cheap finger food, so my old clothes fit again.

And now, at the gym, instead of bragging about my progress to Julie, Robyn and Diane, I use the entire session to thump along on the treadmill until I hurt so bad I get to go home early and soak my ankles while reading health and fitness magazines.

I'm such a perfectly efficient human being now, I think I'm qualified as a time-management consultant to teach others my secrets of making money. And if my mind withers in the process, maybe at least I could have enough money to open up my own convenience store and prey upon all the others out there who are just normal like me.

The Price of Change

I told Steve Haug, my excellent automotive doctor, that his price for a lube and oil change was too high, so he suggested I work in his shop for a day. Since I'm always interested in new and higher-paying jobs for the future when my story ideas dry up, I accepted.

His colleagues, Martin and Dennis, smirked at me when I reported for work cheerfully at Accurate Automotive on Monday morning. I was wearing a pair of over-sized, over-used farmer's coveralls that Darwin, my father-in-law, had given me for encouragement. He told me the aroma of manure and oil and the uniform go well together and would give me that look of experience to put customers at ease. Steve welcomed me with a hesitant pat on the back and had me sign a waiver of liability. Then he left quickly to wash his hands.

Dollars and Nonsense

I was excited when the first customer came in at 8:30 — lube, oil, rotate the tires. She would return at 10 to pick it up. No problem. Dennis was experienced in this procedure, so he drove the car onto the rack. I was a little insulted. After all these years, I had become pretty good at getting my car straight on the rack — except for that one time Steve was pointing this way and that and I got confused and stepped on the gas instead of the brake. He replaced the headlights for free, but *I* had to pay for the bumper repair.

Anyway, I got under the car and started to loosen the nut on the bottom of the oil pan. I liked rolling around on my back on that big skateboard — comfortable, but a tight fit. Dennis suggested I come out from under the car — I was having difficulty seeing with black stuff dripping on my glasses and I couldn't turn the wrench completely because the handle hit the floor.

Dennis is a smart fella. After I stood up, he pushed a button and the car went up. I felt pretty foolish forgetting what the rack was for in the first place. After cleaning my glasses I looked up and realized I had loosened the transmission fluid bolt, so I tightened it back up and moved to the oil pan. I got the bolt off without a problem — but I had to fish around to find it in the collection container.

It took me 10 minutes to remove all the oil and gooey cleanser from my hands. Dennis seemed a little perturbed because I used up six shop rags. He pointed at the lube gun hanging down from the ceiling, then nodded toward the car. I could do this, I thought. When I squeezed grease into a likely hole where the front wheel is attached, Dennis panicked. "That's the brakes, you idiot!" Steve came running over to referee.

I claimed ignorance. Dennis agreed. "I thought it looked a little dry in there," I said. "That's okay," said Steve. "Just take off the tire and wipe the grease off the brake pads." At least Steve didn't call me an idiot.

Dennis, frustrated with his first management role, asked Martin to relieve him. For some reason, Martin didn't seem too enthusiastic. I always did like the sound of the bolt gun and after awhile, I got the wheel off. I wiped off the grease, then removed the other three wheels and set them all down neatly.

I knew replacing the oil was more important than rotating the tires — priorities are important. So when Martin went to the restroom I pushed the rack button and watched the car come down slowly. I first took off all three caps to make sure I wouldn't put the oil in the wrong place. I noticed water in one hole and the other hole wasn't big enough for the oil spout, so I put five quarts into a big whole in the engine.

Proud of my accomplishment, I had a big smile on my face when Martin returned. "Almost done. Just need to put the wheels back on."

I had never seen a face contort quite like Martin's.

"Oh my God! Steve, come quick!"

Steve, Martin and Dennis all stared at the car, then at me. The weight of the car had bent the four wheels — and all the oil was on the floor — I had forgotten the oil plug.

Fortunately Steve was able to repair the wheels in a couple of hours and I cleaned up the oil in an hour. When I returned a week later to pick up my paycheck, I instead got a bill for $145 to pay for the damage. I was grateful the customer didn't sue.

Steve must know what he's doing when it comes to hiring new help. He had me sign that waiver and in the end, he didn't have to pay me anything for a day's work. I paid him. Maybe his prices are reasonable after all.

Darwin didn't want that oily uniform back, so I got to keep it. I might want to change the oil in my own car sometime and save some money and dignity — not mine — Steve's.

PART THREE

Holiday Madness

Flying High for the Holidays

Airlines are finally making some sizable profits — good news for airline employees, shareholders and for the aircraft manufacturers building affordable, new $100-million planes. The bad news, of course, is that if you have to hire a winged limo to visit friends and relatives for the holidays, they'll need to put you up and feed you well to compensate for the higher fares. Budget seats on the red-eye are limited to those next to the latrine, or if you're lucky, behind the wall of first class.

If you can't afford the trip this year, don't fret. Although your friends and relatives will be disappointed not to have the pleasure of your company, a sure-fire way to nurture the relationship is to send them the money you would have spent on the budget fare and give them a call during the dinner hour using your choice of phone company promotions.

I'm not suggesting in any way that sending money can ever replace that warm handshake, hug or the pigfest at the dining table, but after seeing on TV the severe snow storms in Ohio, I'd prefer staying home rather than sliding off a runway. Or worse yet, getting stranded in some airport terminal like Cleveland, Detroit or Buffalo. If, however, you have friends or relatives in Miami, Palm Springs or Hawaii, borrow the money (*from them, if possible*) to pay full fare for your trip. Tell them it's in their interest.

I speak from experience. It was 21 days before Thanksgiving, 1981. I was going from Los Angeles to Newark, New Jersey to visit my cousin Barbara.

157

Holiday Madness

"Thank you for calling Early Bird Airlines. How may I help you?"

"Yes, I'd like the cheapest flight you've got from L.A. to Newark."

"What day will you be leaving?"

"Well, I'm not sure, but probably the day before Thanksgiving. I'd like to leave earlier, but my boss isn't exactly thankful that I'm working for him. He said I could leave early that Wednesday, 'though."

"Well, we have three seats left on a three-stop flight that leaves at 5:15 p.m."

"Not that early. Anything a little later?"

"Yes, there is a flight that leaves at 11:30 p.m. There are two budget seats available, but you must purchase your ticket 21 days in advance, no refund."

"Great, I'm just in time. What time does it arrive?"

"Eight-forty a.m."

"Eight-forty a.m.? What takes so long?"

"Well, sir, it's one of our smaller planes. It stops seven times to pick up other budget passengers and cheap fuel at suburban airports. I assure you, sir, it's the best we can do for this low, discount price."

"Well, I don't have much choice. I tried Pan Am, but they're out of business. TWA required an overnight stay in Cairo and United told me I could only charge the ticket on an American Express Platinum Card. I'll take it!"

I was excited to see Barbara. I got to the airport two hours early. The plane left two hours late, but that was good because I finished reading *Airport* before we took off and was more open to reading the month-old airline advertising magazine.

"Welcome aboard, ladies and gentlemen," the captain said in a tired voice. "We'll be traveling at an altitude somewhat higher than usual, 75,000 feet, to avoid rain. The windshield wipers are malfunctioning slightly, but we don't wish to delay your Early Bird experience any longer." That was one relief.

Holiday Madness

I had drunk too much coffee, so I had to go to the latrine real bad. The seat belt jammed. I asked an attendant to loosen me up. She gave me a drink, but I didn't find her humor appealing. I was about to burst when she finally got the buckle loose. I was lucky I had the good seat next to the latrine, so I didn't have to rub bloated tummies in the narrow aisles with the other big spenders.

After eating the stale rice cake and petrified chocolate-chip cookie, I took a nap. I was so exhausted I didn't notice the seven stops when I heard the announcement. "Ladies and gentlemen, due to extraordinary circumstances beyond our control, we'll be forced to stay in the plane for three hours while the ground crews clear the ice off the runway. We regret the inconvenience and are offering free drinks during the delay."

That was good. After I finished my allotment I didn't care that the turkey TV dinner brought in from the terminal was overcooked. We took off again. I said to the nice fellow sitting next to me, "Well, we might make it yet!"

He looked at me somewhat soberly.

"Buddy," he said. "It's 3 p.m., Thanksgiving Day. We just took off from Denver to go back to Los Angeles. The airline is refunding our fares and giving us gift certificates for turkeys."

I called Barbara when I got home. "Sorry I missed dinner. Something came up."

I was thankful it wasn't the turkey dinner. The holiday hadn't ended yet, so I went over to my friend's house just in time for pumpkin pie.

I sent the refunded airline money to Barbara with a note. "I'm thankful you're so understanding! Hope this covers your disappointment. I'll try to visit you again on Washington's birthday. There are good bargains that time of year."

Sometimes there's more to be thankful for at home, rather than looking for pie in the sky.

Finding the Right Words For Valentine Cards

February 14th is Valentine's Day. This yearly "Guiltfest" is a reminder of our neglect — in an ideal world, romance and affection should be daily events.

But this date has an even more important meaning for me — it's the day I was discharged from the Army — I received no flowers nor a chocolate rifle for leaving, but I was almost forced to re-enlist — as a criminal. I had painted a heart on the trunk of my car with an expletive on the arrow piercing it. I had declared my affections for the military life I loved so much. Back in those days, the military police weren't amused — I almost ended up in the brig.

Gangsters have made this day special, too. The St. Valentine's Day Massacre was quite a spectacle from what I've heard, and red roses were plentiful at the funerals. I'm not sure, but those wise guys might still be active cutting down flowers for this festive and profitable annual occasion.

Cupid, believe it or not, didn't fly around naked shooting arrows of love as you might think. From my limited research, I learned he wasn't all that loving. He liked to practice shooting at William Tell's apple. He often missed, causing me to have serious doubts about his real intentions.

My intentions have always been honorable — I think. I'm somewhat cynical about the results of giving cards, flowers and chocolates as romantic gestures. I've probably given 50 or so Valentine cards and 25 flower bouquets to prospective objects of my affection during my wooing career. (*I usually ate the chocolates myself.*) But in my ancient file of love letters I counted only three cards to me — two from former girl friends and one from my grandmother — bless her heart.

Most of us struggle with the right words to put on greeting cards. We can talk easily of our love for money, food and sports, but lose our way when trying to express affection for those who really matter. We're better at letting others write for us.

Holiday Madness

That's why it was easy to make a few bucks off some comrades in the Army who wanted to be creative. As a budding writer I was able to help them with their love letters and greeting cards. Although I'm rusty, I thought about applying for a part-time Valentine's Day job with Hallmark Cards. What do you think?

From Newt to Bill: "Roses are red, violets are blue. I think of you often, and wish you were through."

For the owners of the Cleveland Browns and Seattle Seahawks to their fans: "We love you dearly, but lost money yearly. Now that we're gone and you yearn for a team, don't be angry, but remember this theme: 'We love to play football for fun and profit, but if you don't pay for stadiums and boxes, don't weep for football because you've lost it.'"

For the IRS auditor: "I don't think it's funny when you take my money. Because I'm forgiving on this special occasion, please take my offer of a 20-year vacation."

To Drs. Mahar and Leonard, my dentists: "When I'm feeling lonely and lost in despair, I think of relaxing in the comfort of your chair. Then thoughts of your work make me aware, it's better to brush teeth than eat chocolate eclairs."

From Billy Bob to Bubba: "You kicked my butt in that poker game, my friend. For this my wife left me, alone in shame. I tried the ponies and lost a bundle, trying to recover but only stumbled. So now that you're rich, a Super Bowl rookie, could you lend me some dough to pay my bookie?"

To my wife: "Your eyes are green like a beauty queen, your skin as soft as velvet cloth. Your heart's as warm as a summer breeze and with talents like these, I'm very pleased, you judge me not by my poetic rot."

From my wife to me: "I remember once on this special day, you promised not, another line. You'd better quit while you're still ahead, or find someone else to lie to instead."

She reminded me of the Hallmark slogan; "When you care enough to send the very best."

Now I understand why I rarely receive Valentine cards.

Turkeys and Pigs Don't Mix Too Well

Thanksgiving Day with the relatives was awful this year.

I was in a disgusting mood. I had locked myself out of the house and couldn't fit through the kitchen window anymore, so I had to run down to the public beach to shower and there wasn't any soap. When my wife returned after buying a home-made pumpkin pie, she asked me to put it in the car. I dropped it on the garage floor — we were late — my fault, as usual.

Usually, the hassles of the long drive, the little brats who think throwing toys and mashed potatoes at you is okay because you're family, and the political arguments among ignorant people, are worth the effort just for the reward of being able to forget your table manners and having someone else clean up after you.

Not this year. I looked strangely at the offerings. The numerous Jell-O and fruit salads, candied yams, slashed turkey and chunks of ham, slabs of cranberries, mashed potatoes and the vulnerable assortment of pies, were a vision from the dreams of an enthusiastic surgeon — or a pig.

That grotesque image lingered for several minutes until I began stirring up interesting conversations to ingratiate myself with my wife's family. They never seem to know what to make of me. That's okay, I suppose, because I encounter difficulty in any mixed company where there's lots of food.

My mood wasn't an ally.

I turned to my wife's grandfather. He's a nice old chap, and at 85 had just gotten a hip replacement after tripping in the yard. "So, I heard you were chasing that young blond next door. Can't run as fast anymore, huh?"

"None of your business," he retorted. "She wasn't a blond. It was my wife," he said with her sitting next to him. I asked my brother-in-law what he thought of the Bosnian peace agreement and the U.S. government's shutdown. He stared curiously at me for a moment, looked at his apple pie, held up his beer and said, "Who cares?" then continued watching the TV football game.

I asked Mike, the family's "Harley Man," how his "Hog" was snorting. He gave me that look I've often seen when asking him embarrassing questions. He smiled anyway — a gesture of family tolerance — and thankfully put the knife he was slicing an apple with, back into his leather jacket.

I passed around the cover of my soon-to-be-published book, hoping to gain some respect. One of the little brats was the only one who thought the illustration of me riding a giant tortoise over a brick wall was at all interesting, so I let him throw his toy baseball at me in return for his admiration, but he didn't miss.

When my adoring mother-in-law came over to ask for my autograph I thought it was a little premature, but I thanked her anyway. She looked at me strangely, then lifted her foot onto my lap. "I want one for my cast." She had recently broken her ankle, so we started talking about everyone's broken bones but it just made me think of the turkey carcass which still had some good pickings on it. She told me about a friend who had an aneurysm, "and when they opened his skull, it popped out and hit the doctor in the face."

I tried to smile while feeling that feeling you get in the stomach when you're about to lose a lot of calories quickly. I went to my wife.

"Honey, I'm not doing well. Same old thing. I don't seem to be having much luck talking with your family and I ate too much."

"Have you asked my uncle about his Alaskan fishing trip? I heard he caught a lot of big bass."

"I don't have the stomach for it now. I want to go home — quickly."

It was an awful sight because I couldn't eat it all, but I took a last look at all the bowls, jars, tins, casserole dishes and serving plates with the leftovers in them.

Holiday Madness

I hate wasting good food — even if it does look like a doctor was doing exploratory surgery. Fortunately I'm not the Thanksgiving patient. But a pig with a bad attitude shouldn't go out in public.

At the Christmas get-together, I promised my wife I'd stay away from the food and talk only about football and the weather. Then I'm going to snatch all the leftovers I can carry to eat at home in front of a friendly and understanding TV.

Turkeys and pigs just don't mix too well.

Never Judge a Cover by Its Face

Halloween was really scary this year, but I wasn't sure why.

I had volunteered at the Walden bookstore to distribute goodies to the kids at the Alderwood Mall and was looking forward to the fun.

I happily thought back to my early days, to Casper, the witches and goblins, vampires and werewolves, Frankenstein and Dracula and my first date. I remembered the white sheet my mother put over me and I was a wimpy ghost afraid of the dark, and the cardboard body box I wore as Robby the Robot and that I couldn't get the goodies in my pocket.

I recalled as a big kid being detained at the Houston airport by vice cops when I was dressed up in a black cowboy outfit with dark glasses. I was on my way to a Halloween party in Los Angeles. (*They told me I fit the description of a drug dealer last seen at* Gilley's *riding the mechanical bull from the movie* Urban Cowboy. *After I explained I was really afraid of horses and* real *cowboys and gave them some candy, they let me go.*)

So, I admit, I was disturbed this year by the sight of so many versions of Gingrich, Clinton and O.J. This wasn't the masquerade I thought Halloween was supposed to be. I asked one little fellow with a Gingrich face why he thought he was scary.

"Mommy said he's a political monster who wants to live in a big white house but somebody else lives there now and doesn't want to move. He's a mean person."

His mother smiled as the kid drooled brown Tootsie Roll juice onto his little white shirt.

"Where's your daddy?" I asked.

"He's with my big brother who needs protection 'cause he's dressed up like the president who daddy thinks is *very* scary."

Of course, some of the standards passed by too — ghouls, vampires, clowns, angels and teenagers with baggy pants and skateboards. Even some of the parents got into the act. There were some Klingons, Captain Kirks and even a few bums came by as themselves asking for handouts. Feeling only a little out of place in my Dockers and T-shirt, I tried to get into the spirit of the things.

As a young mother walked by I said, "Open your purse." Surprisingly she did, expecting to get some candy, but when I said "Trick or treat, give me your wallet," she realized a costume isn't necessary to be scary.

I did scare the pumpkin out of one youngster costumed as the Addams' Family brat. His dyed red hair stood straight up. "Hey, kid, nice hair," I said. "How are you going to get that color out?"

"Mom said it washes out."

I looked seriously into the eyes of his smiling mother, obviously proud of her makeup skills.

"Why did you lie to your kid, ma'am? You *know* that stuff *never* comes out!"

The poor kid dropped his loot on the floor and began sobbing. Everyone was staring at me like I was some perverted scumbag. His mother had no sense of humor either. She didn't even thank me for complimenting her son's hair.

You should have seen the look on this burly father when I said it was inappropriate for his little daughter to be wearing a size 50 double EE bra, high heels and fake diamonds to look like Dolly

Parton. When the wig, beard and biker leathers came off, revealing a very attractive female and she said, "You sexist idiot pig, that's my son!" I realized you can never judge a cover by its face.

There were few other interesting costumes and it began to be boring as they paraded by, so I began throwing the candy into the air and directly at the kids' loot bags. I threw behind my back, over the shoulder and between my legs, trying for 3-pointers. When it didn't land in their containers, I slam dunked 'em home. The kids laughed and had fun, but the parents were apparently controlling their enthusiasm for my antics.

After the 1,500 anxiety-ridden sugar addicts jumped, hopped and skipped away, I realized something was eerily different. It was quiet, and I stood alone. Now I understood why this Halloween was scary. I wasn't a kid anymore.

Next year I hope none of those wonderful little kids asks for a mask that looks like me. I wouldn't want to be in the same category as a politician or grown up who takes himself too seriously.

That's my scary thought for the day.

Truthful Santas: Just for the "Ho, ho," Fun of It

I've often thought about playing Santa Claus.

How wonderful it would be to sit like a magnificent king, pompously and politely telling little white Christmas lies to innocent and idealistic children hoping for ponies, drum sets, cell phones and trips to the North Pole to play with the elves.

I have the necessary requirements — gray beard, large, comfortable stomach, spectacles and experience as a political speech writer adept at stretching the truth.

I probably wouldn't make a good Santa though, because now that I'm older and wiser I can't bear knowing the children wouldn't get what they really wanted. I would have to tell the truth.

Holiday Madness

"No, my little friend. Ponies aren't allowed in apartments, drums won't fit in your room and your parents can't afford round-trip airfare and a Berlitz course in Leprechaunese. How about a Barbie doll and a nice little picture book about the greasy little Christmas pig that got away from dinner?"

Well, I've come up with another idea — celebrity surrogate Santas for grown-ups. There are plenty of innocent and idealistic adults like me who like to fantasize, too. But shouldn't we be able to handle the truth, just for the fun of it?

Dolly Parton: "Hi, Santa. All I want is sugar and spice and everything nice. Can I nap on your lap for a couple hours? I like your pillows." "No you can't, but if you put your hands where I can see them, I'll be glad to sing you a Christmas carol."

Tom Cruise: "Hello, Santa. I've always wanted to be a Top Gun, so can I sit on yours for a few minutes?" "Well, my darling, that's an impossible mission. That awful tabloid article claiming I was sterile has rendered me impotent. Sorry."

Robert Dole: "Santa, my husband said I'm getting tired and boring in my old age. I'd like to get a copy of your secret Geritol cook book with your stimulating recipes that helped you campaign so long." "That's not necessary, sweetheart. Obviously my diet didn't help overcome my image. But I'll see what I can do about getting you a copy of Dr. Ruth's new book, *New-Age Gymnastics*."

O.J. Simpson: "Oh, Santa. I've been really good this year. I didn't buy any of those awful books claiming you're guilty, so I'm hoping you'll bring me a complete set of O.J. Cutlery and several pair of those ugly-ass shoes that are so popular now." "Well, that's flattering, but I have no idea what you're talking about. How about an exciting ride in my specially-equipped Bronco snowmobile?"

Michael Jordan: "I'd like to do a commercial like you so I can get rich and buy season tickets to the Bulls' games." "Ho, ho, hum. Well, if you can take this basketball, roll it down the mall into that department store, make it go up the escalator, roll down the other escalator, go into the athletic department, bounce off the treadmill and into the basketball hoop, nothing but net, I'll get you an audition for a Looney Tune gig."

Michael Jackson: "Oh, Michael. You're so cute in your Santa outfit. Where did you get that wonderful make-up?" "Thank you, but that's not make-up. What would you like for Christmas?" "Well, you're a wonderful dancer and I'd like to get private lessons from you so I can be lighter on my feet." "Sorry, I'm very busy now adding another wing to my house for my kid, but I'll be glad to see that Santa gives you a copy of my new instructional video, *Walking on the Moon with Michael*. It'll teach you how to be weightless when the world weighs heavy on your shoulders."

Montel Williams: "I'd like to get an invitation to be interviewed on your show." "That's wonderful. Why?" "Well, I'm good at telling secrets about how I became successful, I can share my pain, my work is very interesting, my mother murdered my father and I was sexually harassed by one of my patients." "What do you do?" "I'm a psychiatrist."

Dr. Kevorkian: "Doctor Santa. This holiday season depresses me. I've gained a lot of weight and I'm broke. I'd like Santa to bring me a suicide kit." "That's terrible. Santa doesn't do that kind of work. But, if you're good, he might cheer you up with an Ultra-Slimfast eggnog mood elevator, spiced with brandy and Prozac. A CD Christmas version of the *Mash* theme song, *Suicide Is Painless* comes with it." "Thanks Santa. I feel better already just knowing someone cares!"

Bill Gates: "Hi, Santa. I'd like an official Bill Gates Billionaire Plutonium Card to finish my Christmas shopping." "Sorry, but Santa doesn't use credit. Perhaps you'd be interested in a complimentary diskette of my new game?" "What's it called?" "*Windows of Opportunity*. It teaches you how to buy my software for fun and profit." "Yeah, yours, not mine. No thanks, Santa."

Clint Eastwood: "Make my day. Ask for something I can't do." "Gee, Clint, can you do something about your breath? Your mouthwash ain't cuttin' it."

Rumor has it that an *HBO* special will air next Christmas about the experiences these celebrities had while playing Santa for a day. Maybe I'll get screen credit for the idea, making me a better Santa than I thought.

Celebrity surrogates can give bored holiday shoppers something to dream about.

Making the Right Moves at Office Parties

Making the right moves at holiday office parties can be rewarding and entertaining. If you move in the right circles, you can obtain promotions and safely make romantic connections. If you circle around the bar too much, however, the consequences can lead to career suicide.

I'm rusty on the strategic maneuvers I used to have to successfully navigate the typical socio-political situations in a crowded room of cheerful coworkers. I've maintained contact, however, with a colleague I worked with at a large corporation several years ago. He's now a professional party planner and was kind enough to share his wisdom with me.

"Clyde, what's the most important thing people should do at office parties?"

"Plant seeds for future benefits. That's it. And stay sober. Drink too much and you'll say things like 'Hey, ya know what? I've always thought you were a real slob. But I'm feelin' good right now, so I can honestly say I was wrong. You're really a genuine SOB, full of yourself and a lot of bull.' This kind of honest and direct dialogue with management can be a career-ending mistake. Like drinking, it may feel good, but the consequences are deadly. Fill your glass instead with 7-Up and put an olive in it. Mingle slowly at first, then go directly to your boss' boss. Suck up. Most people are smarter than their immediate boss so they just act dumb to avoid being a threat. But now is your chance to make a safe political move. After your boss' boss has had an appropriate amount of Christmas cheer, casually tell her how much you've appreciated working for the company for 25 years and how someday you'd like to run it. Tell her how you'd save money and make people work harder."

"But Clyde, wouldn't that be a pretty direct and obvious lie, especially if you've only been working for the company two years and can't balance your own checkbook?"

"So what? Big bosses don't like listening to details. They're visionaries, looking only for big bottom lines and increasing market share. They prefer cutting to the chase. That's how they got there. When she sobers up, she'll only remember that hard-charging, ambitious and intelligent person who told her what she wanted to hear. When your immediate boss flounders, guess who's going to get promoted?"

"Any other right moves, Clyde?"

"An office party is also a good time to safely plant romantic seeds. During the sobering work days of the year most moves are considered harassment. But Christmas spirits elevate moods, so chances of scoring romantic points increase by the hour."

"Isn't that dangerous?"

"Only if you're dressed inappropriately and drop your olive in something stronger than a soda. Be sure to follow the company's dress code and don't wear any cologne. It's also a good idea to skip your morning shower. No one can accuse you of inappropriate behavior if you can't get too close to your victim."

"Then what's the point?"

"Just like planting the seed for a promotion. If your heart pounds every time you see someone you'd like to spend time with somewhere more interesting than the water cooler, you've got to let your desires be known in a safe and secure environment. Polite innuendoes whispered from a discreet distance will be remembered for a long time."

"But Clyde, didn't you lose your job because you started dating your secretary after the party and your boss found out later?"

Holiday Madness

"Not exactly. First, when we got seriously involved, I fired her to avoid conflicts of interest. Then I got fired because, unknown to me, she was dating my boss, too."

"What happened to her?"

"She married him. Then, when I went to their next Christmas party and told his boss what happened, he got fired, and I got his job."

"I see. So how come you left the company again?"

"I broke the budget. Spent too much money for the next Christmas party."

"Any other suggestions for maximizing office party benefits?"

"Well, if you're really glib, you can tell a coworker you despise, that really you think he's terrific and wonderful. Admit you've been a jerk because of family financial pressures. Ask for forgiveness. Say you'd like to get along better during the next year."

"What for?"

"So he won't come back and kill you."

"For what?"

"When he finds out you ratted on him for bookmaking when he was supposed to be bookkeeping, you can remind him about your party conversation — you're still a jerk, admittedly, but by cooperating with management you got a raise to help with your family problems and now, at least, you won't be a jerk to the person who replaces him."

"Yeah, sure. I can see how that would help."

When Clyde left I realized why I prefer my benefits and obscurity as a writer to having fun at office parties. I always said anything I wanted, so my climb up the corporate ladder ended on the second rung. Now I can say and wear anything or nothing and move anyway I like.

At *my* parties nobody listens and nobody watches — usually nobody shows up.

PART FOUR

That's Entertainment?

Challenged by Bikes

I'm always looking for newer and easier ways to shape up and have fun at the same time. I've always been fascinated with bicycles and the strange people who ride them. Maybe it's something in their genes.

I called Chris Chase at the Mukilteo Mountain Bike Company. I told him I was interested in trading up from my 3-speed Schwinn. He was obviously excited.

"Three-speed Schwinn? I haven't seen one of those in years. Bring it in. We'll fix you right up."

I pulled my trusty old mount out of the garage, and with vague memories of having ridden it when I was much younger, I brushed off dust and cobwebs, put air in the tires and walked it down to his shop three blocks away — no sense in adding wear and tear — on the bike or myself.

"Well," said Chris, "looks like you've got a real classic here — a real dinosaur, actually. I could probably trade you for a Spandex shirt."

"What?" I was indignant. "Are you saying my Schwinn isn't worth much?"

"No," said Chris politely. "What I'm saying is Spandex might help you get the look you're after."

"I see lots of people wearing it who shouldn't," I said.

"You're probably right but let's try it on you anyway."

That's Entertainment?

Chris went on. "I personally think it should be outlawed in public except while riding or worn only by hard bodies, especially females. The typical, inconsiderate Spandex kinda guy is frightening. He comes into the grocery store during prime shopping hours, has a paunch and a farmer's tan and lumbers along in front of you to maximize your shopping experience. Down in Texas, North Carolina, or Georgia, he'd be in big danger out in public. But even in most regular places, he's like an alternative life-form.

"Here. Go see which of these pants, jackets and shirts fit your body best."

I humored him. The dressing room had three mirrors — one made me look skinnier, the other taller, the other more muscular. I came out laughing.

"Those mirrors are pretty clever, but no thanks. I'll stick to my jeans and T-shirt and take a chance on the chaffing. Let's talk bikes now. What kind do you think I need?"

"Depends on what you want if for."

"I need some exercise and alternative transportation when my car isn't running."

"Uh, huh." I noticed him glancing again at my body as he came from behind the counter with a pair of large calipers. He started to put the gadget across my butt.

"What the hell are you doing?" I asked.

"Just measuring to see what kind of seat you need."

I shook my head. "How many kinds of seats are there?"

"Well, there are many. There's the banana seat for narrow-minded beach cruisers, the racing seat for pros and wannabes, the tractor seat for . . ."

"Tractor seat? What's that?"

"Well, it's a safety seat for people who require more balance. You know, they have substantial requirements for their . . ."

I stopped him. "And the gel seat," he said, "is for people who require extra cushioning for the bumps in the road."

Chris handed me the tractor-gel combo seat with a big smile on his face. I got the message.

That's Entertainment?

"What's that metal one for?"

"That's not for you. It's for hard asses. But if you really want to be cool and can afford another mortgage, the Kevlar-covered titanium rail seat is fantastic."

I was slowly beginning to get another message. I still hadn't even looked at the bikes yet, and all I could see were dollar signs.

Chris never stopped. We walked over to the bikes.

"Now, here we have the 18-speed, the 21-speed and the 24-speed models that come with steel, chrome-moly, aluminum, or carbon fiber frames. If you're going to ride for exercise, I recommend the 24-speed chrome-moly."

"Why, Chris? I usually only go one speed — slow. Who needs all those gears?"

"Don't you want to ride up hills with ease?"

"Hell, no. I just want to ride with ease where it's level and with no bumps in the road. What other kinds of bikes do you carry."

Chris' professional smile began to fade. He explained that mountain bikes are for the burly, adventurous types, racing bikes are for pros and serious hobbyists, the cross bikes are for both street and rough road use and the cruisers are for long-distance pleasure riding. I wasn't sure which was for me. He had no idea either. Then he mentioned downhill bikes.

"Downhill? That sounds interesting. My kind of bike — easy riding — I only have to use the brakes. No gears to shift."

Chris finally smiled again. "Those are for the mentally challenged. Anyone who wants to go that fast has a problem."

I didn't think I was that mentally challenged, so I ruled those out. "What about that unusual bike over there?"

"Oh, that's a track bike. It's for people who can't get ahead in life and just like to ride around in circles." Now I was getting excited.

"That sounds good. And what's that one over there? It really looks comfortable." It had a recliner seat, one wheel in the front and two in the back.

That's Entertainment?

"It's called a recumbent bike." *That* one, I could enjoy! It reminded me of my first bike — a tricycle.

I still couldn't decide what was right for me, so I asked about accessories.

"You'd need another spare tire [*pretty funny, Chris*], tool kit, water bottle, speedometer, rear-view mirrors, air pump, rear luggage bag, helmet and a few packs of Gu."

"What's Gu?"

"Oh, that's an instant fast-food. It's really big with bikers. Quick energy — this orange-burst is a favorite. And, if you *really* want to be 'in,' you'll need to buy a Global Positioning System. It tells you exactly where you are at all times — physically, anyway. It costs from $300 to $3,000 — another item for the mentally challenged. It's fun to have but if you think you *really* need to have one, you need more than I can sell you in this store."

My wheels were spinning — too much information, too many decisions, too much mental exercise, not enough physical.

"Look, Chris. I appreciate all your help, but I really wish I still had my childhood tricycle. I knew how to ride it and it was cheap. Unfortunately, I traded it up for the Schwinn a number of years ago. There's no way I'll wear Spandex and I'm really not in shape for any of this. Can you imagine what people would think of me if they saw me riding around town?"

"You might consider what we think of you now."

Chris is a big wheel in Mukilteo and a great spokesman for the physically gifted. But I left his store with my Schwinn, feeling mentally and genetically challenged.

Even Travel Agents Need Vacations!

"Yeah, whaddaya want?" wasn't exactly the response I was expecting. Herbert Hipple, my travel agent, is frequently more polite than that when I call him.

You may remember, Herbert is truly a giant of the travel business. He's six foot six and weighed about 160 the last time I saw him. Living in his relic of a cabin on the banks of the Stillaguamish River in Washington State, he sometimes forgets his manners.

"Geez, Herbert, don't you even care anymore who it is before acting so cantankerous? Some of your clients are going to call you a curmudgeon."

"Don't care. I'm still celebratin' my birthday. Turned 90 last month — need a vacation, not more cheap clients like you. When I got back from that Mt. Everest junket a few weeks ago, I realized my spindly legs ain't what they used to be. Had to walk real slow up the Grand Canyon trail when I got back. Couldn't let those kids down, ya know. So what's up? You want another round-the-world spin on a yo-yo budget? Can't do it. Too tired to call all my contacts. And don't suggest I use that Interwave stuff. Can't afford the 'lectricity for all these new computer gimmicks."

It was three years ago when Herbert gave me fly fishing lessons in the Dead Sea — part of his Mid-East bargain special. Didn't catch anything, but there were lots of flies as he promised. And getting fired in the White House Travelgate Scam must have caused him great grief. He booked 22 Playboy models to join him and President Clinton on an unauthorized golfing trip to Australia.

"Have you recovered from that trip down under?" I asked.

"Not really. Those young ladies keep calling for more. They want me to take them on a private white-water rafting affair and then party at my cabin. Can you imagine their nerve? How is a man my age ever going to get some rest. I need a vacation."

"Well, let's get down to business. After you rest up, my wife and I were wondering if you could figure out how we can get down to Costa Rica for the winter? That whirlwind trip to Europe last winter was just too cold. The only thing we enjoyed was riding the warm trains all day. Loved those free passes you got for us from your friend, what's his name? Oh, yeah, John Majors."

"Hey, keep that quiet. Those were a special favor because I had booked dinners for him with Gates and Forbes. Now that he's out of office, I'm going to have to make friends with that new liberal guy, Flair or something. No telling how he'll react when I tell him I was good friends with William Shakespeare and then ask him for freebies.

"Why Costa Rica?" asked Herbert.

"Palm Springs is a lot closer and less expensive. Besides, I'm an old friend of Bob Hope's grandpa. Yep, shot a few rounds with him during prohibition — boy, he sure could fill his cup. I could probably arrange a golf package including free balls, private use of the entire course, a limo and new nets for the goals."

"Nets? Limo? What's that got to do with golf?"

"Oh. Guess I was thinking soccer when you mentioned Costa Rica. Played a few games with Pele there during World Cup practice. Hmmm. Well, how do you like hang-gliding? I know the guy who operates the Palm Springs Tram. I could arrange free passage to the top of the mountain and free pick-up when you're delivered downtown! Ha! That would be exciting, wouldn't it? Could probably book you in a classy room in the hospital. Hope your health insurance is paid up."

Herbert wasn't making much sense, but he still had his humor. Sometimes it's hard to tell the difference, but this time he was way off his rocker; he doesn't use it much, but he should.

"Listen, Herbert. Maybe you should take more time to think about helping us. I know we put you out all the time asking for so many favors. But you do need a vacation."

"Hey, are you saying I can't do my job?"

"Not at all. I just think it's time for you to get some rest. Maybe you should have that party with the Playboy girls and . . ."

"Forget it. I'll just take it easy at one of those highway rest stops down in Florida — take my old camper. I can advise tired travelers where to find a good travel agent for their next summer vacation while I'm sipping orange juice. I can also practice for the new side trip for my Disney World Adventure package."

"What's that?"

"Gator wrestlin'."

I heard Herbert's muffled chuckle. He's a pretty clever businessman. He knows damn well most of those tired travelers or their relatives have already used his services.

"So what are you going to do this summer?" he asked.

"I think we'll stay home and rest. Sometimes the best vacation trips are none at all."

Anarchist Pitches New Rules for Baseball

I wanted to write something interesting about the presidential campaign this week, but nothing important came to mind. Instead, I talked politics with Eddie. He's the head waiter at the Marco Polo Restaurant where I hang out.

He's a hard-working and caring anarchist with a political science degree. He believes the world's wealth should be spread among us more evenly, so I cleaned my plate of the good Mediterranean food and told him I'd send his tip to Somalia.

Eddie didn't appreciate my humor, so we decided to talk about baseball instead of politics. Anarchists, I learned, don't like authority. Eddie once was obsessed with baseball until The Strike, the introduction of wild-card teams in the playoffs and various other anomalies, ruined the game for him. He's since bounced over to basketball. But he still likes to talk about his 1993, 10-week, cross-country tour of 14 major league baseball parks. In order to afford the adventure, he slept in his Geo Metro, camped out and only occasionally popped for a motel.

That's Entertainment?

He didn't spread much of his wealth around anywhere else either, saving even more money at the games by eating sunflower seeds and taking his own bottled water — tap, of course. He learned much more about baseball, especially after visiting the Hall of Fame in Cooperstown, New York. I lightened him up when I asked if he saw my bronzed Little League glove there. Then I asked him, if he could be Supreme Commissioner of Baseball, how he might change the rules of baseball and become a fan again.

Baseball According to Eddie

Vendors: Peanut and soft drink vendors would be able to eat and drink their wares while on duty, as long as they were licensed. The peanut vendors must pass a two-week, bag-tossing, safety training program and the drink vendors must pass the *Coke-Pepsi Taste Challenge* before dispensing their drink of choice — but only if it's the right one. Wages would be increased from peanuts to Cracker Jacks.

Umpires: Balls and strikes would be discussed with the pitchers and batters when there was any doubt. Discussions would be limited to 30 seconds. If no agreement is reached, a bench-clearing brawl, limit two minutes, would settle the matter. The ineffective umpire would have to leave, and the brawl's winning team manager would call balls and strikes for the rest of the game.

Programs: Printed programs would be interesting — no advertising. Pictures and editorial content must be real, true-life action. The "Get your programs here!" chant would change to "Read all about it!" referring to players' off-field shenanigans, private affairs, contract negotiations and what they really ate or wore rather than what they endorsed. *National Enquirer* reporters would write all the editorial material.

Post-Game Interviews: Players no longer would be restricted to lying when answering boring questions. The old version: "Well, it was a good pitch on the outside corner, but I just kept my eye on the ball looking for something to drive and it went out. I was just lucky, I guess." The new. "I needed a homer to win the game and the bet with my girl friend so I could get lucky tonight. I swung as hard as I could because I'm a damn good hitter and want to make sure I get that $30 million contract when I become a free agent next year." The old version: "My curve ball wasn't working too good, so I threw more heat. Breaking the strike-out record isn't important. Winning the game for the team and fans is." The new: "That team doesn't have any hitters. It needs help. I just had to get the ball near the plate. They'll swing at almost anything."

Player Behavior: Spitting, swearing, crotch-scratching, bat and helmet throwing, dirt-kicking and beanings will be banned to protect innocent children, but only until the 7th inning. Then parents must stretch and take their kids home so the real fans can enjoy the rest of the game. In extra-inning games, tired players can run from first to third if they can escape being tackled by the pitcher. If they hit a home run, they can run straight home.

I'm hoping Eddie isn't really too serious about his suggestions. Baseball needs rules. Anarchy is not good for the game, although it could make it more exciting.

Eddie got me thinking, so I'll spread my wealth around. I got two free bleacher tickets to a game. I hope he'll join me to rekindle his old flame. Maybe he'll carry the water jug if I spring for the sunflower seeds.

Golf for Dummies

Golf began when cavemen learned to roll lizard eggs into holes in front of their caves. It was a competitive challenge and a means for the winners to secure their morning meals. Their primitive clubs made of tree limbs served a dual purpose — to play the game and to smash intruders attempting to disturb their most important social activity aside from hunting and breeding.

Golf remains a delicate social phenomenon. Although modern golf balls are less sensitive to abuse and the clubs are now fashioned somewhat more scientifically, the game has maintained its standing as a major social function in many parts of the world. Its practical side has also evolved. Today, scrambled eggs aren't on the minds of most golfers, but *in* their minds — they play for pride, beer and a few bucks.

Cavemen tolerated savage behavior, but cheating was out of the question. Death by bludgeoning was the accepted punishment. Today's golfers are more civilized. They prefer humiliation to maintain order on the golf course. If you cheat *or* behave like a savage, your companions will restrict your course appearances to when they need a caddy — unless you lose frequently and pay your debts immediately.

I've refused for eight years to be Derek's caddy. He taught me everything I know about golf etiquette. I call him the "Highness of Politeness," but I live far away now, so he has no clue to how I behave on courses near my home. He called recently to ask if my game and etiquette have improved. He mentioned the possibility he might let me play in a tournament with him for old time's sake, although he once swore that would never happen again. I never understood why he got so angry the last time we played when I replaced his ball on the green with a lizard egg.

"No, Derek, I stopped telling strangers that I'm Arnold Palmer's caddy when I tee up. I just say I played a couple rounds with him to make them nervous. It keeps them from offering foolish bets I can't win. I never did learn to say no to you, did I?"

"Has your game improved?"

"Oh, yeah. You taught me not to cheat, so now when I hit the ball behind the trees or in the bushes I use some of my new trick shots. My favorite, even if I can find the errant shot, is to put the ball in my pocket while I'm out of view of the others and toss a new one in a good spot where they can find it when they come to help."

"That's cheating."

"Not really. It's good etiquette. You always told me not to spend more than a minute looking for lost balls if I can't see the green from where I thought it landed."

That's Entertainment?

"Do you count the extra shots you used to forget when hitting out of sand?"

"Sure. I count them all. But once in awhile I forget how many shots it took to get there, so I just round off to an even number. On par 5s, either 4 or 6, on par 4s, either 4 or 6 and on par 3s either 2 or 4. It works out pretty well."

"Oh, geez. Do you still give advice when someone's about to hit?"

"Hell, no. One big dude started to come after me once because he didn't like my advice, so I don't give it anymore unless I'm walking down the fairway by myself."

"What advice did you give him?"

"I told him to dump his wife and trade in his red shorts for a pair of Dockers."

"Are you nuts? What's that got to do with golf?"

"Well, he asked me how he could improve his image and I just did what you always told me."

"What's that?"

"I told him *very* politely and calmly that his bandy legs looked like old tree branches and his wife could improve her game playing with kindergartners instead of us. But I gotta tell ya, Derek, I've really learned to tone it down when I make good shots. Instead of screaming 'look at that one, look at that,' I just tap each guy on the shoulder and point at my ball before he hits his."

"Oh, God! That's terrible. Don't people get tired of you doing that all the time?"

"Oh, no. I only make about two good shots a round, so they don't really mind. They seem glad I'm having such a good time. Besides, I clap really loud when *they* make good shots, so how can they get mad at an avid admirer?"

"And what about standing in people's way when they're trying to putt?"

"I don't do that anymore. Since I've learned to chip so well, I don't have to putt. Whenever I get onto the green, I just pick the ball up and walk to the next hole to advise the group in front how I keep my score low and then critique their swings. I'm so honest now, just like you taught me, I even return their balls that I accidentally hit when I can't find mine."

"Are you still throwing cigarette butts on the green?"

"Hell no. I gave up smoking seven years ago after heart surgery. The doctor said smoking would take several years off my life. So now, to take several strokes off my score, I carry a six-pack with me instead . . . can't remember all the shots . . . and I leave the cans in the bushes to mark where I lost balls so I can look for them during my next round."

Derek was trying to be polite when he hung up. He said he'd let me know about the tournament. In the meantime, I'm writing a golf etiquette book. It's titled *Gorilla Golf*. It will be dedicated to Derek and the original creators of the game.

If you can't win at golf, you might as well humor it.

Dog Training Isn't for Everyone

I received an invitation in the mail to participate in the 1997 Iditarod dog-sled race in Alaska. I was pretty sure the sponsors didn't want to put the reins on me for some healthy outdoor exercise, but I called, just to be sure.

"Yeah, just got the info on your offer to win a free dog-sled ride between Nome and Anchorage. I don't want to put the sled before the dog, but you didn't mean that I would be harnessed with the dogs, did you?"

"Of course not, sir. We're just trying to harness your bid of $500 to sponsor one of the mushers and increase the winning purse. The highest bidders will get to ride in the sled and participate in dog-handling chores."

I could do that, I thought. Cheap thrills and cleaning up after dogs have always been on the credit side of my balance sheet.

That's Entertainment?

The man with the rugged voice explained that the Iditarod commemorates the 1925 event when dog-sled teams rushed serum to critically ill children in Nome, crossing through several rural villages and two mountain ranges. I was impressed.

"So if I bid a lot of money I get a free ride and a chance to win some big money?"

"That's one way of looking at it," the man chuckled.

"How long does the race take?" I asked.

"That depends on how fast and durable your team of 11 dogs is. It also depends on how durable you are and how well you can tolerate frozen TV dinners."

"Well, I once ran a mile with my boots on during Army training 30 years ago."

"I'm sure you could handle it then. Why not make a bid now so you can participate in this adventure of a lifetime?"

I thought for a moment. "Okay, I'll bid $10,000 on Jeff King, the champion mentioned in your publicity."

"Sir, that's very generous of you. Are you sure?"

"Sure I'm sure. I like getting free rides in the snow and ice. My skiing abilities are slipping with age, so I'll just pass up my ski adventure and try this easy one. When do you need the money?"

"By January 31." He was real happy. I was real clever. No way would I spend that kind of money to freeze my butt off and eat only frozen foods. I would get my own team together, arrive unannounced at the starting line, and win the big bucks.

"Great," I said. "The check will be in the mail in January."

I got busy. I hung up the phone and ran over to the four nearby neighbors who have barking dogs. I convinced them to let me borrow their pets and $1,000 for "a great opportunity." I promised them well-trained dogs and a percentage of the winnings. Then I walked around the neighborhood with a new, positive attitude. I looked closely at every dog that yapped at me and considered its size and barking ability to determine if it was equipped and motivated for the challenge. I found seven more healthy specimens and seven people willing to part with their money.

We got some new snow in the nearby mountains, so I borrowed a pick-up and loaded the 11 dogs for the first training session. The rowdy bunch of critters ranged in size from an extra large mutt to a very small poodle. The Polaroid pictures with each of their names on the backs were very helpful when calling out their names every 15 minutes when it was time to eat. Fortunately there were only two Busters and two Daisies. The rest had colorful names like Sandbag, Charlee, Clyde, Blackie, Blondie, Goldie and Silver. I pleased them by feeding and petting them frequently the best I knew how, so they learned very quickly who the boss was.

They kept me in control by occasionally giving me an unfriendly snarl when I tried to keep them from sniffing each other, so I put the females in the lead positions and the males in the back of the pack so they would run faster. I let them bark as loud as they liked when responding to my command, "mush!" The new word must have appealed to them because it meant eating time, which was often. Better than the usual "shut up" and no tasty reward at home.

There wasn't a lot of snow this early in the season, so I kept the workout sessions short and downhill. When they took their breaks and I had to pull the sled up to the top of the hill again, they napped in the pick-up. I was happy to have such smart canines working for me. So smart in fact, that after only two weeks they allowed me to join them for "mushing." Dog food doesn't taste that bad and it would be less time-consuming to eat during a long race — quicker than waiting for TV dinners to thaw out in the cold.

During a dress rehearsal in the third week of training, Blondie bit Goldie and Clyde tried to ride Silver. Charlee had become good friends with Sandbag, so they both laid down to discuss going on strike. I "mushed" and "mushed" but they didn't respond anymore. I had fed them too much. They were lethargic with bloated egos.

The owners thanked me for my enthusiastic, but failed effort, and demanded I return their $1,000 immediately. I tried to get paid something for teaching the dogs to stop barking, but as I was leaving they started up.

When their owners said "Hush," they barked even louder.

Dog training isn't for everyone. I hope the Iditarod people aren't as disappointed in me as my neighbors.

Summer Driving Tips You Don't Want to Know

Travel writers and agents don't tell us everything about summer car trips. I don't blame them.

If they did, we'd stay home rather than fight crowds or try to outsmart the highway patrol or lie awake all night in motels where some people think midnight swimming parties are the best way to avoid sunburns or listen to kids chanting, "Are we there yet?" and "I gotta go . . . *now!*"

I discovered on my own 13,000-mile, 7-week, around-the-country trip, that experience is still the best teacher. Here's just some of what it taught me.

The Truthful Guide for Summer Driving

Auto Safety: Use lots of insect repellent on the windshield and keep a spare roll of toilet paper in the trunk. It's extremely dangerous to drive if you can't see that isolated rest room while passing through America's wastelands. Keep a trash container on the floor of the back seat to keep fast-food wrappers and pop cans from clogging up the spaces between your foot and the brake pedal. Don't play "Let's see how far we can go on *empty*" when your practical and worried spouse starts hollering to pay attention to the road sign that reads, *Next services 190 miles.*

Motels: Always find a motel before dark. If you wait too long, *No Vacancy* signs will force you to settle for leftovers — those with clogged toilets and vacationing maintenance engineers, green scum on green shower walls that fool nobody, economy soap bars

That's Entertainment?

barely large enough to cover critical body parts, and clerks who, with a curious smile, ask if you'd prefer hourly rates. If you want a classier motel with a continental breakfast, but the *No Vacancy* sign is lit, sleep in your car, enjoy the breakfast in the morning and check out with a grateful, "The parking lot was very comfortable."

Evading the Highway Patrol: Exceed the speed limit only when you're between trucks or behind cars fancier than yours. If you're suddenly followed, immediately turn on your own flashing emergency light. Tell the officer you were only speeding to the next town for a repair shop — smoke was coming out of the hood — you didn't want to be on fire in traffic. Offer a complimentary snack and soft drink to the concerned public servant.

Spousal Courtesy: If your spouse is unhappy with the way you change lanes, your speed, your choice of audio programs, when you turn the air on and off, when you open and close the windows, your singing or the driving with no hands while eating a sandwich or applying make-up, smile widely and pull out the one-way plane ticket home that you purchased for just such an occasion.

Map Reading: Modern maps simply indicate with red, black, dotted, green and broken lines, which are the best and fastest roads to get you where you're generally going. Once there, don't be misguided by the old-fashioned locals who draw maps on napkins to get you to the exact location. Remember that many people don't get summer vacations and are envious — but they still get good laughs from practical jokes.

Exercise and Diet: Load your ice chest with healthy fruits, sandwiches, diet sodas and non-fat chips. When stopping at McDonald's to eat the *good* food, lift the box of fantasy foods out of the trunk and put it back unopened. This will satisfy your minimum daily requirements for exercise. Vacations are for escaping reality, not dealing with it.

Washing Clothes: Take few clothes with you, but lots of large plastic trash bags to store your dirty underwear. Avoid the *Out of Order* signs on over-used motel and Laundromat washers and dryers. Instead, take time to explore bargain shopping in small towns for new clothes. Clothes make good souvenirs, too. The bags of dirty underwear won't spoil when next to the ice chest with the other unmentionables — smells a little, but won't spoil.

Traveling with Kids: Take lots of games. My favorite game is, "You'll like staying at grandma's with your cousins instead of going with us just to look at lots of mountains, farms and trees."

Saving Money: Stay home and watch *ESPN*, the sports network. It's safer, saner and inexpensive. You'll see wonderful tourist spots from around the world as commentators tell stories of where the athletes came from and where you might go. To save more money, turn off the TV and take a walk.

Getting Good Pictures: You already know what you and your family members look like, but have a neighbor take a picture of your happy crew in front of your shiny car just before you leave. Buy post-cards of your favorite stops. And to save money, load up on those free brochures you get at the motels and tourist places and cut out your favorite photos. When you return home, have the neighbor take another picture of your weary faces and dirty car.

There! A complete record of your wonderful journey.

When you return from your summer motoring experience, I'd like to hear from you. Your tips can be included in next year's *Truthful Guide for Summer Driving.*

Standing On Your Own Two Feet Isn't Easy

My annual Canadian ski adventure on Whistler Mountain had a new twist this year. I learned the weight of heavy foods isn't conducive to graceful skiing.

We've been taught to believe persistence overcomes any obstacle, enabling us to stand on our own two feet. But when the obstacles are big rocks, trees, wild teenage snow-boarders and slick snow, it's not so easy. But I'm still a believer. Although my ankles are still swollen, it was encouraging that I could still devour loads of good food. The added ballast didn't help me ski better, however.

Someday I'm going to stand up on skis longer than I can sit at a dining table.

Cuz, the owner of Spicy Sports Ski Rental, was glad to see me again.

"How ya, doing, Pinkie," he said. (*I earned the nickname on my first visit after accepting the pink ski poles appropriate for my ability.*) "Ready for another try, eh?"

I got fitted, picked up the pink poles, checked into the hotel and ate a big dinner.

In the morning I ate a big breakfast for more energy and more ballast. Then we went to the top of the mountain where it was snowing — the ground was a white blur. "Bonsai!" I went straight down — it took a few clumsy moments to get out from under the pile of snow, but my wife didn't laugh this time. She slowly wound her way down the mountain, ignoring, without sympathy, my childish, macho antics.

I stopped for a big lunch before my next run. At the top, I took a deep breath, staring down boldly at the challenge before me. I went slowly at first, picking up momentum and confidence — plop! A nice lady in her 70's stopped to help me get my skis back on.

"Son," she said, "if you want to age gracefully, slow down."

Up again, I made slow, wide turns, pushing the edges of the skis hard into the snow. After a few more minutes of painful, burning sensations in my calf and thigh muscles, I fell. I finally got down the mountain successfully, and met my wife and the boys just in time for a big dinner. I told bigger lies about how well I did.

The next day, after a big breakfast, they observed the truth — I fell down putting my skis on. Of course, I blamed the ill-fitted boots, so *Cuz* gave me the high performance type the pros use. I wanted to defy death and whiz down the mountain with unwavering courage. I appropriately exchanged the pink poles for black ones. It didn't work — I almost died trying to keep my body going as fast as my high performance feet. Fortunately, my enlarged stomach cushioned the bumps I encountered on the way down the slope.

On the last run of this year's adventure, I came upon four ski instructors looking at me curiously as I slowly went by. One shouted out, "Whoa! Come here." They were on their afternoon break working on teaching techniques. "How would you like to be a Guinea Pig?" They took me to the top of the lift, assuring me they could solve my problems.

Steve, Mike, Dave and Graham of the Blackcomb Ski School are probably doubting their teaching future. These devoted gentlemen spent the next hour trying to help me get down the mountain with a hint of grace. They failed. When they said "Turn," I went straight and when they said "Crouch" I stood up. When they said "Relax" I did — and fell again. But it was good having them around to help me up. I still have trouble doing that gracefully, too.

My wife, Cory and his friend Scott were grateful I didn't buy the usual illegal quantity of duty-free booze on the way home. We crossed the border this time without the fear of being interrogated again. I still got the suspicious glare from the crotchety border guard, but he was distracted by a nude motorcyclist, obviously more interesting than me, and for sure, a lot *cooler*.

I'm still confident persistence helps us stand on our own two feet. I signed up for more ski lessons next year to be sure. But I also hope persistence helps with my new diet.

I'd like to get off my chair and start walking gracefully again on my sore legs.

It's Time For a Vacation When . . .

Everyone needs a vacation. "Time outs" aren't just for athletes to catch their breath. They're a necessity for everyone to escape the stress of making a living — even criminals go to jail occasionally and politicians get plenty of recesses.

That's Entertainment?

You know when you need a vacation. It's quite simple — your attitude goes south and whatever you do goes with it. You're burned out, kaput, adios—you don't care anymore. This is true for everyone, even humor writers.

Obviously I need a vacation. Just read this column and you'll see I'm brain dead — exhausted. I'm not asking for sympathy — just send money. I'll use it for golf lessons and air fare to any place where I can regain my composure and composition.

I started out trying to write about several humorous ideas this week — criminal bomb cases, the presidential race as an Olympic event, yard care, the baseball All-Star Game, White House files, trees, insurance forms, sex, inaccurate weather reports — I couldn't get rolling on any one topic — my humor began to sour. Here are some examples of what I was thinking.

I don't care who lives in the White House, as long as my name is on the *A* list. I don't care which party invites me, as long as the food is good and the donkey or the elephant don't kick and stomp on my frail body. And the presidential race better not interfere with Olympic TV coverage — especially not those great Coke and Nike commercials. I need a vacation.

The Unibomber and the boys from Oklahoma City and Saudi Arabia, should put on a Fourth of July fireworks show in Death Valley without goggles, gloves or water. And now that the two giant trees in our front yard have been cut down, I'm relieved I won't have 22 large trash bags to fill with leaves in the winter, but I do worry that those miserable crows won't have a decent place from which to squawk while I'm working or sleeping. I need a vacation.

I called my wife last week to ask her if it was okay to stay overnight on a one-day business trip. I had wanted to take the opportunity to play a free round of golf in the morning. She was obviously enjoying *her* vacation; she described her new lingerie, how nice the bubble bath was and how glad she would be to see me that night. Ridiculous choice — lost 12 golf balls in the water the next morning. I need a vacation.

That's Entertainment?

I worry about friends in Texas where the drought has seriously hampered cattle production, but I'm more concerned this week that there will be enough steak and hamburger meat for Fourth of July barbecues. And who cares about that baseball All-Star game? My favorite players aren't playing — Sandy Koufax isn't pitching and Mickey Mantle isn't hitting — some of the new kids haven't even heard of Cooperstown yet. I need a vacation.

When I went through my pile of bills and the other junk mail where I frequently get my funny ideas, I saw the insurance company forms I've ignored three times already — it wants more details about our house, cars and whatever else it can collect premiums for that really isn't worth much. If the company wants to know so much, it should send somebody out to the house to fill out those damn forms — considering those high premiums we pay. After filling out the forms, I decided this was a good idea worth writing about. I need a vacation.

You know it's time for a vacation when nothing goes right. Awhile ago I had a dent in the car repaired at the body shop. And finally, a few days ago, testing this new, extra-strength soap to wash the car for the first time in 12 weeks, I was pleased with the results — even the new paint came off the fender! I need a vacation.

What I really need is to escape from the prison of my mind. The brain cells are burning, my humor is dying. It's so bad, in fact, on this Fourth of July, I'm more excited to see the movie *Independence Day* than to celebrate our country's freedom. The movie is about aliens trying to conquer our entire planet and how we fight back. I'm rooting for the aliens.

Now I'm sure I need a vacation.

That's Entertainment?

This Adventurer Knows His Limitations

The challenge to prove my manhood was too much.

My wife and her son Cory, experienced outdoor adventurers, coaxed me into an exciting, action-packed weekend of white-water river rafting and horseback riding — I had become a wuss in my tranquil life, rather than the wannabe tycoon who once rode down the powerful corporate stream of unconsciousness saddled in a desk chair.

We arrived in Winthrop, a tourist town in eastern Washington that tries desperately to replicate a John Wayne movie set — the gas station, pizza houses, ice cream parlors and espresso coffee outlets were aptly dressed in neo-western garb, but the parking stalls were filled with cars instead of horses.

We checked into our motel where I immediately began demonstrating my manly aptitudes. I jumped onto the inviting hammock, falling to the ground. I succeeded the second time, but was asked, much too soon, to abandon my favorite adventure for the real ones.

We found the Chewack River guest Ranch in an hour. It was only two miles away, but my military map-reading skills had diminished as I navigate the unmarked mountain roads — fortunately my wife pointed out the *Horseback Riding* sign I had driven past before we got to the next country.

Don, our host, gave us basic instructions. They were simple so I didn't pay much attention — the cute barn dog was more interesting and receptive to my coddling than Starla, my 4-legged hostess for the trail ride. I figured, once again, my past experience would carry the day, but this wasn't my day — the pony rides didn't prepare me for this — my foot slipped out of the stirrup — I fell to the ground. Even Starla seemed amused. She made funny whining noises, then walked over to the trough for a drink, allowing me time to regain my composure. The humans smiled politely.

The beauty of horseback riding is you don't have to climb up hills or walk through streams and get dirty and tired. But when I kicked Starla gently in the ribs to show off my manly prowess by galloping past the others, I forgot to stand up in the stirrups. This wasn't good. Although I was able to hang on, and Starla kindly stopped short of the stream, I was scared so much from the near mishap, I had to get off to calm down. The others trotted past me laughing as the muddy water covered my external signs of embarrassment.

The first adventure didn't improve my image, so I became even more determined to prove myself when we met Steve from Osprey River Adventures. He, like Don, gave us survival instructions. Again, I didn't pay much attention. "I'm going to sit on the back of this raft and let you guys do the paddling," I told him, disregarding his admonishment that the back is where the most turbulence is felt.

I had to prove *something*, didn't I?

We slowly moved down the river — very slowly. When we crossed over the first rapids I was disappointed. It was easier to hang on to the raft rope than it was Starla's reins. I wanted to know where all the white water was. As Steve was explaining that the river was at the season's low point, I relaxed, let go of the rope, and almost fell off backwards as we hit a big rock. "Whoa!" is not just for horses.

After two hours of easy rafting, we stopped for lunch on the river bank. It was extremely hot, so Steve jumped into the water. Cory touched it. It was extremely cold. I challenged him to jump in. He challenged me back. Then, just as he was about to splash me with one of the raft oars, I dove into the icy water, determined to avoid another embarrassment. He was amazed at my daring. He and my wife followed my lead. I had proved my manhood!

After floating over a few more easy rapids, the journey ended without further incident. I said brashly, "Nothing to it."

Only after we got home did she tell me, in the most delicate way, that she had lied. It wasn't an intermediate rafting trip — she had called Steve earlier to make sure it was an easy beginner's trip.

My manhood is still intact, but now I'm sure of my adventurous limitations.

I'm still good at riding a desk chair down the still waters of Sleepy Hollow.

Getting Lucky in Las Vegas

I was lucky to leave Las Vegas. I was more lucky my wife didn't leave *me*!

I gained a million dollar's worth of memories and lost weight, too. My pockets were emptied of the quarters I had been saving for months, and my wallet, filled with dollar bills, was much lighter when we left. I maintained ballast, however, by consuming serious quantities of culinary delights from several buffets during the hedonistic week I needed so desperately.

So desperate, I wanted to impress my wife with my unique gambling technique. The clerk at the Hilton VIP desk sympathized with me, I suppose, when I tried to convince him I was a high-rolling celebrity deserving of the 10-room complimentary suite with the private swimming pool. He accepted my autographed book for an upgraded discount room. But my wife was so shocked by the reflection of my body off the mirrored ceiling, her appetite for dinner, among other things, was ruined, so I ate crackers and slept on the comfortable sofa in the honeymoon suite. My gamble didn't pay off.

I wasn't in a great mood the next morning either — not much sleep, you understand, and I was starving. My spirits improved right away when we sat down to breakfast and met Mrs. America hopefuls who were competing at the hotel. My wife didn't seem to mind my sudden burst of energy and curiosity — I am, after all, a writer — until it was apparent I wanted to talk to *all* the contestants. I was invited to watch the swimsuit competition after the breakfast interviews. My wife left in disgust for the shopping

That's Entertainment?

mall. I watched the contestants for 10 minutes but got bored — they were all the same — looked great, but my wife looks better.

That's what I told her later in the day when Verne and Paul, Army buddies I hadn't seen for years, invited me to play golf with them the next day. I lost a lot of golf balls on the difficult course, but the boys were good hosts — they let me off — I didn't have to pay the $1.75 I lost betting. Paul, however, was adamant about getting back the dozen balls I had borrowed and Verne wanted me to replace the two clubs I had lost somewhere in the desert.

As an experienced traveler, I had told my wife it was cheaper to stay at quiet motels off the main strip. But she, too, soon became an experienced traveler. She pointed out we spent more on taxi rides to the streets with lights than the cost of a decent room. I lost a lot of good grace points until we moved, for the third time, to the Hilton. But I gained some credit back when we drove to Bryce Canyon and Zion National Parks. The only thing I lost there was my breath. The incredible scenery painted a picture of freedom and tranquillity that no stingy slot machine could offer.

The buffets were closed by the time we got back to town Tuesday night at eleven thirty. I was disappointed, but at least I could wait for the $1.99 midnight breakfast special. My wife, however, was starving. She refused to wait for the bargain, so we ate the regular fare at a cost of $13.95, no tip. My turkey platter tasted like a TV dinner, so I didn't eat. But my wife savored her BLT — for half an hour! I pouted, thinking of the wasted money I could've used in the nickel slots.

I lost my entire fortune at poker. My better half split to another table, smiling as her pile of chips grew along with my frustration. I left to enjoy the $1.99 breakfast. But just my luck, it turned out the coffee shop was closed from midnight to 6 a.m. — Tuesdays only!

At the airport, I put my lucky quarter I had won in a bathroom slot machine, into the armed bandit near the ticket counter. I lost it. Then I put the other lucky coin I had won in the grocery store slot machine into the slot machine by the trash can. I lost that one, too. But when I put the other lucky quarter I had won in the slot machine by the espresso bar, into the one by the drinking fountain, I won another lucky quarter — something to take home.

I lost a lot in Vegas, but not my wife. I gave her my winnings to show my appreciation for putting up with my childish behavior. She smiled sweetly as I placed the quarter in her palm.

"You're a lucky guy," she said. I agreed with a grin.

I bought her flowers when we got home — some things are still a sure bet.

Academy Awards Reflect Real Life

It's time again for Hollywood's grand Halloween Party. Everyone dresses up as celebrities wearing green tuxedoes, see-this and see-that dresses and hopefully, this year, oversized pants and shirts to impress upon our nation's teenagers that grown-ups can look foolish, too.

The event is fun for the participants. Even if they don't win a statuette, they go to parties to eat and drink the good stuff we can only imagine — with real dishes and glasses instead of paper and plastic. I'm envious because I'm never invited . . . and I was *born* in that city! But that wasn't good enough. I tried to become a member of the screenwriters' *A* List, but the industry was sleeping when it read my classics — I made the *Z* List. I've never understood why.

Here are my annual offerings, hoping someone influential back in my home town will call up and entice me with a multi-million dollar deal — I'd sure like to start earning a living more suitable to my imagined lifestyle.

Ya, Sure, You Betcha: Glen, a famous Norwegian ice fisherman from Minnesota, is on a mission to fish all 10,000 lakes. He observes the mysterious Hilga at one of his many midnight stops. He finally breaks the ice with his crackling sense of humor, dropping a line that she will become the biggest catch of his life.

That's Entertainment?

After he falls through the hole, she fishes him out and apologizes — she's actually a Danish agent doing research for the Department of Fish and Game. Their common interest leads to intense romance and adventure but his love thaws in the spring when he learns the *real* truth — she's just a common cook escaping from boredom. Love is renewed again after he becomes intensely hooked on her pastries, but sours when he forgets to freeze his winter's catch. **Rated PU**.

The Day the Government Stood Still: This remake of the science fiction classic, *The Day the Earth Stood Still*, is remarkably familiar. The aliens inhabiting the White House close down the government, offering citizens an opportunity to visit Planet Opportunity. Ed McMahon stars as the alien Scamo, the universal salesman. He offers subscriptions to out-of-this-world magazines on how to avoid diets, taxes and real jobs. He invites all non-essential citizens to visit his world where each one is a star, and gets to perform their acts in front of political prisoners being punished for refusing to balance an unearthly budget. **Rated one star**.

Divorce, English Style: A British prince, mourning the death of his ex-wife, holds court at the Queen's palace to drink tea with the mistress he's been seeing for years. She wants to break off the relationship out of guilt, but when the prince tries unsuccessfully to kiss her, he reverts to the toad he always was, and croaks. **Rated Two for Tea.**

The Comeback Kids: The story of Michael Jordan and Magic Johnson, who, playing themselves in this documentary saga, divulge their regrets and sadness at not making enough money away from basketball. One comic scene worth noting — Jordan bites his tongue jamming a fistful of thousand dollar bills through the hoop. He can't talk or lick his lips during filming of the "milk does the body good commercial." Magic runs by, steals the bills and makes a no-look pass to his wife, Cookie. She dribbles off court with the cash, anticipating a good shopping day on Rodeo Drive. **Not net rated**.

ER, the Movie: A spin-off from the TV show and another movie. A strange, E.T.-like patient is rushed into the emergency room of a Chicago hospital. When the doctors notice his middle finger is swollen, red and pointing up, they scamper frantically to get their modems and cell phones so he can phone home for *real* help. While critical-care patients are rushed in and out, one doctor falls in love with the alien, two doctors fall in love with themselves, one bleeds to death attempting to shave his two-day stubble without sleep, and another is sued for detaching, instead of attaching, a retina — he was drunk and couldn't read the instructions from the head nurse, who, coincidentally, was just released from the mental hospital across the street after treatment for her aversion to the sight of blood. **Rated UG, with a swollen, red, middle finger up.**

I'm still awaiting that phone call from Hollywood.

PART FIVE

Politically Incorrect

Newt and Willie Do the Super Bowl

I'm always excited about the Super Bowl.

But I keep hoping someone will make the game more entertaining by having amateurs broadcast it — a different perspective. Statistics, game plans and injury analyses are becoming redundant. And the close-up shots of fans auditioning for freak movies with weird masks is a lousy replacement for cheerleaders.

Last year, Hillary, Rush and O.J. were spectacular commentators. Their dialog was educational and timely — their chemistry stirred us all up. This year it's the *Newt and Willie Show.* It's educational and timely, too.

I hope somebody influential is reading.

Newt: "Well, Bill, this should be a good battle — just like ours. I'm excited. And I'm glad we got freebies. Ticket prices are getting out of hand."

Willie: "Come on Newt. Whose hand? You know about Dallas' budget. They bought Dion Sanders for several million and gave quarterback Troy Aikman even more. They cut wages for peanut vendors, groundskeepers and cheerleaders to pay them."

Newt: "Let's not quibble about budgets now. We can do that after the game with martinis — you buy. And don't blame salaries for driving up the prices. You always blame the rich. Do you know how much it costs for health insurance and disabled players' pension funds and remedial classes for rookies to learn to read the play books? Plenty. And players only work four years on average. Just like you. And they gotta get it while they can, just like you."

Willie: "Okay, Newt. Be nice. Maybe if they played without trying to hurt each other, costs could go down. You know, more protective equipment and fewer injuries. They could show their softer sides — play touch football — reduce violence."

Newt: "Sure, Bill. The beer companies would love to pay high fees for commercials aimed at *softies*. Hey, look down there. Isn't that Dion? He's practicing his touchdown dance. See Bill, the game already has its softer, artistic side. We don't need to fund any national artsy endowment programs."

Willie: "Umm, oh. Yeah, she's well endowed all right."

Newt: "I wasn't talking about that cheerleader. But your ratings with men just went up, Bill."

Willie: "Uh-oh. That's not all! Hey, who pushed that button. Are we on the air?"

Newt: "Well, folks, the players are taking the field. The excitement is building. Here comes the ref for the coin toss. Hey, look! He can't find it. Here comes the backup ref with more change. A nickel for the defense, and a quarter and a half-dollar for the offensive backs. The cameraman is taking his place on the 50-yard line and the coaches are . . .oh, my! They're fighting over use of the telephone."

Willie: "I told you this cost cutting wouldn't work, Newt. One ref, one cameraman and one pay phone without a portable head set — it's just not right for a Super Bowl. It's like a superpower — you can't cut everything to balance a budget."

Newt: "Who said anything about balancing a budget. I can't even balance myself. How many beers have I had? Ya know, Bill, I'm starting to like you."

Willie: "You've had too many. Do you think Pittsburgh should use its offensive ground attack or try to win through the air?"

Newt: "Since we've had to cut defense spending to pay for social programs, I'm not sure either can be effective. I guess that's okay. I'll bet the post-game party will be great. I'm getting in the mood already!"

Willie: "Well, here we go. There's the kick. It's long, it's high . . ."

Newt: "Me too! When does the party start?" (*Newt gets a little ill and misses the rest of the game.*)

Willie: "The game's over, Newt."

Newt: "Did I do good? Did everyone see me sitting right next to you?"

Willie: "No. There was only one cameraman — your idea for staff cuts."

Newt: "Who won?"

Willie: "I did. By default."

I'm still hoping for commentators who don't know anything about football. I could enjoy the game and get an intellectual education at the same time.

Pardon Me, But Your Time Is Up

Presidential debates are only slightly more entertaining than election posters that attempt to stimulate us with *Vote For Smith*, and negative TV campaign ads that interrupt the enjoyment of a great football or baseball game.

At least the TV contestants have the courtesy to dress up in suits, have their faces plastered with expensive make-up and mumble interesting things to court our votes. But they don't go far enough. Maybe they should spit and throw things at each other, use expletives and generally provide some real entertainment.

I had a dream. I was a TV moderator for the presidential debate.

"Okay, fellas. You each get a minute to spin your idea and another minute to rebut. The audience applause meter registers from one to ten, and will decide the winner after each salvo. One point will be deducted for every five seconds you go over your allocated time. Understand?

"Okay. On the left is President Clinton, on the right, the challenger, Bob Dole. No, Mr. Clinton. You can't change your mind again and be on the right. Rules are rules. Are you ready now? No, Mr. Dole. You can't exchange your glass of water for pineapple juice, unless Mr. Clinton changes his gin for water. Let's begin.

"Will the audience please stop applauding! No points are awarded for stupidity. Now what, Mr. Dole? No, you can't be excused to change your tie. The rules, remember? Now let's stop this nonsense and get on with the *real* nonsense."

"Good evening. I'm excited to be here tonight. Hillary wanted me to go to a real estate investment seminar, but I can assure you, I feel much more comfortable telling you, the American people, that the best investment you can make in our future is to vote for me." The audience roars. "Since I've served you, I've signed 126 bills into law and . . ."

"That's a lie. You've signed 123, and six of them revoked 87 of those you changed your mind about. If I'm elected I'll . . ."

"That's enough, Mr. Dole. I'll have to deduct two points for the interruption. Continue, Mr. Clinton."

"That rude interruption by Mr. Dole is just a small example of what the Republicans do best. We were on our way to legislating 38 new social programs to make sure every citizen has an equal opportunity to get an education, a job, fall in love, get free tickets to my Hollywood fund-raisers when I couldn't reach them from the White House telephone, and pay their increased taxes through the Internet. Now they're trying to interrupt our attempt to . . ."

"Time's up, Mr. President. Now, Mr. Dole, you have one minute to rebut."

"Umm. Just a minute. (*An offstage gofer wheels a shopping cart full of papers onto the stage.*) This basket contains the work of two subcommittees deciding which committee should be in charge of investigating the ethics of the ethics committee. If I'm elected, (*Dole spills the papers on the floor in Clinton's direction*) this kind of government waste will be eliminated. I will make the government get off the backs of its citizens and . . ."

". . . and let the government share the wealth with the deep pockets of big business and rich individuals and . . ."

"Mr. President, you are warned. One more outburst and I'll deduct four points."

"The Democrats seem to share President Clinton's view that we can't cut taxes 15 percent and still balance the budget. I have here (*the gofer brings in another shopping cart filled with papers*) all the data from the Office of Management and Budget that supports our plan to put more money back into the pockets of . . ."(*a front wheel on the shopping cart falls off, the papers falling to the floor.*) Dole smiles. "Well, it's almost balanced!" The audience roars with laughter. Dole gets a 10!

"Okay, Mr. President. It's your turn."

Clinton takes a sip of gin, a bite of his Big Mac and lights up a cigar. "I'm a firm believer that we must improve health care for our citizens and provide more incentive to live longer, healthier and more enlightened lives. (*He opens a black case and pulls out his saxophone.*) I'd like to demonstrate what I mean."

Just as Clinton puts the reed to his lips, loud cheers are heard. But they're not for him.

"What's going on? Ladies and gentlemen, Ross Perot has just entered the studio." Perot takes the microphone.

"I'm not going to stand around listening to this dribble if I can't speak mine. Elect me and debates won't be necessary. I'll rule for years. I'll make America strong. I'll eliminate the IRS, FBI, CIA, the military, the . . ." Perot gets a 10! Clinton pulls out the gin bottle from behind the podium and offers some to Dole, who accepts gladly. They toast each other, laughing, as Perot is lifted by the two female body guards into the back room.

"Ladies and gentlemen, the debate is over. Perot has won by a landslide. Stay tuned for *60 Minutes*. Those of you on the west coast will see debate highlights, narrated by President Clinton and Bob Dole. Good evening." Good night!

Simple Campaign Reform:
Eliminate Campaigns

When General Powell decided not to play the silly little war games presidential campaigns require, I admired him. I don't know much about the man . . . seems like a nice guy. He must be smart . . . he wrote enough to fill a $25 book. For sure, he's no fool. He pocketed the millions from his book sales and sent his pack of handlers scrambling in search of other puppets. Besides, who would want to be on public display at fund-raisers, forced to mind his manners while chewing the rubber-chicken fat with supporters? His actions illuminate our need for reform.

Although campaign reform isn't as meaty a major issue compared to abortion, health care, budget balancing, Medicare and who gets personal White House parking spaces, it does provide interesting fodder for discussion — just ask Clinton and Gore.

Some campaigners even think reform will help win votes. They say so at *every* fund-raiser. How absurd. We're not so stupid to think the special interest groups like NRA, ACLU, CFC, (*Center for Flea Control*) and BAFO (*Baseball and Football Owners*), will lay down quietly and let politicians run the country.

I do however, believe in the merits of campaign reform, so here's my scheme to save us all the expense of ridiculous, redundant, confusing and mind-numbing months of campaign rhetoric. My plan will save millions of dollars.

The *6-Step Program* would go something like this:

Step 1: Anyone wishing to be president must fill out a job application during the Labor Day weekend. If the applicant can complete the 102-page document without assistance before the 72-hour deadline expires, he or she will be qualified for . . .

Step 2. The applications are then screened and investigated by the CIA, *The National Enquirer*, the IRS, *Hard Copy* and *Mad Magazine*. When interesting, offensive indiscretions are found, the applicant will be qualified for . . .

Politically Incorrect

Step 3. Screening interviews will be held the first week in October. During this process, the applicant's sanity, qualifications and knowledge of job requirements are examined by some ex-presidents, their spouses and a team of unpaid, retired psychiatrists. On October 8th, at 9 p.m. eastern time, (*ratings will be highest*) the 10 semi-finalists will be introduced on *Larry King Live*.

Step 4. Larry will ask them to answer, in only two minutes: 1) *Why they are good candidates;* 2) *What the major issues are and how they are going to solve them*; 3) *What their hobbies are*; 4) *What their favorite movie, book and TV talk show is*; 5) *Their golf handicaps*; and 6) *To give a summary of American political history since Abraham Lincoln*. At the conclusion of the 30-minute special, citizens will have one hour to call 1-800-ELECTME. The five candidates with the most votes, (*to be announced on Halloween*) will be sequestered and advance to the next stage.

Step 5. With only seven days until the election, suspense will be at fever pitch, much like the O.J. verdict. A special panel of their peers will have interviewed the finalists and narrowed them down to three. The panel will include a diverse, non-partisan group of respected and impartial personalities; Louis Farrakhan, Howard Stern, Barbara Walters, Rush Limbaugh, Whoopi Goldberg and Kermit the Frog.

Step 6. With two days until the election, a live White House press conference will be held announcing the three finalists. If they don't trip at this step, each will have 10 minutes at the podium to plead his/her case to the TV audience. The ratings should break all records, so 10-15% of the advertising revenues should be plenty to pay for the entire election process, including air fare home for the losers — perhaps with enough left over to balance the budget.

On election day, instead of wasting time and money on ballots, the Internet will be used to tally the popular votes. The candidate getting the most, wins.

The entire process would eliminate millions spent on campaigns and prevent voters from becoming confused by rhetoric. A *cut-to-the-chase* election — suspenseful and entertaining.

Politically Incorrect

The only two problems with this scheme: 1) Preventing voters in Iraq, Somalia, Cuba and Arkansas from jamming the Internet lines. (*Although spreading world-wide democracy is an important part of America's mission*); and 2) Amending the Constitution. (*Our founding fathers didn't know about* CNN *and the Internet.*)

If you're over 35, somewhat sane and a U.S. citizen, the application is available from DOA (*Department of Applications*), Washington D.C. It's only $75 thousand, plus $3.95 shipping and handling. Tax deductible, of course.

The best campaign reform is no campaigning at all.

An Unconventional Convention Speech

I received a nice "thank you" note from Bob Dole for the speech I recently wrote for him. He declined to use it, although he said it was better than the worldly one his regular writer wrote. I know Mr. Dole prefers simple words rather than 50-centers, but he found my 2-centers not worthy of my usual fee — nothing.

I'm hoping to have better luck with President Clinton. He's more loose-tongued than Mr. Dole, so he can eat his words more readily without getting indigestion from the little white (*house*) lies he tells. If he uses this customized, no-focus speech, he'll reward me with a cushy writing job in the Capitol, I'm sure.

"Good evening. I hope you're enjoying the Big Macs and fries donated by my favorite sponsor. Please throw the trash in the proper receptacles for recycling, so Vice President Gore can do his job. You all know Bob Dole is trying to get me out of the White House into the outhouse by trashing Hillary's and my character. This is inappropriate dirty politics. If that wimpy old man continues making Jack Kemp throw inflated economic footballs at my tax record, I'm going to retaliate by having Al fill his political plate with the environmental waste those fat elephants don't talk about.

"Now, my August vision for the future. It's about the same as April's, a bit more precise than May's and a lot more exciting than June's. The economy has grown considerably and unemployment is down since we made a legitimate investment in White House real estate. That's because we've hired lots of good, easy-going government employees to crack down on those businesses that try to make too much money. I'll take some credit, but my Hollywood friends deserve more of it.

"I'm always amazed at the special effects work in those thrilling, violent movies. Movies brought in millions for us in tax revenue, which I've used to put more cops on the streets and in the movies. This kind of creative expression and use of tax money for the good of the country is what I'm most proud of.

"I've kept most of the promises that I can remember — welfare is reformed, health care has been administered to and we've stopped the fighting in Bosnia, Haiti and Somalia. We've also made some good trade agreements with Japan, Canada and Mexico.

"And tonight, I'm proud to announce a major breakthrough with Cuba. I've convinced my buddy Fidel to sell us cigars in exchange for Big Macs and Nike jogging shoes. As you know, I don't inhale, but a good cigar and a jog after an arduous Cabinet meeting is — well, that's a pleasure hard to beat.

"Abortion is important, too, so I'm stretching my position on the distribution of condoms in the classroom to include sex-education teachers who work earnestly to prevent teenage pregnancy. They could set good examples for casual sex like I occasionally do . . . OOPS! What I really mean is I'd like to be remembered as your education and environment president — someone who truly understood the need for sexual restraint and population control.

"I see a strong America where everybody has equal opportunity to make enough money to eat well, live in big houses, play golf and travel around the country in style. If people work hard and are smart enough to avoid my tax policies, or can tell good stories and become politicians, the American dream will once again be possible to obtain.

"I can't remember what my last promise was on family values and the military, but I do recall a 'don't ask, don't tell' policy that includes gay marriages, discreet extra-marital affairs and a powerful military that protects me from being overthrown.

"I hope you'll enjoy the Madonna concert we've sponsored. I'm excited she's invited me to play with her . . . the saxophone, I mean. I'm fortunate I can now face the music. Hillary got upset at me when Madonna referred to me as her father figure. Well, enjoy the concert and remember one important thing. Voting for me is an endorsement for good entertainment for America — something Mr. Dull can't provide. Thanks for the nomination, good night and God bless Hollywood."

I'm looking forward to hearing President Clinton's acceptance speech. I hope he uses mine because it's more unconventional and informative than the others.

The American people deserve the truth; I deserve more than I get — nothing, as usual.

Party Politics No Fun at Inaugural

Getting invited to a Washington party isn't easy. But if you can sing, tell bad jokes and good lies or have an extra few thousand bucks lying around designated for lost causes, it doesn't hurt your chances.

If you knew an arrogant friend who dreamed of power, influence, free golf, unlimited Big Macs and a private 747 and he becomes the president, you're sure to get an invitation.

So don't be dismayed if you were snubbed for the Inaugural. Your name was misplaced in the IRS or FBI computer files instead of on the "A" List, so sooner or later, you'll be notified to appear in

Politically Incorrect

Washington anyway — at government expense, not yours. Sometimes there's a silver lining in the clouds over Washington.

I've tried many times to procure invitations to White House parties by sending bad checks to political campaigns, impersonating Boris Yeltzin or Yasser Arafat (*quite well, in fact, but my accent gave me away*) or by streaking in the snow down Pennsylvania Avenue, an athletic ability worthy of presidential recognition.

I haven't been successful thus far, but I figure the anticipation for these elite parties is probably more exciting than the events themselves — too much politics, not enough beer. But the planning is fun. You get to think of ways to look good in tuxedoes that don't tuck you in or dresses that reveal too much or nothing at all. It would be more practical to throw your own party — if no one shows up — more food for you and less stress trying to be polite.

At least you feel important in the process. It's better than spending money to rub stuffy noses with people who would tell you how interesting you are when all you can talk about is your hometown weather, bowling trophies, meeting the local mayor and recipes for apple pie, chili and tuna casseroles. Although these topics are more important than what some of those pompous people discuss, your status will always be "voter" rather than "player," no matter how hard you try to fit in.

For more insight on Washington parties, I called Bill Gasman. He's a high school buddy who once had presidential aspirations, but now works for a private security agency guarding government office buildings. An ethics committee once halted his bid to obtain a senate seat because he tried to steal it after hours. He was rewarded when the Nixon folks hired him as a temp to be a Secret Service agent for the 1972 Inaugural.

"Bill, you must've had a pretty good time."

"Ha! At the State Department gig, Kissinger was sitting in a big, soft chair pontificating on world affairs. People listened politely while that cigar smoke and intellectual babble snuffed out all the party spirits."

"What did you do?"

215

Politically Incorrect

"I was hired to prevent physical harm to anyone, so I made sure the men curbed their aggressive behavior and didn't ruffle the women's feathers."

"Sexual harassment at an Inaugural?"

"No, no. Some of the guys just jostled the women in the crowded room trying to shake Kissinger's hand. They wrinkled those foo-foo dresses and then, when apologizing in languages I've never heard, smudged the women's designer make-up with those double and triple cheek kisses."

"What did you do then?"

"Nothing. Just watched. The women left to powder their noses, but I suspect they went instead to another party — probably at the Treasury Department where Donald Trump, the Sultan of Brunei, Ross Perot and Georgio Armani were special guests. So suddenly it was a stag party — pretty boring until one guy spilled champagne on another guy's pants leg and tried to wipe it off. The guy with the wet pants smiled — you know, that special kinda smile, and the two went off somewhere alone."

"What then?"

"Well, I became suspicious when Bob Haldeman and John Erlichman came in the back door with their arms around each other. I had heard they didn't really like each other that much. I was hoping it was booze from the Oval Office party down the street working its wonders and not something else. For a while I thought maybe I was at one of those guy bashes. But when Kissinger got up and demanded some more women, I was relieved."

"Then what?"

"The two guys involved in the champagne incident returned and were quickly approached by John and Bob. The boys had just come in to take care of business. Turned out the two men were democrats who crashed the party to gather information on Viet Nam strategies. The champagne was just a ploy to talk privately."

"What did the boys do?"

"Not much at first. Just told a few bad jokes. But when I saw John take out one of those little tape recorders and start asking questions of the two democrats, I knew trouble was brewing. As I reached for my assault weapon, Nixon walked in with several of my colleagues. He yelled to John and Bob, 'I can use that,' and put the recorder in his pocket, then invited the men to join him and the ladies in the Oval office for some dancing."

"What a party!"

"Not really. Pretty boring. As soon as I got off duty I joined several other temps — waiters, cooks, gardeners, housekeepers, secretaries, spin doctors and a few old congressmen — for a *real* party. Denny's had a fabulous $1.99 all-you-can-eat buffet to honor the president. Now *that* was a real bash!"

I'm sorry I'll miss the next Inaugural, but it'll soon be time to try for the Academy Awards again — perhaps a temp job as a look-alike for a star that doesn't come out at night. I could do Matthau or Dangerfield, but would rather do Cruise or Gibson.

Oh well. At Washington or Hollywood parties it's difficult to distinguish the actors from the real people anyway.

Settling Differences Behind Closed Doors

I was exhilarated when the government went on strike. I called my accountant right away.

"Hello, Dianna. Isn't this great? How much tax money will I save now that we don't have to pay all those *non-essential* workers that got laid off?"

She disappointed me. "Those *other* non-essentials are still getting paid," she explained, referring to the politicians and IRS agents, no doubt.

The humor of this whole debacle is extraordinary, but it's also very serious and frightening. It scares me to think these two gray-haired foxes are leading innocent flocks of followers into a terrifying den of trouble. Do you really believe Gingwitch and Slick

Politically Incorrect

Willie didn't talk about the budget on Air Force One because they were too depressed returning from Rabin's funeral? America shouldn't be worrying about enemies from afar. America's potential economic death is more critical. If our leaders can't get along, how are *we* supposed to? "We have seen the enemy. It is us."

It's best to settle differences behind closed doors.

I'm invoking my Constitutional right to drive with an editorial license while under the influence. My source overheard the following presidential dialogue between Willie and Newt in the executive restroom of the White House.

Willie: "I refuse to cut Medicare or Medicaid. I care about the elderly."

Newt: "Come on, Willie. I know you're worried about aging and your pending unemployment, but we gotta think about the big picture; we gotta look good. I want my face on a stamp someday, too. Just look in the mirror. We're losing it. The stress."

Willie: "Well, you might be right, Newt, but except for your big business friends, nobody is going to gain much from your ranting and raving about tax and spending cuts."

Newt: "Let's see what you think after you get 10 mil for your presidential memoirs and have to pay eight mil in taxes. You'll have to get a big part in a movie to make up the difference. But you have the right connections, so I wouldn't worry too much."

Willie: "Maybe. But what am I supposed to do about this budget thing? It's not the shoestrings I'm worried about breaking anymore, it's the people's impression that I'm not doing anything to protect their shoes."

Newt: "Well, *that's* an obscure analogy. What the hell are you talking about?"

Willie: "I don't know."

Newt: "Hallelujah! The truth shall set you free! Look, I'm not sure what the hell to do *either*, but when I was watching *Sesame Street* the other day, one of those little puppets observed that when two little pigs disagree, one little piggy's slop shouldn't be mixed with the other little piggy's, because then *everything's* a mess."

Politically Incorrect

Willie: "What are you saying? We're both little piggies?"

Newt: "Are we? I do think we've gotta clean up our acts. I got a lot of media play for pretending to be snubbed on Air Force One. I had to say something . . . I didn't think it was appropriate to tell them you couldn't talk to me in the Jacuzzi — what a story *that* would've been!"

Willie: "Whew! It would. How could I explain that? Hey, you're really a pretty thoughtful guy, Newt — guess I haven't been very affable with all this budget stuff going on. Maybe we should go on *Saturday Night Live* together — let loose a little — I'll play the sax and you dance around in those striped boxer shorts. We'll show America that we're regular guys . . . that we take off our pants just like they do — assure them we're getting down to the serious, non-partisan process of balancing this budget."

Newt: "Shhh! Somebody's in that stall down there."

Willie: "Hey, who's in there?"

Woman's voice: "You're in the wrong toilet, fellas."

Newt: "Oh gosh! Hillary!"

Willie: "Don't worry. She supports the 'don't ask, don't tell' policy."

Newt: "Listen, I'm glad we got to know each other better. Let's get outa here. By the way, if I support your budget proposal will you let me ride up front on Air Force One next time?"

Willie: "Deal — another martini, Newt?"

Hillary: "I'll take one, please!"

Important matters affecting millions shouldn't be debated on public TV. There's too much ego at stake. Adversaries should be able to settle their differences behind closed doors.

And sitting behind the wrong doors is better than not opening any at all.

Profiting From Dirty Laundry

There's substantially more than dirty politics going on in the White House these days.

Rumors indicate an illegal White Sale is bringing in millions to fund democratic campaigns and to pay off the Lincoln bedroom maids to keep quiet.

Airing dirty laundry, it turns out, can be quite profitable. Basically, those who sleep in Lincoln's bedroom are not only expected to contribute large sums of money, but autograph their dirty sheets and undergarments. The guest items are then sold at very private and very silent auctions. A Barbra Streisand autographed bra was rumored to bring in $25,000 in Saudi Arabia and a pair of Steven Spielberg leather underwear soaked up another $50,000 in Tokyo. Soiled celebrity sheets are a specialty item bringing in between $500 to $10,000 each, depending on the kind of stains found. Popcorn butter and pizza stains are worth less than others. In return for their generosity, guests are encouraged to steal the authentic White House soap, towels and "official" Al Gore recycled toilet paper.

Incredible? My source, wishing to remain anonymous for obvious reasons, has it all on tape. She said she recorded it all while working in a Washington laundromat specializing in delicate fabrics. (*Her experience in delicate matters later led to a high-paying job at the only Victoria's Secrets store in Provo, Utah.*) Here are excerpts from the secret tapes allegedly recorded behind the headboard in Lincoln's bedroom to authenticate the merchandise used in the White Sale.

Guest: "Here's our dirty sheets. My wife and I signed them with the official White House Guest Pens, but they ran out of grease before we could sign our underwear. Could you replace the pens so we can have them as souvenirs?"

Maid: "Yes, sir. But you'll have to autograph one of your personal checks made out to me for $1,000. That will include my silence, but you'll also have to autograph the two mint candy

220

wrappers on your pillows. I get about $50 for those. You know how much it costs to put three kids through college these days? Are you staying another night? Check-out time is noon."

Guest: "That depends whether or not the president can do something about our room service tab. These prices exceed my charitable contribution limit and I don't know how to sing the blues."

Maid: "That's not my department. Call extension 1315. Maybe they can help."

Guest: "Hello. Concierge? Yes, I was wondering if the president comped our Air Force One seats to Disney World and the Madonna concert at the Kennedy Center. No? Geez. How much was that again? Thank you."

Guest to his wife: "Well, honey, we could ask Madonna if she wouldn't mind sharing the bedroom with us tomorrow. We could buy extra underwear for her to autograph. Selling those could offset our contribution commitment for the tickets."

Wife: "No way. Politics may make strange bedfellows, but I'm not sleeping with any woman, especially her. And neither are you! She can make Lincoln's ghost happy, but we're checking out!"

Another Guest: "Hello? Guest services? Listen. I appreciate the president's gift, but I can't seriously take this cat with me on my trip to Asia with the senators to visit their friends. It wouldn't be politically correct. He made a mistake. He meant to give me a regular white kitten, not a real white tiger cub. Could you please ask him to give the critter to a zoo instead of leaving him in here with me? It's chewing up the linens and I'm losing my shorts paying the maid to replace them."

Guest Services: "Well, sir, if you contribute just a little more, we could take the cub back to one of your hotels. But you would have to comp the president and his entourage again for that wonderful show at your hotel."

Guest: "Okay. But please tell him I'd appreciate it if he autographs more than just a towel, a set of sheets and a pair of his shorts at my hotel. I think it's only fair after all the free chips I donated to his cause during his last visit. And I'm not speaking of the potato variety. Also tell him I can't get Chelsea into that midnight show . . . birthday or not. It's against the law, you know."

The voices on tape sounded like a singer that wears one glove and a fat cat who owns major hotels in Las Vegas. But I won't gamble on speculation. I could get in trouble.

The shenanigans between the White House sheets are staining the moral fabric of our society. But dirty politics and dirty laundry usually come out in the wash.

It's just a matter of when the Tide comes in.

Too Much Talk, Not Enough Food

I like the local elections in Mukilteo because I get to go to all the campaign parties, (*almost everyone gets an invitation*) and nobody notices that I really throw only pennies in the collection box. Instead, the hosts have to keep their eyes on me around the food table, in case someone else shows up to eat.

It might be fun to be a mayor or city council member. I like parties, but I couldn't afford campaign advertising or posters larger than cereal boxes. I'm good at making up important things to say, so I'd get free publicity in the local newspaper.

Just for the practice, I went to John Sharkey's campaign party last week at Riley's Pizza Parlor. I wanted to check out the food and catch up on all the local gossip. The current mayor, Klem Klopper, who owns the place, obviously never was much good at fund-raising — his slush fund wasn't big enough to pay for the pizza and beer, so I settled for the free broccoli and carrot sticks and a couple of chicken wings on the side. The food wasn't so hot, but the gossip was.

Sharkey is a City Council member and has a reputation for being stingy with our tax money, so why would he change his image

Politically Incorrect

feeding cheap freeloaders like me with gourmet food? He's a smart politician.

Now Sharkey's opponent, the formidable Mira Scruthenthalmer, hasn't yet sent me an invitation for her party. I suspect she'll spring for better food, because the gossip I heard is, she's full of beans, and will probably beef up her reputation by feeding *her* freeloaders prime rib and horseradish. I'll be there.

As you know, I believe everything I read in the newspaper, especially what I write, so when I read in an interview that Mira had said she was more qualified than John because 1) she had higher moral standards; 2) had more life experience; 3) got along with everyone; 4) knew more about budgets, infrastructure and police activities; and 5) had better ideas for our community's growth, I was, of course, impressed. I like well-qualified candidates who are confident and honest.

However, the interview really ruffled some feathers in town. The natives feathered the newspaper with several *Letters to the Editor* condemning what she implied about John's moral standards not being as high as hers. So when I asked John's wife, Claudia, about John's moral standards, she said, "There's nobody as high as John."

Well, I couldn't just take her word for that, so I went over to the bar to ask John if he agreed. He held up his mug and said with conviction and a giggle, "I'm always high on life." He offered me a taste, but I declined. I don't like root beer.

Mira also had said she would have more time than John to spend as our part-time mayor because his "plate is too full" with his regular job. When I asked him about that, he showed me his plate of broccoli and carrots. When I asked him what he thought of Mira and her comments in the article, he just smiled. "Did she say something?" Of course, I knew he was lying. He's a politician.

To become a fair and more informed voter, I'll ask Mira about her side of the story at her party when I'm not eating or talking. There's always a possibility she was misquoted in the newspaper about what she thinks of John's moral standards. But frankly, I'll be more interested in the quality of the food and if I can have seconds. If I can, I'll know her standards for parties are quite high. Who cares about morals while I'm eating?

All this may seem obscure and insignificant, but I'm sure, if you're like me, you haven't gone to many fund-raisers. If you have, you probably spent more time mingling with people you know rather than discussing real political issues with the candidate. Most of us don't know what the real issues are, other than if the drinks are on the house and if the food is any good. So we must read the newspapers to find out.

It's difficult to know what each candidate really thinks, not only about the issues but also their opposing candidates. Leaving it solely to what we read isn't fair to any candidate. There should be more parties so we can sort out the gossip from the truth.

If I ever run for office I won't much care what my opponents say about me. I'll have the kind of fund-raising party where the only slinging that matters will be the money my freeloaders throw in the box so I can pay for the steaks and lobster.

PART SIX

Healthy Sicknesses

Clinton Recipes Stir Up Depression Diet

In the Kitchen with Bill is a new recipe book which honors President Clinton and his eating habits — it's full of bull as well as fat. It's insensitive to those like me, who have suffered heart attacks and been administered the "eat healthy" gospel by hypocritical government bureaucrats. But Bill is his own man. He eats what he pleases — role model be damned! Touting his appetite for lethal, fatty foods, is another example of his waffling; butter, syrup and all. It's a sticky issue to be digested carefully.

Smokers and drinkers are penalized by lawmakers through exorbitant "sin" taxes because tobacco and alcohol are hazardous to our health. I gave up cigarettes, but still smoke a pipe — I learned from Bill not to inhale. But isn't dietary fat equally dangerous? So why isn't Bill the laughing stock of the pig farm? Does he really believe he's promoting the reduction of health-care costs by refuting the laws of clogged arteries?

Admittedly, I'm envious of his eating abilities — I'd love to join him at any pigfest. Prior to my heart surgery, I could have easily competed with him at the dinner table. But I'm not a strong man anymore — I can no longer partake with reckless abandon.

Therefore, I'm angrily opposed to the flaunting of bad eating habits. If there were justice, there would be "sin" taxes on ice cream, butter, bacon, chocolate and other essentials. It's unfair and it's depressing, but so is life. So I've cooked up a few healthy recipes. I hope they depress you as much as they do me. It's my "counter" offensive to politically-incorrect eating habits.

Healthy Sicknesses

The Politically Correct Depression Diet

Dainty Dunkin' Doughnuts: In a non-stick pan, fry six skinless mountain oysters in celery or carrot juice for 10 minutes. Remove the nuts. Roll them into a mixture of powdered rose petal and carnation flower. Arrange in a baking dish with two or more bananas and bake 15 minutes. Remove. Add eight ounces each of Rum, Tequila and Vodka. Removes stress and increases need to call in sick for work.

Tainted Tuna Meltdown: Leave left-over tuna casserole uncovered on counter overnight. Add one cup of non-fat motel or cottage cheese, two balls of non-fat, wadded string cheese, a pint of Tabasco and too-hot tamales. Mix in blender 30 seconds. Skim the scum off the top. Nuke until microwave window is completely covered with slime. Serve immediately with Kool Aid. Eat it, or apply to thighs or belly for quick weight loss.

Groasted Stuffed Chicken and Riled Rice: Remove whole, raw chicken from plastic bag. Marinate one hour in Geritol, then roll in Cackling Oat Bran mixed with one small can of smashed chick peas and a pint of Cognac. Stuff cavity with sugarless bubble gum, then tie legs together with mint-flavored dental floss. Bake 60 minutes. In a separate saucepan, cook minute rice for 30 minutes until grains are listless. Add one cup of prune juice and stir. Add two handfuls of freshly captured fleas until rice is sufficiently riled up. Remove chicken from oven. Cover with two cups of melted, chocolate-flavored Ex-Lax. Provides 900% of the USRDA for digestive system cleansing.

Nocturnal Nightmare: Place two, long asparagus spears in boat-shaped glass dessert dish. Cover with three equal blobs of day-old, congealed Cream of Wheat. Cover with a combination of crisp, chocolate-covered night crawlers, strawberry yogurt and creamed coffee beans. Sprinkle with chipped eggshells. Guaranteed to keep you awake or put you to sleep forever.

Healthy Sicknesses

If this healthy menu depresses you as much as it did me while it was stirring in the fatty tissues of my brain, you're probably on the way out for ice cream or a copy of *In the Kitchen with Bill.*

I apologize. I just wanted to make the point that "sin" taxes on tobacco and liquor aren't justified any more than they would be on what the president and most of us like to eat.

So far, the government hasn't banned books and magazines on pipe and cigar smoking or tending bar. Mr. Clinton swears he never inhaled the forbidden smoke, (*perhaps he prefers grass brownies*) but he sure doesn't hide the fact that he ingests just about any kind of unhealthy food.

"Sin taxes" should be eaten by those with forked tongues.

Exercisers Build Muscles in the Wrong Places

There are too many exercise machines on the market — Solarflex, Thigh Disaster, Bowloflex, Tummy Tucker, Dreadwalker, Ab Cruncher, Staminator, Arminator, Backabreaker, Abductor, Butt Buster — so I consulted an expert before I took the plunge.

With a body mass like mine, I'm an easy target for those mass-market geniuses who display those impossibly great bodies working out on their equipment — those TV shopping channels and infomercials are stretching our minds with so much encouraging information, muscles in our heads are being built up where they don't belong.

On one recent show, a 67-year-old lady called in. "I've lost four inches around the middle. I was so excited I bought three more Abductors for friends. It really works. All you have to do is work out 15 minutes a day."

Abigail was so convincing I called the 800 number quickly to get the extra discount before the 10-minute window of opportunity expired. I wanted the free Cindy Crawford and Sharon Stone video demos.

Healthy Sicknesses

I hung up just as quickly when the smooth lady on the phone told me the guarantee was valid only if I lost all 10 inches of my gut muscle within the advertised time frame of 90 days and if I promised to endorse the product. I figured it was time to consult with Greg, my friend and trainer at the local gym. He's advised me well, but apparently I don't remember much of what he said. My taste for food and wine is more developed than my physique.

Before I called Greg I went to an exercise equipment store to see some of these machines and get some customer referrals. The manager asked me politely to get off the Cyclizer because the store's insurance policy didn't cover abusive wear. He did give me several numbers, however.

"Yes, we're very pleased with the Dreadwalker. It's lasted six months without any problems. Our family uses it all the time, but sometimes it's frustrating because there isn't enough room on the rails to hang up all of our clothes."

"Of course we're pleased with the Abductor. It was a real steal. We got it on sale from the TV shopping channel. And my stomach is feeling much better now. My wife says I'm much more appealing, too. After my surgery for strained abdominal muscles, I can't eat as much, so I've lost about five inches around the middle."

"Well, I can't really say enough about the Butt Buster. Like the advertisements say, it fits well in any closet, under the bed, in the garage, the bathroom, the attic or under the office desk. So we weren't really upset too much when we couldn't find it after two or three workouts. Our kid finally fessed up and said he and a friend had taken it to the park and used it for a skateboard rack. It really holds up well, he assured us."

"We've bought three Solarflexes so far and will probably buy more. They make great New Year resolution gifts. And each year during the annual town garage sale, we sell them at half price to neighbors and deduct the loss from our taxes as charitable contributions to the handicapped. And we always keep one in the basement for our workouts when it's not being used to hold our hanging plants."

I was beginning to get the picture.

"Will the Staminator really increase my stamina if I use it like you did?"

"Sure thing. But be careful. You should replace the rubber on the pedal regularly. I worked out three hours a day until I slipped and broke my back. I was trying to lose weight like that 350-pound fella on the infomercial who looked like Arnold after 90 days. But I didn't follow the directions . . . worked out more than the recommended 20 minutes a day!"

I called Greg. He suggested coming back to the gym.

"Why not use the equipment you already pay for?" I like a man who has brains to go along with brawn.

So I agreed. I kept the 28 free video demonstrations that came with the several pieces of equipment I returned under the money-back guarantees. I use the films for inspiration before eating big meals and after listening to Greg's lectures about control.

Exercise machine ads have developed strong muscles in my head. They may be in the wrong place, but now it's easier to avoid those with perfect bodies that try to make me believe it's a realistic goal to make a rock out of a turnip.

Health Care Needs More Than Patients

My healthy friend Derek faxed me a joke to cheer me up after I had told him about my experience with a new, streamlined, cost-effective health-care plan.

There were three doctors at the Pearly Gates. Saint Peter asks the first doctor what he does. "I'm a heart surgeon at Valentine Hope."

"Go right in, you're on my list." The next doctor says he's a brain specialist at Thoughtful Care Hospital. "Okay, come on in," says Saint Peter. The third doctor says he's with Superior Health

Healthy Sicknesses

Maintenance Organization Number 131. Saint Peter looks in his appointment book.

"Yes, you're listed. You can go in, but you have to check out in two days."

Real funny! Here's a better joke. I had to get an appointment with Dr. Smithers to get his permission to see a cardiologist, a psychologist, a nutritionist, a physical therapist and an internist, each of whom works for the same company. Never mind that all the extra paperwork for the referrals cost more hours for the nurses and doctor than the cost of my session with him.

It was difficult saying good-bye to all of the good, trusted doctors who made a decent living keeping me alive despite my efforts at self destruction. *(Bad eating, attempts at setting world records for uncoordinated fitness activities, etc.)*

I needed a tranquilizer, so I went to see Mr. Pibbs, my wonderfully delirious pharmacist. I couldn't get my regular medications, so I started leafing through the exciting, *Pharmaceutical Digest: 10,000 Drugs You Never Heard Of.* Mr. Pibbs explained the insurance company would only cover Brand X and Brand Y pills because the name brands cost too much. When I complained that I prefer Mercedes over Chevys when it comes to my health, he phoned Dr. Smithers to appeal to the insurance company on my behalf, which, of course, would take several days. Dr. Kevorkian would be too late to do me any good by then, so I accepted one Brand X and one Brand Y for the sake of variety.

Well, so far, I've only seen the new psychologist. Peggy was pretty good, but I had to reveal to her my personal history from scratch, so here we go again. Of course, I also had to fill out the obligatory health forms, too, which I hope the other new doctors understand I can't do — I get anxiety attacks filling out bureaucratic forms, especially those due in April. It's one of many reasons I need a psychologist in the first place.

This new corporate medical system is good for the people who manage and monitor the doctors and technicians. Now they too, with their higher incomes based on how much money they save, can

Healthy Sicknesses

afford the nice cars and homes the doctors have. But I'm not sure the doctors are pleased about mandatory time management and forms processing in lieu of medical training and patient relationships.

Soon we'll see surgeons watching time clocks during operations. If they can't get the job done properly in the allocated time, they'll be forced to let the patient die so the next victim can get on the table before the 5 p.m. quitting time. Good family doctors waste too much of their time directing patients to specialists rather than discussing and treating the illness and its emotional stress.

Doctors spend years in school, work for peanuts as interns and residents before qualifying to practice their trade. They deserve to be paid well for their skills and merits based on competence — determined by the patient, not by a bunch of bureaucrats. Would entertainers and sports stars tolerate such perverse standards for judging *their* skills?

Do we need insurance companies in the medical business? If you need to see a doctor, pay him $10 for a visit, pay him $5 for a shot and pay him $1,000 for surgery. Or trade his services for a pig, a chicken or World Series tickets. It worked in the old days, why not again? A good doctor makes money based on skill and reputation. I don't think insurance companies have any business determining what good health care is and isn't. I'll risk my doctor's judgment.

Perhaps new technology, like the Internet, will soon allow us to punch up our symptoms on a computer, get an analysis, advice and a cost estimate on what needs to be done — something like auto body estimates. It's certainly competitive, could reduce labor costs and let people have more say in managing their own health care.

I'm out of patience with this absurd idea that managed health care will keep costs down. Just like the growing government, new programs to cure social ills require the hiring of more and more ignorant bureaucrats just to monitor the programs, thus eliminating any savings they might have claimed.

Managed health care needs more than patients. It needs surgical removal!

Truth in Advertising for Personal Ads

I went sulking into my designated doghouse. My wife got mad at me again for leaving beard trimmings in the sink. I was just trying to look civilized for her new friend who was coming over to visit in a few minutes.

In the discomfort of my cluttered and stuffy office, I started pondering how great it would be to be single again — no toilet seat, hair in the sink problems; no hassles about spending grocery money for golf fees or nagging to clean up after cooking; no lawns to mow, remote controls to surrender, or good jobs to get.

I opened my secret file and pulled out the promotional piece I once used to lure unsuspecting women when I was a member of a video-dating service in Los Angeles. It brought back lots of memories — and made me *very glad* I was still married.

Being single had lots of advantages, of course. I dated the world's most beautiful women when I slept enough to get some good dreams going. I was always charming, well-dressed and well-groomed when I dated — it's easy when you only have to do it a couple hours a month. And my living quarters were always comfortable except when a lady came over — there wasn't enough room on the floor for more than one person to share space with my golf clubs, wardrobe, magazines and newspapers — and I wasn't lucky very often, so my bed was always a good place to hide dirty ash trays, empty beer cans and smelly fishing tackle.

Los Angeles differs from most cities because the selection process is less complicated. There's more to choose from. If you had the bucks you got good women. If you had the looks you got some, too. If you were kind, loving and interesting, you could always snag a few. With all those traits you could get them all — so why be married?

Healthy Sicknesses

The video service was perfect for me. I was a good actor in front of a camera and could write good ads — it was my profession. "I believe being kind, gentle and romantic are excellent traits for a man who cherishes women like I do. I also think that my future in advertising and public relations could provide a deserving woman with the means to which she'd like to become accustomed."

I said that in front of the camera and wrote it next to the other lies on the promotional fact sheet accompanying the video.

I had lots and lots of first dates — sometimes four a week. It didn't take long, however, before the truth set them free. One lady actually saw me for four months straight. No marriage, though. She caught me leaving the back door of the unemployment office.

So when I left Los Angeles and moved to a more civilized place in Washington, the only lie I told my present wife was that I was going to get a good job. Other than that, she accepted me with the traits you share only with your dog or cat.

I really sympathize with the single folks today who advertise on the Internet and the personal sections of newspapers. I looked at some of them, just to be reminded how lucky I really am.

"I'm a SWF, tall, slender, well built, intelligent, irresistible, energetic, fantastic lover and desperate to find a man of my equal."

"I'm a SBM, strong, handsome, rich, potent, smart and very, very popular."

"I'm a stupid, ugly, fat, and unemployed MWM, who loves long walks on the beach at night, working on computers all day and discreet late-night dinners where friends of my wife can't see me."

The third one will probably succeed. Honesty usually does. The other two are hopeless romantics, lunatics or both. I suggest that Truth in Advertising be applied to personal ads as they are for credit cards and loan documents. It's a good policy to make the buyer beware. Here are suggestions to improve personal ads.

Wrong: "I love candlelight dinners at good restaurants, romantic walks along the water, cuddling by the fireside and exciting roller-coaster rides."

Truth: "I like eating at Burger King and Pizza Hut with discount coupons. I love walking by the water with someone who knows how to swim, and cuddling by the fireplace with a good book. I also love wild arguments."

Wrong: "I'm seeking a gentle person who appreciates country music, nature, children and the theater."

Truth: "I'd like to meet a kind but dominating SOB who can keep my tantrums under control, who understands Pakistani folk music, can live comfortably in a tent, likes children who belong to someone else and can act nice in front of my friends and family."

Wrong: "I'm looking for someone who doesn't care about money, but cherishes beautiful things like love, flowers, poetry, butterflies and cats."

Truth: "I want somebody who has lots of money so I don't have to worry about it, thinks love is a good idea if it improves my sex life, likes to smoke poppy seeds while reading Edgar Allen Poe and likes to press butterflies and skin cats."

Wrong: "I'm interested in a person who likes to travel, drink good wine, go to the right restaurants, wear fashionable clothing and lives in a very large house."

Truth: "I want somebody rich and famous."

When I came in to meet my wife's new friend I turned on the charm. When the friend left, my wife sent me back to the doghouse. She prefers the truth, too.

Divorce — Telephone Style: 900 Reasons for Happiness

Once again, my wife accused me of running up the phone bill with $689.22 charged to "900" numbers. I said it was a phone company error. We argued for several minutes, as usual. I admitted my temptation to call those sexy women who help men become better lovers for their spouses, but I would *never* call those psychics who claim they can tell your future or a horse's for $3.99 a minute. I assure you my future isn't worth that much — not anymore.

She gave me two 900 numbers to call, then left for work.

I called the first. "Hello. You've reached the law firm of Smith, Smith & Smith, America's favorite family law firm. Your divorce is our family business. Have your Social Security numbers ready before the free, five-minute consultation begins. After then you'll be billed $3 a minute. Please hold while a legal specialist . . ."

I hung up and called the second 900 number. "Hello. Divorce Hot Line. Your free, five-minute consultation will begin when a licensed counselor can devote full attention to your problem. Please hold." The recording sounded less threatening, so I held.

"Hello. My name is Sally Smith. How did you hear about us? What's your name and what's your problem? You have five minutes, starting now, to determine if you will need further help at $5.50 a minute."

"Hi, my name is Joseph," I lied. "My wife gave me your number. I guess she's pretty mad at me. She also gave me another 900 number, but I hung up when they answered. She must be pretty serious about divorcing me."

"Was the other number for Smith, Smith & Smith?" Sally asked.

"Why, yes. How did you know?"

"Just a marketing question. That's our affiliate. Now, what's your problem?"

"Well, my wife is always nagging me about smoking cigars in the house, leaving dishes in the sink, not sharing the remote control and yelling at her every morning."

"Why do you yell at her?"

"Because I don't have to get up when she does. After the alarm goes off she just lays there for half an hour and I can't get back to sleep, so I get cranky."

"Why does she get up earlier than you?"

"Because somebody has to have a job."

237

Healthy Sicknesses

"I see. And why don't you? Then you could smoke your cigars somewhere else and there wouldn't be dishes in the sink?"

"Listen, Sally. I tried work. . . always compromising, doing what you don't want, when you don't want. Nobody appreciated it — least of all, me."

Sally told me why it's important to compromise, be honest, kind and considerate to my wife. Then she said coldly. "Your five minutes are up. Do you wish to continue?" I had no choice. I was hooked.

"Sure," I joked. "I should talk for a couple hours just so the bill will go up and my wife will think I'm taking this seriously. Hey, I just heard one of those phone companies has a new promotion — free calls on Monday nights. I'll call you then!"

"I'm sorry. We don't have a relationship with that company."

"How come? My wife works for them. Maybe she can get you a good deal, too."

"Let's get back to your problems."

"Okay. I really love my wife. I don't want to get divorced. I stay with her because she puts up with me most of the time. But I put up with her, too. She doesn't mow the lawn or help take out the trash. She doesn't agree with my politics or help me change the oil in the car. She always bugs me about losing weight while she eats chocolates and she doesn't know a touchdown from a home run."

"Why not divorce? Perhaps you're not right for each other?"

"Sure we are. We're honest and respect each other and . . . okay, I'll get a job."

"Good," said Sally. "And you won't lie to her anymore about making 900 calls?"

"Well, okay."

Sally gave me another 900 number to call. She said I would enjoy it. I hoped for a sexy voice — and got one!

"Hello, you've reached Smith Phone International. My name is . . ."

"Honey, is that you?" My wife laughed.

238

"Yes. Did you enjoy talking with Sally? Did she straighten you out?"

"How do you know her? That was a great prank."

"Her husband owns the company. We have lunch together. She's been married to John 25 years — he's a real pill, just like you. We talk a lot."

I finally laughed, too. "So how come we can't get a deal on those . . . OOPS! . . . 900 calls?"

Shop Together, Stay Together

Body parts and shopping skills are the two most scientific differences between men and women. They are both good topics for discussion, but shopping is less likely to get me in trouble than describing what I know about anatomy.

Body parts attract men and women to each other. Shopping together divides them. The hunter-gatherer theory must be right. Men prefer bagging all they need quickly and with aggressive recklessness, while women shop carefully for building materials for a cozy home before filling their bags with closet stuffers.

Men believe it's important to support our president. When Mr. Clinton said the economy was doing well, I got excited and went to the mall to spend the money he said I have. It was also an opportunity to show my wife that I could be a helpful assistant.

Apparently lots of people support the president. The place was buzzing with excitement. I told my wife I would only spend money on important things, so I quickly found the food court and left her alone to enjoy her kind of feeding frenzy. I wasn't really worried. She's an excellent shopper — only buys what's on "special," which means, of course, it's marked down to what it should have been in the first place.

I returned to the clothing store in an hour. She hadn't bought anything yet — no surprise — because the "specials" didn't fit, weren't the right color or the right price. I pointed at several blouses on a rack. "These look great. What's wrong with this one? Hey, this green one goes with your orange one."

For some reason, three ladies nearby looked at my wife sympathetically. I thought I was being supportive.

I started getting that impatient, jittery feeling, so I went to get a strong cup of coffee to calm down. Then I took her over to the "exclusive" department. I knew we couldn't afford anything there because everything was priced for exclusive people. She suggested I needed more food, but I didn't go for it. I needed to score some marital points so I gave her a hug and told her I would stay behind her 100 percent.

So I followed her back to the "special" department. This time I just stood there without commenting while she fingered every item on the swivel rack. She found something she liked. I got excited. "Great! Go try it on." She returned. "What do you think?"

I thought for a long time before lying.

"It looks good on you, but makes you look a little dumpy. I think you should get something a couple sizes smaller that flatters your great figure." It worked!

She returned the loose, ugly, yellow-striped blouse and bought the nice tight black one that made me very happy.

I kept my promise and stayed behind her 100 percent. I followed her back to the "exclusive" department. She tried on one of those fashionable skirts — the kind that hang loosely over the entire body exposing only the top of the feet.

"Great! Very fashionable." I lied again. "But I think it hides your great figure and that flower print makes you look more like a little girl than the elegant woman you are." It worked! She took the piece of garbage back and bought another short, tight, black skirt which I liked.

I was feeling good. I have my own theory that it's easy to go shopping with your spouse if you use the right strategy. We went to the shoe department where men can test their mental endurance. I saw a great pair of legs on a woman sitting on the chair across from us. "Excuse me, but those shoes you're wearing certainly compliment your legs. What kind are they?"

The lady glared at me. My wife glared at me. My face was red. "I was just trying to help you find the right pair," I said feebly. I had just lost the points I had gained earlier. I excused myself and returned to the food court for dessert. When I returned a half hour later, my wife was sitting in the same chair with six boxes of shoes in front of her. I smiled. "You have such great legs, I want you to take your time to get the right pair."

The store was closing. "We'll take all of them."

I got my points back.

Men know as much about shopping as we do anatomy. And it's definitely a safer topic.

The truth shouldn't offend anyone.

'Til Death Do Us Part: I will, I will, I will

My wife and I had an argument over who would inherit my trophy wine collection should I kick the bucket while table dancing at the New Year's Eve party.

The discussion ended quickly and very cheerfully. We drank the two bottles instead. But when we talked about her antique clothing collection, we couldn't settle our differences. I thought the Salvation Army and she thought more like the Smithsonian.

It was time to make a will, one of those resolutions we postpone every year. My faith in immortality had died recently when I lost an arm-wrestling match to her, so I called Mary, the estate-planning attorney, for an appointment.

Dying isn't funny, but the antics of the heirs are. I remember when my mother died. It was sad for a few days until my brother and I fought over who would get the furniture, the car and the silver dollar collection. So we had to hire an attorney to interpret the will. I got the silver dollar collection and some money, which I spent quickly to buy a used VW from the junk yard. We're still in disagreement over our mother's real intentions, so I haven't spoken to my brother since.

We went to Mary's office.

"I want to give everything to my wife," I said to Mary, "except my cigars, pipes, the autographed baseball, my *Playboy* collection, my Official Super Bowl coffee cup and the boxes of books I wrote still stacked in the garage. I want it all to go in a museum in my name."

"What if you both die together?"

"Then we want to put everything into one of those trust things. You know — no taxes and the kid can't touch the money until he's responsible enough to handle it."

"How old is that?" asked Mary.

"Sixty would be good."

My wife was stone-faced.

"Now let me be clear," I said. "The kid is 14 now, so if anything happens to us we don't want him getting anything until he graduates from college. Then he can have some to get his Master's degree, then a little extra to help him get his Ph.D."

"Oh, good. What is his career interest?" asked Mary.

"Rock guitarist. Spends his time listening to Nirvana when he's not riding the skateboard. We think a Ph.D. in music will be good career insurance, then he can get our money in his later years when he's unable to rock except in his chair."

"How about giving him a portion when he gets married?"

"No way. Why give a kid incentive to marry for money?"

"What about a gift when he has a child?"

"Why give him an incentive to have a kid? There's plenty of them around already."

"What if he doesn't go to college?"

"Then he doesn't get anything until he's sixty. That's incentive to get a job."

My wife sat quietly. Mary looked at her sympathetically.

"What does your husband get if you die first?"

Healthy Sicknesses

"What does your husband get if you die first?"

"He only gets the pots and pans, lawn mower, power tools, stereo, TV and VCR." Mary interrupted with a puzzled look.

"There's a community property law in this state," she said.

"Well, I've earned almost everything, and I know the law. He's supposed to get half of everything we've earned together. I just want to make sure my son is taken care of and my husband doesn't go out and buy that Ferrari he's always talking about."

"Honey, I wouldn't do that!"

"Put that in writing," she said to Mary.

"What about personal property?" asked Mary.

"I want them to go to charity."

My wife shook her head bewildered. "What charity is going to take those old clothes, that Kodak Instamatic and your Casio watch? All you have of any value is your mother's silver dollar collection."

"Nope, not the silver dollar collection. It was part of the agreement with my brother that I had to will it back to him when I croaked."

Mary seemed amused. "Well, it looks like my work's cut out for me. I'll get back to you in a few days."

"Okay," I said. "By the way, what's your fee?" She whispered the figure quietly.

"Yikes! What's left for our estate?"

"How much do you have?"

My wife and I looked at each other and smiled. "Not enough to pay you."

Just enough to drink another couple bottles of estate wine; a resolution we intend to keep.

Healthy Sicknesses

Sleep Survey Results Are In, and . . . zzzzzzzzzzz

An important *U.S. News/CNN* survey indicates 26 percent of Americans who get less than six hours of sleep per night, get some of it while driving. And the survey didn't include teenagers!

This is frightening. That's a lot of car wrecks.

If the results are true, maybe drunk driving should take a back seat to sleeping as the major cause of auto deaths. If the stats *aren't* accurate, maybe it's because of the pollsters. After stopping for naps in their cars, (*the survey was taken in rural towns, no doubt*), they arrived late and weren't too welcome at the homes of the 817 crabby pollees trying to sleep at one o'clock in the morning.

Assuming the survey is fairly accurate, and as a concerned citizen who gets less than six hours of sleep a night, (*I often get 15 during the day*), I spent some time talking with locals about this startling information on "Sleep Drivers." Of course, I only interviewed close-by neighbors so I didn't have to drive.

"Oh, hell yes, I've fallen asleep at the wheel several times," said Bill. "Never thought much about it, though, until you mentioned it. But where else can you get a decent night's sleep when your wife throws you out and you're too drunk to drive?" Bill wasn't much help.

"Hey, Paul. Got a minute?" Paul was getting into his car.

"Sure. Just a minute. Gotta be at my brother's before midnight."

"Have you ever fallen asleep at the wheel?"

"Yeah, a few times. But just for a few seconds. Almost got myself killed a couple times so now I'm very careful. No-Doz and a jug of coffee. No problem."

I pointed at the bottle of water on the floor.

"That? Oh, I splash my face every 30 seconds after the caffeine wears off. Works real good with the window wide open. Loud music helps, too. Those insects, though . . . that's another big problem."

"Doesn't your brother live a long way from here?"

Healthy Sicknesses

"Yeah, but it's only six hundred miles. I've still got six hours. No problem."

"Right. Have a nice trip."

I stopped by at Mildred's, a school-bus driver and our neighborhood's favorite grandmother. She was in her rocker listening to rap music.

"Yes, I fall asleep many times during the day, but not behind the wheel. The bus ride is only 10 minutes each way. It's not a problem. Wouldn't want to hurt any of those children, ya know. I just can't stay away from those darned midnight Bingo games. They just go on forever."

"How many times do you think you nap during the day? Mildred? Mildred! Wake up, Mildred!"

I stopped by to see Martin, a Hell's Angel who runs Devil's Beauty Salon when he's not headin' down a highway, lookin' for adventure or whatever comes his way.

"Hell yes, I sleep on my bike! Me and the *Hog*, we're like soul mates, man. We live and breath together. She's my babe. She keeps me calm. It's tough to find peace when you're born to be wild. On the open highway, I'm relaxed, man, takin' in all that fresh air 'an stuff. Hey, wanna tattoo?"

Lonnie said he sleeps a lot at the wheel, "but there's not much traffic and the new, computerized auto-pilot and cruise-controls work real well." I shook my head in disbelief. I won't fly Trans-Pacific if I ever go to Tahiti.

I stopped by to see psychiatrist Dr. Doze, the world-renowned sleep doctor. I wanted to know about any recent cures for the "Sleep Driver." We shared a bottle of bourbon while he read some passages from his new book, *Sleepy Tales From Dreamland,* and listened to *Rock-a-Bye My Baby* on the stereo.

When I awoke I realized how clever Dr. Doze really is.

His adult-only storybook has pictures of politicians and their campaign speeches. It's got nude photos of celebrities Roseanne, Dr. Ruth, George Foreman and Rodney Dangerfield. It's got details about raising and selling Tsi Tsi flies for sleep and profit, several articles on the federal budget, wiring diagrams for the space shuttle Columbia and several air-head brain teasers.

When I was leaving he gave me a relaxation audio tape that comes with the book. I played it while driving home. *It* worked too!

I told the police I'd gladly pay for the telephone pole if they arrested Dr. Doze for malpractice.

Sometimes a cure is worse than the affliction.

Wonder Vitamins for Wonderful People

The wonderful folks at the One-A-Day vitamin company are popping out a new vitamin for 50-year-olds. In a survey, the company reported consumers chose basketball star Kareem Abdul-Jabbar and actor/dancer Gregory Hines as the two role models in the best shape for half-century old people. President Clinton only tied for second with Cher. Strong vocal cords, I assume, are considered attributes of fitness.

The survey also revealed that 50-year-olds feel better and more self-confident about their states of mind than they did when they were 30, but don't feel as good about their sex drive. Finally, an accurate poll — except for the state of mind thing.

I'm always alert for new wonder drugs that can keep me looking and acting younger than I really am. Like everyone else, I'm a wonderful person, and deserve to stay that way. I'm no fool — I don't buy them. There's something more honest about the laws of nature and capitalism that keep me away from these miracle solutions. To lose weight, I should eat less and exercise more. It's that simple. Most good nutrients can be found in healthy foods like lettuce, broccoli, spinach and ice cream, so who needs vitamins? So, who eats healthy foods? No wonder I struggle.

Just being older than 50 is a healthy sign — you've survived four decades of false hope thinking you were going to live in a big house, drive a luxury car and vacation around the world. No new pill

Healthy Sicknesses

is going to make you feel better when you're living in a meager apartment complex, driving an old Chevy and spending your summer vacation in Detroit or Death Valley.

Most people are still looking for hope and magic. The street hawkers who once sold snake oil cure-alls from the backs of horse-driven carriages, are now living the good life in corporate offices pitching their wares from TV, and on the backs of newspapers and magazines.

We've come a long way to modernize the process, but the process still produces lame antidotes for the human condition. However, if I knew anything about chemistry I'd make and market a Decade(nt) Vitamin. I could use the money. It would improve my state of mind and give me the energy to vacation in Bermuda. It may even improve my sex drive when I become more popular.

Decade 0-10 Vitamin: Shaped like little animals. Taken once a day, they would reduce crying, diaper rash and hyper-activity. Twice daily reduces the stress of over-protective parents, ridicule from peers and TV addiction. Taken three times daily, they would prevent Toy-throwing Syndrome and I Want This-I Want That Disorder.

Decade 11-20 Vitamin: Shaped like Jeans and sports cars. Swallowed once a day with Coke or Pepsi, they reduce laziness, fatigue and aloofness. Increases ability to perform daily household chores and bathe regularly. Taken twice a day with milk shakes, the benefits are significant changes in regularity and manageable hair. If dose is increased to three a day with pizza, sex drive and the compulsion for unusual clothing will be reduced. Cooperation with authority figures and a reduction in Invincibility Syndrome will be observed.

Decade 21-30 Vitamin: Shaped like $100 bills. Ingested once a day with alcoholic beverages, reductions in delusions of grandeur and superiority will be obvious. Taken twice a day with alcoholic beverages, the effects include superior tolerance of authority figures, young children and in-laws. Doses of three per day with tap water increase stamina for child-care, mortgage and car payments. Accompanying reduction in sex drive would also reduce sleeping disorders.

Decade 31-40 Vitamin: Shaped like little mansions. One a day reduces mental strains caused by political rhetoric and spousal unrest. Two a day increases tolerance for mental abuse by teenagers and a decrease in appetite for fast, fatty foods. If taken three times daily with bottled water, renewed desire for fruits and vegetables increases chance for survival into the next decade.

Decade 41-50 Vitamin: Shaped like fashion models and miniature Mercedes. Taken once a day improves mental ability to cope with hair, muscle and tooth loss. Twice a day improves sex drive and reduces the stress of activities involving cost of loans to children and their weddings. Taken three times a day, a noticeable reduction in gardening and TV watching will be replaced by the desire to actively participate in athletic activities. Doctor approval recommended.

Decade 51-60 Vitamin: Read directions on One-A-Day's 50+ vitamins.

Decade 61+ Vitamin: Shaped like hearts and tombstones. One a day, taken with Geritol, prevents irregularity and increases sex drive. Twice a day with Geritol increases sex drive with regularity. Three times a day with alcohol reduces sex drive and decreases chance of getting lucky at all. Taking none reduces my profits but proves you don't need my product.

No new wonder vitamin will make you a wonderful, healthy person. It's naturally wonderful just to be alive.

Smile! There's a Bright Side to Visiting Your Dentist

When I was a little kid I remember singing *All I want for Christmas is my two front teeth.* Well, I got them, but used them to bite off probably more than I should have chewed during the past

Healthy Sicknesses

few decades. Now, as a grown up little kid, I'm singing the blues —
I just got fitted for new teeth. It seems I didn't chomp on the right
kind of gums to keep my own healthy. Maybe not enough brushing
and flossing, either. So now I'm paying the price, a high one at that,
to my dentist, Dr. Molar.

Dr. Mahar, my periodontist, did all she could to save the
molars that have been on death row for years. I tried jawing my way
around for possible solutions to save them, but there was no chance
for a reprieve. She didn't seem too excited about my suggestion for
tying wires around the loose fellas to hold them up. (*It worked on
my back yard fence.*) Finally losing them made me aware I had
taken them for granted too long.

I did some reflecting. Maybe dentists deserve more credit
than they give to us. (*Just try getting a trade-in credit for your old
teeth.*) I've learned the most dreaded of all appointments to keep are
even more dreadful if you don't keep them. The results are painfully
obvious, but there are some positive aspects to a dentist visit.

Clever scheduling isn't publicized much, but everyone
knows it's a legitimate excuse to get off work for a couple hours;
and if you're a really good actor, the emotional trauma of the
experience and the effects of Novocain can get you off for a whole
afternoon. Remember when you were very young, you got little
candy prizes for bravery if you kept your mouth open wide without
crying? Although the goodies were seen as incentives for good
behavior, they were really just clever insurance for the benevolent
dentist that you'd be coming back for more and more treatments.

Later, during the teenage years of heightened self-
consciousness, dentist visits were rewarded with a bright smile and a
day off from school. Oh, the pain! For some lucky few however,
braces were a symbol of self expression, depending on how many
food particles you could show off after eating.

In the primary years of adulthood we began to feel the pain
of more costly treatments because *we* suddenly had to pay instead of
our parents. And as the years go by, root canals, bridges, supports
and cement begin taking on more negative meanings than a civil

engineer might find enjoyable. Replacements are the ultimate disaster, especially if you like to sing the Bobby Darin classic about the "shark biting, with his teeth, dear," but you have nothing of your own to show.

Personally, I enjoy my dental visits early in the morning. That chair is so comfortable I can get some extra sleep. Except for one adult-only dentist who once had some interesting, provocative art on display, I can usually doze off while looking at little Teddy bears and happy rabbits running along the ceiling. Lidocaine, Xylocaine and Novocain are also excellent pacifiers if you keep your eyes closed while the dentist brings that long needle from behind his back before he sticks it where you think it's going to come out through your nose. I prefer drinking a couple of Hurricanes before the visit — if someone can drive me home.

I'm fortunate that Dr. Molar makes my visits educational as well as fun. He explains quite clearly, and with a sense of humor, that Amalgam is that high-tech mixture of chemicals like glue and tooth paste, used to make fillings. Those amazingly effective toothpicks and drills are called scalers, burs, explorers and probes. And masculine teeth are more square and bulky than feminine ones which are more narrow with softer corners.

One of his customers, an elderly fellow, was complaining that his wife wanted him to talk more. Dr. Molar, always up on important current dental research, informed the man that women use 40,000 more words per day talking than men do. (*Nobody has talked to me about this important fact. I'd prove it wrong in less than an hour.*) So the man requested women's teeth to help him get along better with his wife.

Dr. Molar is one of the few medical professionals I've met who doesn't make me suffer by reading old magazines while waiting in the lobby. He's always punctual. This helped explain why he refused my request for the feminine teeth. He has trouble making me stop asking him so many questions, so he can get his work done, and get to the next customer.

But I believe in talking a lot in the chair before the work starts so the dentist suffers as much as I do. It's a lot more fun that way and I always leave with a bigger and brighter smile.

The Real Tobacco Hypocrisy

Spitting venomous words at these helpless, persecuted little companies that can't advertise and must now pay large sums of money to such innocent victims of nicotine, is as unsavory as a dirty spittoon — and just as tasteless. It's hypocritical to chew on tobacco companies just because their products are addictive and deadly. It's just a smoke screen for discrimination at its highest level.

Current science proves that obesity and dietary fat are *equally* as deadly as nicotine — and try telling me that you don't know someone addicted to cheese and ice cream, pizza or even cooking oil. And smokers are *far less* numerous than overweight citizens. It doesn't take a Mars scientist to deduce that the number of advertisements for exercise equipment, diet books and low-fat foods far outnumber those for tobacco. And what good can we possibly say about the quantity of ads promoting full-drip bacon cheeseburgers, pizza, ice cream and other delicious but lethal foods?

Politically-correct hypocrites are worried only about the advertisers getting teenagers hooked on cigarettes. What happened to the lofty concept of setting healthful examples for our children? How can our forked-tongue president gleefully stuff Big Macs and cigars in his mouth while he uses the same body orifice to espouse healthy living? What are we doing to protect all the truly helpless, small children who are bombarded constantly with ads for unhealthy sugar-laden breakfast cereals and fat-laden candy bars before they're barely old enough to chew them? Something is wrong here.

If the tobacco companies have to endure the rabid hypocrisy of our intrusive government in the courts, then I propose we sue for this one too.

251

Healthy Sicknesses

"Court is now in session. Mr. Candy, you may proceed."

"Thank you your honor. I'm about to bring 187 dying witnesses to the stand, but I'd first like to request a wider witness chair for their comfort. We intend to prove beyond a doubt, that the relentless advertising by these ice cream, pizza and cooking oil companies have contributed to my clients' illnesses and the deaths of 150 million citizens since 1960. Additionally, we intend to prove that . . ."

"Objection, your honor. Mr. Candy is inferring that my clients intentionally coerced their customers into clogging up their arteries and consuming and becoming fat. He's also speculating that their products are addictive."

"Objection over-ruled. Sit down Mr. Snakeoil. Mr. Candy, you may proceed."

"Your honor, I've had two heart surgeries. I smoked two packs and ate a pint of Haagen Dazs a day, four KFC chickens and two extra-large pepperoni and cheese pizzas a week. Since my surgery I've given up the cigarettes, but I haven't yet shaken the need for my fat fixes. I've . . ."

"Mr. Candy, the court isn't interested in your personal history. Proceed with your first witness before I hold you in contempt for making me hungry."

"Mrs. Brady. Isn't it true that you've gained over 125 pounds since you became depressed after quitting smoking? Is it not true that you feel better watching pizza commercials on TV only if you're eating one at the same time?"

"Yes, it's all true. But I'd like to add that . . ."

"Thank you Mrs. Brady."

"Mr. Snakeoil, You may cross examine."

"Mrs. Brady. I regret your plight. However, isn't it also true that your doctor told you to exercise to burn off the fat calories? And isn't it also true that you didn't follow his advice?"

"Well, yes, sir. But . . ."

"That'll be all, Mrs. Brady."

Healthy Sicknesses

"Your honor, my next witness is 15-year-old Billy Wobble. Billy, have you ever seen tobacco ads? And did they make you want to go out and start smoking? My second question. Have you ever seen pizza, ice cream, hamburger and fried chicken commercials? Did they make you drool and want to eat?"

"Like, no. I've never smoked. It's a dirty habit. But like yeah, I always go for those cool food commercials. I don't think I could go a day without a pizza, hamburger or fried chicken."

"Well, Billy. Would you say you're addicted to these foods?"

"Like I'm not sure what addicted means. But, like I think I'd rather die than not be able to eat them."

"Objection, your honor. Mr. Candy is trying to compare food with tobacco. We all need to eat, but we don't need to smoke."

After 97 witnesses the judge was removed from the trial — conflict of interest — he owned shares of stock in KFC. Mr. Candy and Mr. Snakeoil were also relieved of their duties. They owned shares in General Foods and R.J. Reynolds.

The re-trial of the class-action suit against the fatty food companies is pending. Mr. Clinton has appointed a special, portly, PR panel to determine whether he should give up the Big Macs before he has the FDA limit fats in foods as it is now doing for the nicotine in cigarettes.

It may be politically correct to be a hypocrite. But if you're going to chew on the tobacco companies, don't chew the fat in your food. This is a discriminatory and deadly issue. It can't and shouldn't be solved through regulation.

Personal choice and responsibility are the only healthy solutions true to the American spirit.

253

Employee Benefits for
the New Century

Employee benefits have always been an issue of great concern for both employees and employers. Employees want it all; health care, pensions, maternity leave, savings plans, holidays, four-week vacations, sick leave and big paychecks. Employers would prefer the complete elimination of benefits — just common sense to many of them.

This may sound extreme, but I've gotten pretty angry lately, discovering that few employers give their employees any significant discounts on merchandise and services aside from paper clips, pencils, personal phone calls and scraps of food. Just the other day I was at the check-out counter of my local supermarket. I asked the cashier how much discount she gets on groceries. "None." Why not? At a new car dealership employees get a discount that reduces the monthly payment from $350 to $348, but no free oil changes.

Even employees working at the local sewer district just get a bunch of crap when they ask for discounted service for doing their dirty work. Employees at telephone companies get nothing but long distances from their supervisors when they ask for bigger discounts than regular folks like you and I can get. How much would it cost the company? Military personnel can't buy used tanks, assault weapons, submarines or jet aircraft. Instead, like the groceries, the old stuff is given or sold to food banks and potential enemy countries. Diamond miners, risking their lives every day clawing the soil, don't even get to keep the little shavings they dig up and hide under their fingernails.

This isn't fair. When I worked at one of the first McDonald's 35 years ago, I was the night manager and cooked up quadruple cheeseburgers, shakes with real ice cream and then brought home the unsold burgers and fries, lying under the heat lamp, to feed the family. This was completely acceptable then. When I got fired for throwing a raw hamburger at a drunken customer who stuck his obstinate head in the order window after the grill was closed, (*he asked for a* fresh *one rather than one under the heat lamp*), the generous day manager gave me a huge bag of burgers, fries and ice cream for severance pay. Not a bad deal considering my salary was $1.35 an hour.

I've heard the excuses from employers, especially at fast food places, that if employees could eat all they wanted during work hours, it would be like a leaky faucet — a little bit adds up to a lot.

That's a puddle of gunk. A hamburger costs about 40 cents to make, I suspect. If 10 employees each ate 10 burgers, that would be 100, a total cost to the establishment of $40. Do you know anyone who can eat that many? Do you think $40 would hurt your local hamburger joint if it had dependable, happy and well-fed employees?

Conventional benefits are indeed extremely costly to an employer, so what we need is an unconventional new concept for the next century. I've come up with a plan that is less costly and certainly more practical — steeply discounted products and services for those who produce them. The actual cost of producing goods and services is only a fraction of what a consumer pays, so why shouldn't employees be given the opportunity to save considerably on what they produce instead of getting costly benefits which shouldn't really be an employer's responsibility anyway? Harsh? Not necessarily.

Where I live, for example, the Boeing Company makes commercial jets. If the company eliminated all conventional benefits, it could probably offer its $150 million 747 jumbo jets to employees at cost; about half price, I'm guessing. This could certainly make the employees more excited and productive. The thought of owning a private 747 like the president's would be a lot classier than dreaming of having a new car, and they could even live in their new plane when it's grounded — if they could only afford the parking space. The company wouldn't suffer because nobody could afford one anyway. After all, it's the thought that counts.

Nike employees should get those $100 Michael Jordan shoes at the $10 it costs to make them in China, and then they could

Healthy Sicknesses

run at a healthy pace from Nike Town to their bank to deposit their savings they'd certainly enjoy.

I think IRS agents shouldn't have to pay taxes. If most of them were laid off instead, I can assure you none of us would complain, and those left working would be very pleased they had a job at all. I believe prison guards should get free room and board in empty cells and school bus drivers should be allowed to take the buses home on weekends and holidays for vacation campers.

I would like to see those folks working in sweat shops get free clothes, shoes and athletic equipment. Those poor souls sitting or standing for hours assembling computer chips and mother boards should get a few big bytes off the cost of a new computer and those who manufacture cars should get a free one if they can ride out a good year of hard work without being absent more than a month.

Doctors and mechanics should get free spare parts and politicians and clowns should receive similar costume allowances. People who harvest corn, wheat and tomatoes should get free tortillas and pasta, along with sauces that go with them. Grape pickers should be allowed to drink all the wine they want during working hours to get them through another hard day.

Politicians should get all the benefits they provide their constituents — promises that they'll be re-elected if they do a good job of lying.

The problem with my suggestion is I haven't figured out why most people who make products or provide services would even want discounts on something they're sick of seeing or doing everyday. Perhaps, like the leaky faucet or the trickle-down theory of economics, my idea may be clogged by a little dementia.

But I still think there should be such a thing as a free lunch for those who prepare it. It just makes good sense.

PART SEVEN
Almost Serious Reflections

The Child in the Mirror

Most people equate growing up with growing older. I see it all around me while I'm having fun — usually in the strange facial expressions of those who take the time to watch or listen to me.

Recently, in the elevator of an office building, I quipped to one of the mannequins that moved only to push a button; "I haven't found a bathroom that doesn't need a key. Which one is the lucky number?" The well-dressed, distinguished gentleman replied with a snicker, "Grow up," as he turned his charm to a young woman in the elevator with us. She wasn't impressed, and I felt better.

Normally I don't take such an insult too personally, but I was in a bad mood — I had almost cried when I had to pay $5 for parking. That was my lunch money. When I finally got to the 15th floor to meet Jim, a tolerant friend who has a regular job, yet still talks with me, I whined that I was broke and wouldn't be able to pick up the lunch tab.

"I planned to pay anyway," he said. "You'll never grow up."

Jim and I had a good lunch. But when the waitress came by to ask if everything was all right, I couldn't help myself; I put on one of my happy grins and said, "No! I think the bartender left the alcohol out of my drink, and the fly in my soup wasn't dead, so I'm getting a buzz in my stomach instead of my head."

Jim was embarrassed, of course, but the waitress giggled. "Haven't heard that one before. Would you like another bowl of soup or another drink on the house?"

"No," I replied. "I'm afraid of heights." The waitress cracked up. I got the attention every child deserves.

Well, at least I thought I was funny. Jim just looked at her and rolled his eyes the way so many others do when I'm playing my silly games.

Later, while I was saying good-bye to Jim, I noticed that the same young lady from the elevator was shoveling papers all over the reception desk. I realized she was trying to look busy in front of her boss. "I used to do that, too," I said, "but once I got my computer I couldn't fake it anymore. You do a great job of it!" Of course, she blushed at the truth, and again Jim gave me the rolling eye routine. And, just as I turned around to leave, the young woman said, "Nice to meet you. You're sure more fun than most of the dull people who come in here asking for appointments or the bathroom key."

Again I felt worthy of my childish antics.

In the elevator again, I ran into another group of walking mummies. I had to get them "unwrapped," if you know what I mean. "Hey, does anybody know which floor has a bathroom I can use that doesn't need a key? I've got an immediate problem here. There was a fly in my soup today, and now it's heading south — fast."

This group of elevator deadbeats came to life quickly, so it was good that they got off on the next floor. I was able to chuckle at my success rather than suffer more insulting remarks.

I had so much fun on the elevator, I stayed on for a few more rides to practice my childish behavior and make people laugh or wonder. Some of my routines were real crowd pleasers, others weren't. I was lucky enough to meet the distinguished gentleman again. "Hey, how ya doin'?" He sneered back.

"Shouldn't you be in school today? Does your truant officer know where you are?"

I gave him one of my sheepish grins.

"You know, when I bumped into that nice young lady you were flirting with in the elevator — you know — your boss' secretary, I asked her if she knew you. She said, 'oh, yes.' Apparently a lot of other nice young ladies do, too."

"And what did she have to say?"

"She sneered. 'Dirty old man.'"

Almost Serious Reflections

I don't understand what's so great about growing up. My morning mirror certainly reflects weary eyes sinking deeper into their sockets and skin that's getting saggier around the chin and neck. But I like to make faces in my mirror, temporarily changing myself into a little kid. It's good for laughs, it's fun and makes it easier to live with more courage and a helluva lot more enthusiasm.

I'm not growing up, just growing older. What's so bad about acting childlike to feel that adrenaline rush you only get by acting out the innocence and freedom of youth?

I prefer reflecting on the child in the mirror to contemplating the bleak illusions of growing up.

An Exaggerated Dose of Nostalgia

I just got off the phone with Beverly. She was my ninth-grade crush 38 years ago, but I didn't let her know until today. I figured it was okay to call her now that it was safe, both of us being married and all, and living far apart.

I was revisiting my past recently, glancing through old yearbooks and at pictures stuffed in a cigar box. According to the autographs, I was quite a guy back then. I looked pretty good in the pictures, too. Not much has changed, I thought.

Bev was that girl you once knew who wore the drab, frumpy clothes covering everything but hands and bobby socks, but had the beauty and charm reserved for saints. She was very smart and unpretentious. I didn't talk to her much in high school because I had bet friends that one day she would wise up and marry me. I was playing hard-to-get. I lost a lot of money when she left without saying good-bye after graduation, but it wasn't the $5 that hurt. It was pride — humility wasn't one of my strong points back then.

"My goodness," she said. "How nice to hear your voice."

Almost Serious Reflections

I was relieved she didn't ask why I was calling, because I wasn't really sure. "Just thought I'd see how your life turned out," I explained awkwardly.

"You bet money that we'd get married?" she asked curiously. "How flattering. How come you never told me?"

"I thought you'd chase me like all the other girls, but you were too shy," I said.

"Why are you telling me now?"

"I'm not sure."

I told her about all the great things I've accomplished — straight "A's" in college, the Congressional Medal of Honor for service in Viet Nam, the Pulitzer Prize for writing columns, a contract to pitch for the Los Angeles Dodgers, (*until I broke my arm saving a child's cat from a tree during a windstorm*) writing scripts for *Seinfeld*, advising Presidents Bush and Ford how to beat the Democrats and tutoring Bill Gates in computer technology.

"I always knew you'd do well." She was always kind.

"Really? Then how come you didn't chase me?"

"Because I felt so inferior. You were so good looking and smart and popular that I never thought I had a chance."

"Yeah, but don't you remember the kissing party at Jeannie's house in junior high?" I asked. Beverly giggled.

"You were the best," I said.

"But Jeannie was the sexy one, wasn't she?"

"Well, I guess. But her lipstick got all over my face and it smelled bad." Bev had a good memory.

"And you left early and walked home after kissing me, didn't you?"

"Well, yes, but I had a couple other girls waiting for me and I wanted to give some of the other guys a chance with you."

Bev didn't respond.

She told me she had earned three Master's degrees and had worked as a librarian, teacher, media specialist and syndicated movie critic. I wasn't surprised.

"What else do you remember about me in junior high?"

"Well, you wore baggy pants and your hair was oiled down with Vaseline and you hung out with Darryl, Gary, Marty and Victor."

"I remember them," I said. They were the school's smartest guys and best athletes. That's why they always wanted me around. I was good for their image. And Victor — he was the guy you foolishly favored over me."

"Yes," Bev said quickly. "I remember that your imagination was always healthier than reality. I see you haven't changed much."

I was silent for a few moments. She wasn't fooled by my stories. I could feel tears forming. "Bev, you were my first love, you know."

"I always suspected so," she said, "but I didn't want to hurt your feelings. I knew I wasn't right for you."

I'm glad I talked with Bev. She was always honest and practical. The truth is painful sometimes, so maybe that's why I prefer telling tall tales — it's easier to enjoy the fantasies.

I thought of tracking down some more old friends for nostalgia's sake. But after thinking for awhile about my conversation with Bev, I realized that my imagination many times serves me better than the truth.

I really was quite a guy back then. Humble, too.

A Course in Art Appreciation

For years I've been wondering how to pay homage to the best neighbor anyone could have. I couldn't find the appropriate contest to submit his name to, so I decided to vote him into the Schwartz Hall of Fame. This honor won't get him any monetary rewards, but perhaps he'll find some gratification knowing I learned a lot about art appreciation without going to art school.

Almost Serious Reflections

Art Smith lives two houses up the street. I met him after getting married. My wife had casually told me how kind he had been during her divorce, and what large shoulders he had to cry on for a man five-foot-seven.

He's about my age, works as an electronics technician and has two sons. Russ is a talented teenage artist working long hours to become a famous cartoonist. Sean, the elder, ranks high in being a hard-working young man with a talent for mimicking Buddy Holly and detailing cars and trucks. (*We get a discount.*)

During my first crisis I was hesitant to ask Art to come over after knowing him only two weeks. It was quite embarrassing to explain to him how the toilet got clogged, but I would've been in deep do-do with my wife had I paid a plumber to fix my accident. Art didn't hesitate. I was saved. Two weeks later, he fixed a shorted-out light switch. Then he assembled our kitchen fluorescent lights.

In five years he's helped build my office, fixed our VCR twice, my portable tape recorder three times, lawn mower twice and hauled dirt in his truck for landscaping. Once when I was away, the water heater blew, and sure enough, he came over to help my wife buy and install a new one.

On several occasions he's driven us 40 miles to the airport and picked us up when we returned. He's listened to me complain about everything that doesn't work including my writing, but he claims he can't help me with that. He's probably just being modest as usual.

His most significant and caring deed was during a vicious weather front at home while we were in Europe during Christmas, 1996. A significant amount of snow fell, followed by heavy rain. We read about it in a European newspaper. We worried. When we returned to see our front street covered with silt and sandbags, I quickly imagined our garage must be a disaster, too. It wasn't.

"Well," he said when he walked over to visit the next day, "I was concerned, so at two in the morning I came over and discovered the heavy rain was rapidly melting the snow and it was beginning to flow into your garage. So all I did was clean the gutters

264

and dig a trench to divert the water somewhere else. I was finished before breakfast."

That is the kind of man he is. We're not close friends and we don't have much in common except trust. We'd like to be considered a good neighbor by him also, but so far all we've been able to do is take care of his cats, give him a ride to pick up his car or truck when they're being repaired and enjoy an occasional dinner with him.

Few people are in my Hall of Fame. If I had a museum for it, his picture would loom large at the entrance. After all, he'd probably be the one who framed and mounted it, built the structure and kept the utilities functioning properly. The best that we can do is let him know we appreciate his overwhelming kindness.

Since I can't build my own Hall of Fame, I had a small plaque engraved for him to hang somewhere in his own home. *"A good neighbor respects our privacy. A great neighbor honors us with appropriate intimacy. Thank you, Art Smith."*

Tribute to a Special Friend

It was the 40th anniversary of Cory Hovander's birthday this week. You probably didn't hear or read about it in the news because he is a closely guarded secret. There are many selfish people like me who don't want to share him.

He's a real gem — hard as a rock, smooth as glass and glitters with personality. I'm roasting him because I want to embarrass him in front of everybody when I read this out loud during desert at the little French dive where we're taking him to celebrate his birthday.

Cory is also like a good cheese. He has aged gracefully with good taste, is soft and well textured but smells somewhat better. (*He needs cologne.*) He appreciates gourmet food, his old Mercedes-Benz, his Beatles' memorabilia, fine clothes, fine women, sports trivia and is in excellent health and very athletic. (*Remember, he needs cologne.*) He's also been known to lift a whole case of beer, one can at a time, without even the slightest strain. According to Cory, his many female admirers think he's "drop-dead" good-looking, but to me he's just a friend — the kind we all need.

I met Cory when I first moved to Washington. He manages an RV park. We became real friends very quickly. I've always said a real friend does three things — helps you move, takes your calls at two in the morning and helps you paint. We hit it off because we could exchange obnoxious insults with ease and had the same high-class tastes with a low-class budget.

I was impressed that he helped me move my belongings from the storage unit into my first apartment. He rushed to the hospital when the nurse called him at two in the morning, after I awoke from heart surgery. His generous smile always makes me feel better — when I'm broke, not feeling well, bragging about the sexual prowess of my youth, had a lousy day at the golf course or when I'm constipated. He had even cheered me up when the drunk woman at Billy Bob's country-western bar punched me in the chest for refusing to dance with her just three weeks after I left the hospital.

"Don't worry about it," he said. "If you have to get your chest redone, I know a good lawyer. I also know her probation officer. Her ex-husband is still in the hospital."

I was delighted Cory knew important people and was willing to share.

As further proof of our bonded friendship, he climbed our roof to paint the trim. (*I fear heights on sunny days.*) I didn't even mind picking up the beer cans when he was finished. He didn't tell me until later that he would have preferred Beatles' music rather than the Chopin I played for him while I was sunning myself below.

Cory says he's intelligent, too. He knows the secrets of politics and economics. One day I asked him why he spent so much money on a first date with one of his followers.

"Life is politics," he said. "If you want to win over a woman, a congressman or a country, it's all the same. It's important that you impress upon them that you have the money to get them what they want. Show them they're important to you. Show them you care. Make it a win-win situation. Take 'em to Billy Bob's!"

I asked him where he got the money.

"Leverage. I learned to use other people's money instead of my own. I have six credit cards and I keep them all up to their limits. That's good economics."

Always the adventurer, he once joined me on a fishing trip. He doesn't like to kill anything, but will eat almost anything that's dead. So when I was about to throw back a six-inch trout I caught while he was finishing off a six-pack as our designated drinker, he smashed the poor fish against the rocks to prove he was a real hunter. Then he took a picture of the bloody rock to remember his deed. It's still framed on his kitchen wall. He's never fished since, and I still remember dining out on fish and chips after the big catch.

I've obviously exaggerated Cory's character and deeds. My purpose was to make him smile that big smile, not to cry in his soup at dinner.

He's been one of my inspirations to keep living. He's there when you need him, and even when you don't, but always cheerful even if he's secretly hurting inside. His generosity is saintly, even if he isn't. Happy birthday, Cory.

You're another decade old, and even more decadent.

To Be or Not to Be? That's Indeed a Question

To be a writer or not to be is my current dilemma. As a humorist, I can assure you it's no laughing matter.

Hamlet, too, asked himself in a time of crisis; "To be, or not to be?"

Almost Serious Reflections

"Am I, or am I not?" This disturbing question has been haunting me for several months with some ghostly thoughts unworthy of stone monuments.

". . . 'Tis nobler in the mind to suffer the slings and arrows of outrageous fortune, or to take arms against a sea of troubles and by opposing, end them?"

I've been seriously pondering the thoughts of Shakespeare's tragic character. But I am just a character with no outrageous fortune and with a mind that's lost its noble cause. My sea is just down the street, and rather than trouble, my sea provides the only stage where I can contemplate my crisis in peace. I'm not interested in being a tragic hero; but it would be nice just to be a hero to someone, if only myself.

The irony lies in my struggle between laboring at real work that's necessary, or just loving the labor of writing that's not. Humor was never my intended course, but I do find it funny that the Great American Novel was my majestic dream. Patience is not my great virtue, if I have any at all. I'm feeling dry. No inspiration, no perspiration.

As I ponder the future, the torment increases as my a ho-hum existence settles into a long-term reality. There's little glamour in writing, but I find the dignity of real work less satisfying. Fortunately, my editor is compelled to remain in my employ — not for the meager wages, but because he's a masochist with a sense of humor who thrives on mending my words without mincing his. So instead of trying to force a funny column, I shared my struggle with him, hoping to uncover some answers to my problem.

Editor: "So, what kind of job are you thinking about?"

Me: "Returning to public relations. Make lots of money and work with movers and shakers again. I miss the camaraderie and stimulation."

Editor: "You're thinking of promoting a strip joint and a menagerie? How are you going to explain away the past seven years at your interviews?"

Almost Serious Reflections

Me: "Well, I could tell the truth. I've been writing books, planting grass and learning to cook. But I'm afraid any astute boss will see right through me."

Editor: "What do you mean?"

Me: "My only T-shirt has my tortoise logo from my column. It shows through a dress shirt. Sure giveaway I may not be the fast-laner they're looking for. Maybe I need new T-shirts with a Roadrunner printed on them."

Editor: "Get some regular T-shirts. But how are you going to get dressed early every morning and drive the crowded freeways to the city? You'll fall asleep at work."

Me: "No problem. Once I lose 30 pounds I'll fit into my custom-made clothes. Then I'll buy a new car with an automatic transmission, temperature control and a stereo system. Then I'll buy a new health club membership near the office and . . ."

Editor: "Whoa! You said you wanted a regular job to make more money. Now you're spending it all on things you don't need."

Me: "Yeah. Well image is important out in the real world. It's okay to wear my robe around here all day and talk and act weird and shower only when my wife can no longer tolerate me. Writers are expected to be eccentric."

Editor: "So what makes you think you're really ready for playing in the business world? You'll have to follow rules again, go to meetings, get along with people and make reports on your work progress for your boss."

Me: "I can do all that if I have to. But I'll be so busy doing the wheeling and dealing with the really important people that I won't have time to talk to my colleagues and the boss. I always got great results before. And I can take naps during the meetings if I sit in the back."

Editor: "Don't you remember getting laid off and fired time and again?"

Me: "Sure. But that wasn't my fault. The system doesn't provide the right atmosphere for creativity and independent thought. There's always somebody that thinks they know more than me."

Editor: "I think you know what to do. Go walk by your sea."

Me: "Yeah. You're probably right. I need to write some good columns, sell more books and take more showers. Then maybe my true boss will give me a raise."

Editor: "Now you're talking. Now go do it."

I had played Hamlet in college and knew the role well. Shakespeare said that all the world is a stage and we're just actors. I agree. Sometimes it's just difficult to remember our roles.

Ay, there's the rub!

My Life in Mukilteo

I'm so grateful to be alive, I cry sometimes while walking alone on 5th Street during the dreary Northwest months between November and April. The gray clouds, fog, mist and rain crowd the sky, but after wiping the moisture from my eyes, I can clearly see the whitecaps hopping across the water of Puget Sound.

Across the Sound, Whidbey Island provides a remarkable background for the two white, almost luminous ferries that carry hundreds of cars and passengers between the crowded docks.

The large blasts from the ferry fog horns, the clanking sounds of the local train carrying parts to the nearby Boeing Company, lonely dogs barking for attention and children playing are diversions more welcome than the sirens and honking horns of the city I once called home. When spring air and sunshine open the flowers to introduce the new season of color, warm weather and just a hint of the tourist season, I smile. I'm reminded of my good fortune to be alive in Mukilteo, not dead in Los Angeles where I suffered a heart attack and much disillusionment. If I believed in the after life, this would be heaven. I do believe in dying and this is where I'd like to do it — I just hope it takes awhile.

Almost Serious Reflections

I abandoned the excitement and complexity of city life to find the kind of peace where I could grow without peer pressure. But I'll always have city blood. Fortunately Seattle is only 25 miles south when I need a fix. I don't go there except to sell books or attend an occasional concert or play. Most frequently it's to take visiting friends to experience Pike Place Market and Pioneer Square.

Mukilteo is a hearty meal for the soul, but sometimes I do miss the cultural diversity and associations I had with the power brokers of Los Angeles. I felt important there. Now I feel nothing when remembering the meaningless ingestion of political, material and natural pollution.

I've attained a new power base here thanks to Paul Archipley. Another Los Angeles emigrant, he started Mukilteo's first weekly newspaper, *The Mukilteo Beacon* and included my *Life in the Slow Lane* column. It's given me, along with my first book, a hint of celebrity, but mostly notoriety. I don't notice it unless somebody comments on something I wrote, which is less frequently than I would like. I've been able to let go of my custom-made suits and shirts, and have found a comfortable existence within the loose confines of my robe, Dockers, jeans and a few bargain shirts from K-Mart and Costco.

Mukilteo is a native American word for "good camping ground" and our little house and large yard make it feel that way. It fits Old Town, the area near the ferry dock where we live. Back in 1861 the Washington Territorial government established Snohomish County and made Mukilteo its county seat. Now we have a city of 15,000, but no skyscrapers. Politics here are like anywhere else, I can only suppose, because I don't participate — my irreverent humor doesn't earn me much respect on serious matters. Our city council does its best not to alienate us with tax increases for things we want but don't want to pay for, and our police are friendly if you don't break the law too much and support the idea of someone opening our first donut shop sometime soon.

We don't have a Main, or a Maple or an Elm Street, but we do have our archaic, Mukilteo Speedway. It takes us from one end of town to the other, although the 35-mph limit for a speedway can make an intelligent person question our city's rational thinking. I get sad sometimes when driving slowly up the 5-mile stretch of strip malls, new housing construction and fast-food stores. The resplendent beauty of the distant snow-capped Olympic mountains, the orange-red sunset reflections on the water of the Sound and the stark, natural outline of Whidbey Island are slowly becoming a vague part of the background to progress, rather than the calming equalizers they once were for weary workers returning home.

At the water's edge is the ferry dock, lighthouse and our own state park — there's not much there except parking spots and a boat launch, so I feel special when I take many walks down there to air out my stale mind after being cooped up too long in my stuffy office. I always regret it, breathing heavily on the way back up the hill to home. Our operating lighthouse next to the park is a tourist attraction, so I paid to have my name engraved on a floor tile there. I'm hoping people will see it and remember my literary contributions to the city.

I once dreamed of being a famous author so I could have an excuse to hang out at bars, wear whatever I wanted and sleep only when necessary, not scheduled to a job. But I don't drink, except for an occasional glass of good wine. I'm fortunate that just two blocks away is my favorite hangout, the Marco Polo Restaurant. It includes a delicious view of the Sound to go with its good food. I'm usually greeted by Eddie, the anarchist waiter with a political science degree, who serves up great political conversation to challenge my conservative thinking. Karim, the owner and chef with a golden heart to match his culinary treasures, keeps me off the diet wagon but welcomes me as family, not just a customer. Shireen, the waitress, reminds me kindly that it's not important how much I leave for a tip, as long as I leave. She has great humor — I hope. None of them comment on my food-stained shirts — probably because it's mostly their food, but when my wife joins me, they remark how nice I look in clean clothes.

Almost Serious Reflections

A hundred yards up the street is the Mukilteo Coffee Company. This is the popular eatery where Gary, the owner with the great first name, roasts and brews his own special coffees. Across the patio is Riley's Pizza, another popular eating hole where former mayor Brian Sullivan serves up his micro-brewed beer and heart-stopping good food. But he obviously didn't learn much about creative campaign fund-raising — he lives across the street as just another good neighbor. Arnie's, The Buzz Inn, Ivar's and Cheers Two are other nearby feeding holes which I frequent rarely because I can't afford too many hangouts on a hanger-on budget.

When I run people off by ranting about my cynical views of the world, or complain about the barking dogs keeping me from my work (*always a good excuse*), and when I can't find someone to rant at, I always find a ready audience at the nearby Boeing gymnasium. Julie, Greg, Robyn and Diane are good listeners because they're trained and always ready to answer the questions I've repeated so many times when I run out of interesting things to say. "How many calories does it take to lose 20 pounds? How many times a week do I have to do this stuff? Does golf count?" Karim's Sunday buffet is always a good excuse, but I get no sympathy from anyone.

When I do go up the hill from my house, it's usually to the post office where Tom, the postmaster, and his coworkers Karen, Lynda and Berit, humor me when I disregard the *No Soliciting* sign and sell my book anyway. Near the post office is the Lotus Restaurant, where the cheerful, hard-working Melissa serves up my special combination lo-mein to perfection — not much oil, low in salt and lots of vegetables to go with the noodles. I always stop there after going to the bank — if I'm fortunate enough to have a deposit for my book account. Melissa doesn't see me as often as I'd like.

At the bank, Kim H. and Kim B., Heather and Diana treat me like a real celebrity — no free samples, but they do ask for my autograph again and again — depositing checks or to open my safe box. They were among the first to buy my book, so I like to give them the same interest as they have given me.

273

Almost Serious Reflections

Mickey runs the best clip joint in town. He's the barber located next to Riley's and the Coffee Company. I got a good clipping by him a couple times, but then discovered Andie. She operates another clip joint a couple miles away and is better looking than Mickey, so I prefer her to stroke my hair.

At the south end of town is Harbour Pointe, the new ritzy area where large homes and the Harbour Pointe Golf Course have changed the rhythm of our lives. I hear there are some bad feelings between Old Town residents and those of Harbour Pointe — something to do with who pays the most taxes and who gets the most benefits. Nothing unusual. But Boeing, our wealthy neighbor, seems in a good position to provide some steady jobs to ensure our city's survival in spite of the trivial rivalry.

When I first moved here in 1991 I was depressed. Many said the rain and overcast skies would send me running home to Los Angeles. They were wrong. I like being despondent in a rainy environment. It encourages me to write, and when I write well I feel well. And when the sun invites me out for golf, fishing, work in the yard or just to gaze at the magnificent sights of this paradise, I'm always reminded of my good fortune. I feel alive among so many people who share my views.

I hope paradise remains (*in the minds of others*) a fantasy island where warm breezes caress the leaves of tropical foliage, and lightly clad, tanned people live in harmony eating pineapples and sipping sweet drinks found beneath umbrellas in tall glasses.

That image will preserve my place here in the real paradise.

THANK YOU:

FOREIGN COUNTRIES

Canada
Michael & Leslie Dawes, Richmond
Robert & Carrie Johns, Surrey
Mary-Ann Adrian, Surrey
Margaret Gansner, Comox
Darrel & Jill Haines, Langley
Sally Lever, Surrey
Emily Scott, West Vancouver
Bill Taylor, Victoria
David & Ita Bayne, Tsawwassen Delta
Rod Foley, Abbotsford
Vivian Fuerst, Vernon
Margaret Jenkins, Victoria
Marianne Kasperson, Coquitlam
Gordon & June Litster, Nanaimo
Joan Schneider, New Westminster
Tina Vayda, Toronto

Mexico
Alejandro Guerrero, MD, Merida
Jim & Carol Burry, Puerto Vallarta
Norma San Miguel de Wyse, Ajijic
Cesar & Maru Madero, Granjas

Saudi Arabia
Marjorie Burnell Dhahran

England
Dave Shaw, Rochdale
Gareth Hemming, Wales

New Zealand
Jacqueline Bale, Hatfields Beach

Germany
Kevin & Susan Casey, Heidelberg

Australia
Ennio Morello, Batemans Bay
Susan & Tyler Goss, E. Melbourne

UNITED STATES

Alaska
Marcy Green, Haines
Bill & Bonnie Mehner, Anchorage

Alabama
Thierry and Tracy Ross, Dothan
Todd Walton, Birmingham

Arkansas
Barbara Nelson, Almyra

Arizona
Heidi Anderson, Phoenix
Lori Daigle, Glendale
Julia Morgan, Mesa
Al & Doris Nemite, Quartzsite

California
Suzanne Alexander San Mateo
Robin Austin, San Francisco
Glenn & Marilyn Back, Santa Maria
Marilyn Baehler, Grass Valley
Erma & Walt Becker, Fresno
Bernie Blau, Chatsworth
Celia Blum, Los Angeles
Irma Boucher, Sherman Oaks
Jane Calavano, Burlingame
Merri Beth Callender, Santa Rosa
Pat Carlson, Sacramento
Mary Carney, Redlands
Clytia & Bob Chambers, Studio City
Marshall Chericas, MD Los Angeles
Yolanda Ching, Citrus Heights
David E. Cocking, Whitehorn
Kathy Coleman, San Jose
Ted Conde, San Mateo
Derek D'Sa, Los Angeles
Heidi Davis, Los Angeles
Deborah Davis, San Francisco
Ron & Barbara Davis, Visalia
Judy & Geoff Dettlinger, Walnut Creek
Tina Dickson, Sacramento
Pat DiGiorgio, San Francisco
Aileen DiMiru, Reseda
Freddie Dirks, Roseville
Bette Donagher, Sacramento
Linda Dotson, Los Altos
Edward Duran, San Mateo
Kyle Everett, San Francisco
Barbara Falconer, LaHabra Heights
Toni Ferrara, Long Beach
Christina & Seth Frankel, Eureka
Rich Fybel, Rolling Hills Estates
Kathleen Gibbons, Danville
Mr. & Mrs. Robert P. Glasson, San Rafael
Marian Goldman, Burlingame
Gary Gregory, San Francisco
John Gusoskey, Pittsburg
Ted Hammam, San Jose
Laurie B. Hann, Los Angeles
Ed Hess, Torrance
Susie & Brett Hesse, Visalia
Charlotte Hill, Los Angeles
Maureen Hjoith, Los Angeles
Alison Hoyer, Granite Bay
Larry and Lori Jacobs, Sacramento
Barbara Jacobs, Sunnyvale
Herbert Jaffe, San Francisco
Cathy Johnson, Chico
Philippa Jones, Napa
Peggy Kanehann, Malibu
Royce Knibb, Calistoga
Dick & Frances Lambert, Orange
Pat Lindstrom, San Jose
Beverly Mangus, San Francisco
Charles McDermott, Lakewood
John McMillan, Antelope
Pam Middlebrooks, Folsom
Dick Miller, Lawndale
Wade Mishimoto, San Pedro
Mark Mishkin Los Angeles
Richard & Jeanine Moore, Chula Vista
Arnold Morgan, Encino
Dina Morgan, South Pasadena
Sandra Mulligan, Acampo
Debbie Myman, Los Angeles
Khosrow Noorbackhsh, Belmont
Philip & Klina Oberti, Madera
Earleen Olken, Sacramento
Tim Olsen, Simi Valley
Rudy Ovalle, San Francisco
Mike & Elve Peck, San Mateo
Janet Person, Camino
Vicki & Cali Rashkin, Solana Beach
Jim Rawlins, Santa Ana
Rashell Reneau, Sacramento
Garth Reynolds, Gold River
Bertha Rodriguez, San Francisco
Melanie Rome, Tarzana
Manuel R Rosario, San Leandro
Stephen E. Roulac, Larkspur
Gerald Rubin, Tarzana
Aiko Sandberg, Camarillo
Terri Sasse, Citrus Heights
Andrea Scarborough, Burlingame
Dick & Ruth Schwartz, Nevada City
Geri Scopesi, Daly City
Wayne E. Seel, Foster City
Beverly Shniper, Beverly Hills
Jerry Simek, La Jolla
Maria A. Simons, Granada Hills
Roy and Cynthia Snider, Folsom
Bernice Somberg, Hillsborough
Jim Spes, San Francisco
Nancy Steensma, San Mateo
Robert M. Stone, Rancho Cordova
Dawn Strickler, Fairfield
Mr.&Mrs. Darwin Strobel, Orangevale
Mark Sweeney, Martinez
Jerry & Vanessa Tennies, Grass Valley
Ron Verner, Los Angeles
Carrie Watson, Rancho Cordova
Olga Weiss, San Francisco
Bonny Williams, Rancho Cordova
Jeannie & Scott Wood, Manhattan Beach

Colorado
Theresa & Richard, Banta Denver
Villa Mae Crick, Howard
Jim Farver, Broomfield
Carvel Glidden, Steamboat Springs
Lyle Hetterley, Bailey
Tom Knapp, Littleton
Judy Lightfield, Denver
Jerry & Duskey Mallory, Evergreen
Jan Purdy, Longmont
Beverly Jane Robin, Greenwood Village

Florida
Katie Bancroft, Chiefland
Tom Bradley, Chattahoochee
Virgie Brown, Tavares
Millie Cortez, Clearwater
Wynelle Ethridge, Sneads

THANK YOU:

Jennifer Knapp & Chris Falanga, Archer
Perry and Janeeta Fischer, Chattahoochee
Leon Foster, Marianna
Danilo Gelabent, Tallahassee
Darrell Goodier, Chipley
Guy Green, Marianna
Yvonne Hindman, Quincy
Alice Jo Johns, Chattahoochee
Michelle Kelling, Cedar Key
Linette Lash, Chipley
Venice Martin Greensboro
Heather McAanal, Chiefland
Deidra McDaniel, Grand Ridge
Anne Graham Miller, Cedar Key
Jim Mills, Largo
Jan C. Morris, Chipley
Frank Pringle, Chattahoochee
Cynthia Remley, Clearwater
Donna J.L. Schuetz, Cedar Key
Kathleen Slater, Coral Gables
Kate & Don Thibodeau, Cedar Key
Harriet Thompson, Cedar Key
Roger Twitchell, Tallahassee
William G. Viertel, Cedar Key
Jerome Whiddon Sneads
Mary Leah Williams, Sneads
Bill Worthington Jr., Chattahoochee

Georgia
Lisa Adamson, Hampton
Craig Bush, Bainbridge
David Decker, Stockbridge
Mike Fowler, Jonesboro
Bonnie Gaudet, Peachtree City
Adrian Gillespie, Conyers
Wendy Green, Atlanta
Kelei Griffin, Jonesboro
Teresa Guinn, Folkston
John & Gail Hayes, Atlanta
Joe Hiett, Riverdale
Dave & Sue Jacobs Villa Rica
Cecilia S. Koby, Jonesboro
Roslyn Neely, Bainbridge
Beverly Reece, Lake City
Mary Sivert ,Lake City
Jack Smith, Thomaston
Herb & Sarah Starzer, Atlanta
Lee Walker, Covington

Hawaii
Phil & Rosalie Corbett, Mililani
Mike Manoske, Honolulu
John White, Kailua

Idaho
Bill Britt, MD, Coeur d'Alene
Rhonda Hendrix, Twin Falls
Jerry Kress, American Falls
Wanda Maes, Jerome
Mike McEnulty, Hayden
Mary Raffety, Coeur D'Alene
Jackie Sawyer, Payette
Bob & Dana Stovern, Pinehurst

Illinois
Randy & Denise Amundson, Chillicothe
Tom Austin, Urbana
Beth Ann Close Pontiac
Evelyn Glosecki, Irving
Kay Grill, Irving
Ken Hackbarth, Aurora
Jim Harris, Pontiac
Pete Hillier Kewanee
Kay Kelly, Odell
Bill & Diana Keway, Galconda
Edna Kruse, Colfax
Bruce & Rene Lauer, Wheaton
Jennifer Lawless, Strawn
Carol Martino, Pontiac
Tony McGuire, Chicago
Terry McGuire, Naperville
Mary Ann Nelson, Monmouth
Jerry Newburgh, Wataga
Betty Pouliot, Pontiac
Steve Rider, Kewanee
Gloria Smith, Kewanee
Joe Webster, Rockford
Nina White, Irving

Indiana
John Bonar, Evansville
Emily June, Lafayette
Brad & Connie Meeder, Leesburg

Kansas
Dan Buxton, Topeka
Tom Smarsh, Colwich

Kentucky
Doug Widner, Lexington

Louisiana
Ronnie Comeaux, Plaquemine

Maine
Janice Halteman, Aurora

Maryland
Bob Brennan, Baltimore
Susan & Peter Grube, Millersville
Rita Hofbauer, Rockville
Rob & Linda Losey, Monkton

Massachusetts
Ken Usher, Chicopee

Michigan
Richard Chulski, Lansing
Allison Ebner, Marshall
Brenda Ferries, Houghton
Mike Marn, Rockford
William A. Porter, Grayling
Dr. & Mrs. A. Sitchin, West Bloomfield

Minnesota
Deb Biggar, Brewster
Randy & Nancy Dale, Burnsville
Kathryn & Erica Jordahl, Albert Lea
Kathleen Keath, Braham
Jan Mattson, Saint Paul
Patricia Moore, Brooklyn Center
Marit and Jason Peters, Maplewood
Jack & Lynn Stansfield, Winona
Bill Patty & Megan Waugh, Albert Lea

Missouri
Lois Urnes, Bridgeton

Montana
Mary Roberson, Superior

Nebraska
Tom Jones, Papillion

Nevada
Keith Chestnut, Reno
Gerald Gordon, Las Vegas
Judy Jacobson, Las Vegas
Deanna Khal, Las Vegas

New Hampshire
Jacqueline Hill, Salem

New Jersey
Elizabeth Coan, Lindnwold
Marc Fine, Edgewater
Jim Gatens, Spring Lake
Donna Grove, Pilesgrove
Pam Lopes, Manalapan
Tom Morgan, Blackwood
Barbara & Marty Wolf, Marlboro

New Mexico
Jill Acheson, Ramah
Marietta Ackerman, Albuquerque
Adam Armijo, Santa Fe
Jim Augeri, Albuquerque
Edward Baca, Albuquerque
Gay Bailey, Rio Rancho
Melanie Barry, Rio Rancho
Kane Bieri, Rio Rancho
Tommy & Cristina Case, Albuquerque
Theresa Chacon, Santa Fe
Peg Conn, Albuquerque
Rob Dean, Santa Fe
Jason Divenere, Santa Fe
Betty Dudding, Corrales
Barbara Fike, Santa Fe
Helen Garner, Santa Fe
Paul S. Gilman, Santa Fe
Lily Gonzales, Santa Fe
Serena Hutchins, Aztec
John Paul & Betty Jones, Albuquerque
Suzanne & Neal Keiper, Santa Fe
Marty & Wendy Leathers, Albuquerque
Karen Manning, Tucumcari
Jacob McManaman, Rio Rancho
Veronica C. Montoya, Santa Fe
Naomi Murphy, Gallup
Dee Newman, Conchas Dam
Peggy Pick, Santa Fe
Diana Roach, Rio Rancho
Kirk E. Roberts, Rio Rancho
Karen Rutledge, Albuquerque

THANK YOU:

Dina and Norman Sassone, Santa Fe
Jerry Schmidt, Los Lunas
Elaine Shoemate, Albuquerque
Patricia Soldow, Santa Fe
Deborah Sonnenmoser, Tucumcari
Ken St. Germain, Albuquerque
Jean & Gene Stark, Santa Fe
William Thomas, Albuquerque
Marla Truitt, Santa Fe
Charlene Wheeler, Tucumcari
Janet Windsor, Albuquerque
Al Winkeljohn, Albuquerque
Beverly Wright, Albuquerque

New York
David Alber, Wynantskill
Cristy L. Caracane, Mohawk
Catherine Nevin Chu, Fayetteville
Roxanne Congdon, Little Falls
Judith Cooper, Cooperstown
Jim Duggan, Brooklyn
Marcia Iris Feldman, New York
Mary Frost ,Brooklyn
Lori Greenstein, New York
John Hanley, Brookville
Bob & Bobbi Heinkel, Rochester
Terry Landau, Brooklyn
Mary Loewenstein, Little Falls
Sally McFarland, Brooklyn Heights
John Moore, Astoria
Carrie Oliver, New York
Michael Robles, White Plains
Michael Towers, Brooklyn Heights
Becky Yarnes, Great Valley

North Carolina
Kitsy Birdsong, Dunn
Melissa DiChiera, Dunn
Joe Edwards, Dunn
Maxine Frisbee, Linden
Jimmy Gaines, Dunn
Hazel Godwin, Dunn
Leamon Hall, White Oak
Robert & Celia Henkens, PhDs, Beaufort
Stanley Johnson, Dunn
Rachel Poe, Dunn
Sally Skaggs, Dunn
Cathy Wood, Erwin

North Dakota
Kari Janz, Carrington

Ohio
Frank Adams, Fostoria
Sean and Patti Barrett, Beavercreek
Nick Barrett, Bowling Green
Kathy Bumgardne,r Fostoria
Pat & Toni Colman, Martins Ferry
Alyssa Cool, Bowling Green
Gayleen S. Dachenhaus, Bowling Green
Penny Day, Fostoria
Kim Fox, Beavercreek
Gail Geroff, Fairborn

Patricia Graves, Pt. Clinton
Maril & Kathy Hague, Northfield
Sue Leggett, Beavercreek
Barbara Luehrs, Dayton
Diana Melocik, Painesville
Gayle Mitchell, Beavercreek
Doris Ann Norris, Fostoria
Greg Peltier, Fostoria
Cody Roth, Fostoria
Patricia Sauber, Fostoria
Bob Sears, Tiffin
Annette Shaull, Fostoria
Kathy Spencer, Pierpont
Joe Stearns, Fostoria
Bob Sterbank, Lyndhurst
Michael Teggart, Fostoria
Don & Donnie Van Brackel, Defiance
Judy & Larry Werner, Cincinnati

Oklahoma
Jim & Jimmie Nolen, Del City
Bruce & Shirley Spence, Oklahoma City

Oregon
Gary & Gay Abendroth, Portland
Connie Ainsworth, Clackomas
Nancy Barker, Oregon City
Mike Barrows, Portland
Jody & Allen Buie, Portland
Bette Van Buskirk, Portland
Patrick Dearing, Hood River
Lonny & Barb Deffenbaugh, Salem
Gracie Dellett, Troutdale
Judy Echert, North Plains
Bob Erickson, Beaverton
Ralph F. Fear, DDS, McMinnville
R.W. Ferris, Portland
Chrissie Forbes, Eugene
K. Franssen, Gresham
Lenneke Garza, Portland
James Hendricks, Beaverton
Mark Jaquette, Portland
Dan Johnson, Vale
Mrs. Phyllis Koppen, Clackamas
Sharon Krebs, Clackamas
Verne Kreutz, Portland
Ted & Rita Mae Kurrus, Seaside
Linda Lawrence, Albany
Cheri Lerma, Cannon Beach
Margaret Macaulay, McMinnville
Emma Magee, Springfield
Cathleen & Rodney Mazour, Portland
Ann & Gary McAdam, Portland
Marguerite K. McNair, Beaverton
Connie O'Harra, Weston
Connie Barr & Ron Parsons, Hillsboro
Tom & Barbara Pelett, Roseburg
Porfirio Pena, Portland
Tiffany Perle, Portland
Timothy J. Roberts, Portland
Cameron Shaw, Portland
Leah Sideras, Portland
Leonard Thornton, Milwaukie

Mike Uhlig, Estacada
Yern-Linda Usher, Gresham
Bernie & Anita Verbout, Portland
Tony Wright, Roseburg

Pennsylvania
Mary G. Campbell, Canton
Ric Caprara, Monroeville
Jennifer Howard, York
Elizabeth Morris, Turbotville
Brenda Mott, Canton
Vincent W. Plaza, Coopersburg
Christina, Jacoobus
Dorothy A. Schrader, Danville
Betty Scott, Malverne
Johanna Shubert, Elizabethtown
Susan Stull, Canton
Debbie & Kurt Weber, Pittsburg
Michael Wheeler, Canton
Rich White, Canton
Don & Pam Fredeen, Derrick City

South Carolina
Angie Swiecki, Belvedere

South Dakota
Mrs. Glen Bovill, Baresford
Pat Miller, Rapid City

Tennessee
Andrea & Jim Brewer, Nashville
Jim Conner, Crossville

Texas
Debbie Avery, Boerne
Laura Bailey, Laredo
Marvin Berry, Seguin
Carmella Birdwell, Lewisville
Carol Bishop, Dallas
John Bokel, Coppell
Cathy Bowen, Laredo
Stan Brudney, Coleman
Kenneth Carnes, Gonzales
Lorina Chaffin, Irving
Laurie Cheatham, Seguin
Cindy Cockerham, Seguin
Mrs. Luther Cockrell, Woodlake
Linda Crisp, Artesia Wells
Tommy Csatari, Dallas
Stephen Doerr, Seguin
Rodney S. Doyle, Groveton
R. Gayle Eason, Fair Oaks Ranch
Kathryn Eyerman, Carrollton
Robert Faltysek, Laredo
Alynette Farley, Austin
DeWayne Finn, McAllen
Laura Gardner ,Carrollton
Laura Gardner, Dallas
June Shaver & D'Ann Gimenez, Houston
Julie Gordon, Amarillo
Terri & Monica Guerra, Laredo
Danny D. Gunn, Laredo
Peter Harrington, Dallas
Ed & Rhonda Haynes, Richardson

THANK YOU:

Carol Hernandez, Seguin
Susana Hinojusa Laredo
Lea Ann Holmes, Groveton
Eric Jensen, Seguin
Brigitte Johns, Carrollton
Beverly Johnson, Carrollton
Janice Jolly, Garland
John Jones, Boerne
Billie Klein, Seguin
Darla Martin, Carrollton
Benny McClain, Groveton
Barbara McCune, Dallas
Kay McKenzie, Laredo
Connie McMinn, Weatherford
Martha Mericle, Groveton
Stacy D. Minor, Richardson
Michael,Karen,Brian Mitchell, Carrollton
Eleanor C. Moore, Seguin
Clara Moreno, Laredo
Heather Morin, Amarillo
Marilyn Morris, Victoria
Manuela Murillo, Laredo
Eddie Perez, Laredo
D. Brent Phillips, Groveton
Sherry Poe, Gonzales
Richard and Barbara Pulaski, Huntington
Sylvia Rendon, Laredo
Sandi Rockne, Highland Village
Estella Rodriquez, Laredo
Homero R. Sanchez, MD, Laredo
Ernie & Sally Sears, Houston
Shay Shelton, Valley View
Dot Smith, Irving
Dennis Smith, Plano
Maria De Lourdes Soliz, Laredo
Rosalinda Soto, Seguin
Bill & Esther Stewart, Laredo
Nancy Stucky, Shenandoah
Scott Summers, Laredo
C.T. Taylor, Coleman
Lynn Teeter, San Marcos
Jane Titus, Dallas
Faye Titus, Seguin
Linda Trimmier, Post
Marie E. Tyson, Lewisville
Chris Wagner, Dallas
Mike Wagner, Laredo
Tommy Warren, The Woodlands
Frankie Weikel, Jr. Laredo
Billy R. Wilson, Dallas
Glenda Winchester, Dallas
David L. Wygant, Amarillo
Shirley Zoboroski, Seguin

Utah
Lesley Lawrence, Coolville
Gary Lee, Tooele
Carl Mahon, Monticello

Virginia
Margaret Frary, Blacksburg
Glenn Glassburn, Fredericksburg

Alton Kimball, South Hill
Mary Glenn Mancini, Herndon
Edith (Eadie) Nanney, South Hill
Peggy Prevatt, Richmond
Beth Puryear, Carrollton

Washington
Greg Abbey, Edmonds
B. Joan Abbott, Seattle
Jeanette I. Abelsen Seattle
Paul Achuff, Edmonds
Joyce Acker, Shoreline
Bonnie Ackerman Edmonds
Robin Acohido, Kingston
Tom & Vicki Adams, Sequim
Kathryn Adolphsen, Seattle
Farrell E. Adrian, Shoreline
Vicki Ahlgren, Seattle
Al & Elaine Akers, Green Acres
Irene Aksnes, Edmonds
Carol Albanese, Edmonds
Germaine Fitzgerald & Scott Alberti, Seattle
Donna Albertson Issaquah
Karen L. Alessi, Lake Stevens
Anita Alexander, Everett
Jan Allan, Seattle
Laura Allen, Anacortes
Charlie Allen, Kingston
Amie Allen, Seattle
Jack and Doris Alloin, Bainbridge Island
Kari Alskog, Stanwood
Donna Amos, Everett
Jane Anastasi, Mukilteo
Dan Andersen, Everett
Steve Anderson, Everett
Mark Anderson, Everett
Gail E. Anderson, Kirkland
Nona L. Anderson, Lake Stevens
Allen Anderson, Lynnwood
Judy Anderson, Marysville
Wallace & Elizabeth Anderson, Stanwood
Dawn Anderson, Woodinville
Shirley & Roy Andrews, Mukilteo
Dan Anic Auburn
Gay Ann, Seattle
Shirley Archer, Kirkland
Jeani Archer, Langley
Susan and Mike Archer, Vancouver
Gary Arford, Mukilteo
Arlene Armatage, Bothell
Carol Arnold, Federal Way
Sue Arnts, Des Moines
Yvonne Ash, Mill Creek
Glen Atkinson, Kirkland
Janet "K" Atkinson, Seattle
Wayne & Glenna Atwood, Port Ludlow
Larry Augustine, Bothell
Kathy Aversano Mukilteo
Ingrid Axtell, Mukilteo
Craig Axtell, Woodinville
Sherri Ayers, Everett

Steve Bacon, Mukilteo
Carmell Bailey, Everett
Rita Bailey, Kirkland
Leslie M. Bailey, Seattle
Dorothy Bailey, Seattle
Joanne Baker, Blaine
Paul & Jeannie Baker, Woodway
Janet Bakker Seattle
DeAnna Baljz, Ritzville
Charlotte Balza, Renton
Maureen Bangs, Edmonds
Gordon Swenson & Vicki Banks, Tacoma
Jack & Sheryl Barbre, Mukilteo
Barbra Barlow, Everett
Joy Koeppel Barnes, Everett
Cindy Barnes, Snohomish
Roger Barnett, Shoreline
Gary & Marie Barrett, Freeland
Marsha Barrow, Bothell
Paula Barta, Lynnwood
Teresa Barthol, Everett
Lynne Bartholick, Port Angeles
Brenda Bary ,Bremerton
Stacey Baskaran, Sequim
Phyllis Bauer, Kingston
Cynthia L. Beardsley, Puyallup
Shelly Beaudet, Everett
Jo Ann Bell, Shoreline
Judy Bendixsen, Seattle
Natalie & David Bendsten, Bellingham
Judi Benjamin, Edmonds
Walt Bennett, Kingston
Tonia M. Benson, Everett
Amy L. Benson, Everett
Greg Benson, Shoreline
Rick & Leslie Bereiter, Bellevue
Bob & Katie Bergan, Port Orchard
Marlene Berggren, Lynnwood
Edward Bergsagel, Shoreline
Mary Berry, Spokane
Bernie Bezdek, Lynnwood
Dave & Vicki Bezold, Mukilteo
Dina Biles, Mukilteo
Rosemary & Dave Bingham, Mukilteo
James & Gael Birkenbuel, Edmonds
Karen Birnie, Edmonds
Dee Biscoe, Battle Ground
Margie Black, Woodway
Barb Blacker, Everett
Marshall,Julie,Erin,Heather Blakemore, Kirkland
Susan G. Blanchard, Bothell
Wyatt Blanchett, Mountlake Terrace
Al & Charlie Blunt, Shoreline
John Boettner, Seattle
Greg & Jenny Bogard, Fife
John & Laura Bogen, Bremerton
Jamie & Bob Boldman, Edmonds
Sandie Bollinger, Port Orchard
Suzanne Bond, Mill Creek
John R. & Gretchen Bond, Shelton
Norma Bonner, Everett
Margo & John Bonner, Seattle

THANK YOU:

Parveen Bonyadlou, Mukilteo
Mary Boock, Everett
Bruce Borst, Medina
Evelina Bosi, Seattle
Thia Nu Botley, Lynnwood
Howard Botts, Black Diamond
Marge Bouchard, Renton
Tarry R. Boudreaux, Arlington
Roger Boulch, Everett
Dianna Boursaw, Stanwood
Richard W. Bowen, Everett
Earl & Kasey Bower, Lynden
Ann M. Bower, Seattle
J.A. Bowers, Mukilteo
Charline Bozek, Bothell
Jim & Carolyn Brady, Bellevue
Christopher Brady, Marysville
Kim Brady, Snohomish
Heather Lynne Braley, Everett
Paul Brandhagen, Lynnwood
Diane Brandt, Everett
Linda & Jamie Branha, Kent
Dolores Braun, Lynnwood
Pat Bray, Shelton
Joe Breit, Bellevue
Tonjia Brendle, Issaquah
Becky Bressler, Arlington
Bob Brickner, Mukilteo
Margret Bridwell, Bremerton
Ronda & Lindsay Broatch, Kingston
Karen Brockway, Kelso
Lee & Karen Brodniak, Mukilteo
Gary Brooks, Shoreline
Kathy Gillespie & Beth Brothers, Olympia
Larry & Glenyce Broweleit, Seattle
Marjorie A. Brown, Bellevue
Robert A. Brown, Clinton
Alane Brown, Everett
Doug Brown, Longview
Diana Bruland, Everett
Bob Brunton, Greenbank
Carl Bryant, Mercer Island
Brandi Bryant, Silverdale
Megan Bryson, Marysville
Tim & Tara Buchanan, Mukilteo
Dianne Buck, Bothell
Rhia Bucklin, Edmonds
William Buell, Mukilteo
Joseph L. Bundrant, Edmonds
Terrie L. Bunnell, Clinton
John Burgess, Everett
Crystal Burke, Seattle
Judy Burnett, Bellevue
Daniel Burnett, Bothell
Mary C. Burns, Everett
William Angdahl & Helen Burns, Mukilteo
Liz Burrell, Mercer Island
Larry Burton, Burlington
Carolyn Maia, Burton Seattle
Roger Bushnell, Bremerton
Susan Bye, Mukilteo
Bruce Byers, Lynnwood

Jodi Cable, Everett
John M. Calkins, Edmonds
Bob & Jane Callahan, Sequim
Pat Cameron, Mill Creek
Jean Camp, Everett
Bob & Shirley Canterbury, Quilcene
Chuck & Bonnie Cantoni, Mukilteo
Robert L. Card, Ferndale
Shannon & Joe Cardinale, Bellingham
Gayle & Richard Cardwell, Ph.D, Seattle
Linda Olson & Paul Carlson, Lynnwood
Scott Carlson, Poulsbo
George & Margaret Carlson, Shoreline
Dawn Carluccio, Lynnwood
Dennis Carpenter, Bothell
Lynn Carpenter, Shoreline
Rebecca Carreira, Mukilteo
Julie & Lee Carter, MD, Mukilteo
Dawn Cartmell, Bellevue
Jan & Dan Case, Bellevue
Michael Casey, Lynnwood
Jeannie Cashman, Bothell
Julie Caudle, Everett
Marie Cave, Lynnwood
Bill Center, Rear Admiral USN, Everett
Larry Challain, Olympia
Derek & Jana Chapman, Renton
Chris Chase, Mukilteo
Nola Cheff, Seattle
Norm Cheney, Everett
Sherley Chester, Marysville
Vicki Chiappuzzo, Lynnwood
Maurie Lund Chiswell, Brush Prairie
Linda Chittim, Lynnwood
JoAnn Chrisman, Renton
John & Lisa Christensen, Everett
Greg Christiansen, Bremerton
Royce Church, Mukilteo
Linda Clark, Everett
Vicki Clark, Marysville
Donna Clayton, Woodway
Dan Clements, Everett
Joan Clemons, Bremerton
Sheila & Sean Cline, Lynnwood
Yali & Tony Cockburn, Bellevue
Hearst Coan, Bellevue
Jeaneane Coffman, Everett
Kathy Colby, Tacoma
Rosie Collins, Hoquiam
Brian Collins, Marysville
Florence Connelly, Lynnwood
Gerri Conrad, Lynnwood
The Conrans, Redmond
Michael & Karen Constant, Mukilteo
Susan & Ross Cook, Bothell
Randy Cook, Everett
Steve Cooke, Seattle
Jenny & Will Coombe, Silverdale
Tom Cooper, Aberdeen
Gladys Corbin, Marysville
Virginia Corcoran, Everett
Norma Corcoran, Kirkland

Lois Corley, Bothell
Carol Costello, Kirkland
Sue & Mike Costello, Mukilteo
Stanley James Covell, Everett
Nancy Cragin, Edmonds
Bob Creamer, Mukilteo
Walter & Myra Creasey, Maple Falls
LaDonna Cress, Everett
Kay Crisler, Stanwood
Diane Criss, Arlington
Sally Cristopher, Kent
Claudia Cruz, Snohomish
Leslie Cullers, Kent
Tish & Dennis Culp, Olalla
Don & Nancy Cumming, Vashon Island
Bill Cummings Seattle
John Cunningham, Edmonds
Victoria Curry, Edmonds
Phyllis Curry, Seattle
Lynn M. Curtis, Garfield
Gary Cushman, Granite Falls
Ben Cutts, Everett
Mike & Leah Daffron, Mukilteo
"Fast Lane" Daltons, Bothell
Robert & Bet Danley, Bothell
Mary Darden, Oak Harbor
John M. Darnielle, Bremerton
Dan & Marie Davenport, Lynnwood
Cathy & Randy Davis, Marysville
Jolyn M. Davis, Mill Creek
Bill Davis, Mukilteo
Geraldine Davis, Shoreline
Dee M. Davis, Silverdale
Chuck M. Davis Jr., Everett
Lisa & Clay Dean, Mukilteo
Kristin N. Decker, Marysville
Donna Dehn, Edmonds
Beverly Dehnert, Kent
John Demeroutis, Edmonds
Bev DenBleyker, Lynden
Dirk & Beverly DeRooy, Marysville
Rik & Kim Deskin, Kirkland
Adrienne DeVere, La Conner
Polly Diafos, Edmonds
Del Dickinson, Bothell
Mary Didzun, Edmonds
Janet DiSalvo, Mukilteo
Tammy W. Dittoe, Everett
Mark and Kathy Divelbiss, Kent
Evelyn Dixon, Everett
Jenny & Frankie Dobrenski, Newman Lake
Ron Dodge, Granite Falls
Mike & Gaye Dodge, Seattle
Diane Doern, Everett
Bob Dolan, Bothell
Kathleen Dolan, Southworth
Robert Doll, Edmonds
Pete Donahue, Seattle
Kathy Donaldson, Coupeville
Robert Donaldson, Seattle
Mark Doneen, Shoreline
Carrie Donohue, Marysville

THANK YOU:

Eunice Doolittle, Lakewood
Rose Marie Doran, Mukilteo
Don & Candi Doran, Mukilteo
Wilma Dougherty, Bellevue
Carol Douglas, Sequim
James P. Downey, Kent
Lance Dozier, Lake Stevens
Ardis Drain, Seattle
Barbara Drollinger, Everett
Sharon & Ed Dryden, Greenbank
Jan Dugan, Monroe
Sally Duncan, Everett
Suzanne Declemens & Mickayla
Dunn, Everett
Tom Duren, Edmonds
G. Duval, Bellevue
Nancy E. Dye, Seattle
Richard Eadie, Shoreline
Scott Earnhart, Friday Harbor
Gay Easter, Seattle
Robert & Bonnie Eaton, Mill Creek
Leslie Eaton, Sequim
Wes & Maureen Eckhardt, Marysville
Evelyn Edeen, Snohomish
Beverly Edwards, Anacortes
Dick & Jan Eichler, Mercer Island
Carol Elgin, Bellevue
Vicki & Don Ellen, Lynnwood
Audrey Ellenwood, Lynnwood
Kathryn Ellicott, Everett
Ella Ellingson, Mukilteo
Marcia Elvrum, Seattle
Ron Elwood Mountlake, Terrace
Mark & Linda Embrey, Mukilteo
Gary Emerson, Kent
Judy Emmett, Seattle
Jon & Renee Engwall, Everett
Dorothy Erbstoesser, Poulsbo
Glenda Erwin, Mercer Island
Barbara Escandon, Edmonds
Marty Estergreen, Lynnwood
Nicole Estes, Stanwood
Sandi Evans, Everett
Cindy Everhart, Edmonds
Sam Ewing Jr., Mukilteo
George Fair, Mukilteo
The McCluskey Family, Gig Harbor
The Harper Family, Mukilteo
Peggy Fargo, Seattle
David Farmer, Freeland
Anna Farr, Seattle
Frank Emil Faruolo, Vancouver
Anita Maria Faulkner, Bremerton
Lynne Fay, Brinnon
"Doctor Bob" Feasel, DDS, Mill Creek
Rick Ferrell, Vancouver
Mary Ferrier, Everett
Dee Fincher, Kent
Mary & Gary Finkelstein, Kirkland
Bill Finley III, Lake Stevens
Sara M. Fischer, Renton
Lorell Fisher, Arlington
Dick and Patti Fisher, Mukilteo
Teresa Flanders, Marysville

Randy Flannigan, Tacoma
Florine Fleck, Roche Harbor
Leslie Fleury, Everett
Jim Flickinger, Mill Creek
Tina J. Floresca, Everett
Jerry Flynn, Bellevue
Lara Flynn, Lynnwood
Lin Fogg, Everett
Mark Forbes, Freeland
Gary Forbes, Seattle
Carol Foss, Marysville
Marge Fossum, Bremerton
John Foster, Lynnwood
Thomas H.D. Foster, Mill Creek
Jane Fought, Edmonds
Chris & Autumn Fowler, Everett
Anita M. Franett, Seattle
Judi & Jim Frank, Bellevue
Mrs. R.K. Frank, Everett
Marilyn Frank, Maple Valley
Sharon Franks, Everett
Gary Fredback, Bremerton
Bev Freese, Seattle
Dianne Freethy, Sedro Wooley
Caryn Frey, Seattle
Fred E. Friedel, Issaquah
David Froines, D.C, Edmonds
Jean Frost, Sequim
The Fryes, Mukilteo
Kim Fuller, Aberdeen
The Family Fuller, Everett
Tracy Fulton, Bothell
Gale Gallagher, Everett
James L. Galvin Jr., Seattle
Frank Gandarias, Langley
Lynette Gardiner, Mukilteo
Jamie S. Garner, Bremerton
Nancy Garr, Bellevue
Harold A. Garrett, Bothell
Char Garrett, Lynnwood
John & Michelle Gaska, Edmonds
John Gaskell, Olympia
Terri Gauthun, Sequim
Fred Gautschi, Edmonds
Carol E. Gazarek, Port Orchard
Chuck Gazarek, Seattle
Carol Gehbauer, Mukilteo
Pam Gehrig, Bellevue
David Gehrke, Des Moines
Jim & Toni Geiger, Mukilteo
Shaunae Gelbach, Lynnwood
David & Cindy George, Mukilteo
Crissy Georgelas, Everett
Anne M. Gerbing, Bothell
Ingrid Gerdon Everett
Sid & Jean Gerling, Lake Forest Park
David Ghenov, Edmonds
Joseph Giannunzio, Bothell
Ron & Diana Gibson, Bremerton
Roberta Gibson, Oak Harbor
Jo Gideon, Pt. Orchard
Suzanne Giftai, Seattle
Anne Gilbert, Mountlake Terrace
Ron & Kathy Gillespie, Yakima

Shelly Gillett, Everett
Karen Gilliland, Mukilteo
Adrienne Gillis, Lake Stevens
Teri Gladfelder, Kent
Lauretta A. Glover, Seattle
Lee Gobernatz, Mukilteo
Don & Diane Gockel, Medina
Barbara Goldman, Monroe
Lisa Golesch, Mountlake Terrace
Dan & Julie Golich, Mukilteo
Beverly Gonzales, Edmonds
Craig Goodmanson, Kirkland
Linda Gordy, Quilcene
Linda L. Goring, Friday Harbor
Robert A. Goryns, Everett
Robert & Lorri Gottlieb, Mercer Island
Karolynn Gould, Mukilteo
Edward Graff, Kirkland
Jacklyn A. Graham, Edmonds
Dave & Serena Graham, Mt. Vernon
Carol Grant, Alderwood Manor
Helen Graves, Federal Way
Randy Gray, Seattle
Carol Greco, Everett
Conrad Green, Poulsbo
Rick Greenhow, Puyallup
Lisa Jo Greenshields, Arlington
Carol Greenwood, Seattle
Steve & Cindy Gregg, Everett
Rosemary Gregory, Shoreline
Carolyn Grossheim, Blaine
Roger & Monika Gruberman, Brier
The Three Sisters Grzelewski, Seattle
Lillian Gundersen, Port Orchard
Joyce Gunderson, Bellevue
Jo Gunn, Lynnwood
Marlena Gutierrez, Friday Harbor
Patty & John Guza, Everett
Bob Haas, Mukilteo
Marilyn Horton Hackney, Mountlake
Terrace
Dwight Hagan, Arlington
Norm Hagen, Seattle
Bridget & Leslie Hagey, Langley
P.A. Haight, Bothell
Liz Hale, Everett
Karen Hale-Tessaro, Marysville
Cal & Zenda Hall, Bellevue
Dr. Roger Hall, Lynnwood
Dwight Hall, Lynnwood
John Halpin, Seattle
Beverly Halvorson, Bellevue
Judy Hamel, Lynnwood
David & Bridget Hanning, Lynnwood
Kristine Hansen, Everett
George & Jean Hansen, Sequim
Herdice Hanson, Shoreline
Denise Hanson, Shoreline
Lucinda & George Harder, Kirkland
Jean Hardman, Lynnwood
Karen Harms, Kent
Sandra Harrell, Lynnwood
Mike Harris, Everett
Diane Harrison, Lynnwood

280

THANK YOU:

Ginger & Walt Hart, Everett
Glenna Hart, Kirkland
Emily Harter, Everett
Ray Hartman, Shoreline
Matt Hartwick, Snohomish
D J Sackett & Glenn Hathaway, Lynnwood
Steve Haug, Everett
Gary Haugland, Mukilteo
Shannon & Micheal Haven, Bremerton
Roger Hawkes, Shoreline
Beverly & Paul Hawley, Edmonds
Kimberly Hayes, Edmonds
Bill & Barbara Hayes, Friday Harbor
Ceridwen & John Heath, Bremerton
Gary Hebert, Lynnwood
Melanie Hecla, Arlington
Ron and Mary Hedges, Bellevue
Brenda Hedrick, Colville
Bob and Karen Heer, Sequim
Ed Heidel, Everett
Luan Heinz, Mukilteo
Cindy Heit,Lynnwood
Ruth Helem, Everett
Carla & Tim Hendrickson, Bothell
Magic Hendrix, Lynnwood
Gerrie Heneghen, Seattle
Judy Henry, Marysville
H.Erika Henze, Mt. Vernon
Jeff Herbert, Marysville
Larry Hermann, Brier
Irene Herring, Friday Harbor
Karl Herrmann, Seattle
Merrick & Patt Hersey, Vancouver
Marta Hester, Port Angeles
Gordon Higgins, Shoreline
Barbara Hill, Everett
Bob Hill, Kingston
Stan Hill, Mercer Island
Kathy Korst & Scott Hill, Union
Laura Hilley, Brier
Jan Hinchliffe, Everett
Edna Hindman, Ritzville
Mark Hinkelman, Bellevue
Judy Hinrichs, Mukilteo
Jill Hitzemann, Seattle
Kim Hodkinson, Snohomish
Dennis Hoelshe,r Seattle
Erik Hoerauf, Mukilteo
Scott & Jennifer Hoffman, Edmonds
Maxine Hoglund, Arlington
Candi Holland, Everett
Caryl Holmquist, Kent
Bob & Melody Holsten, Everett
Patti & Reed Holtgeerts, Edmonds
Kim Holttum, Lynnwood
Robert Hondel, Graham
Linda Honer, Camano Island
Stephanie Hoover, Edmonds
Sheri Hoover, Everett
Johnny Horner, Edmonds
Cory Hovander, Arlington
Randy Howard, Mukilteo
Ilese Howe, Edmonds

Mary & Stephen Howe, Mukilteo
Judy Howell, Edmonds
Mary & Don Hrutfiord, Blaine
Don & Roxanne Hubert, Carnation
Vickie & Don Huey, Rochester
Beverly J. Hughes, Mountlake Terrace
Julie Hull, Medina
Jean C. Hunt, Everett
Dan Hunter, Everett
Jan Huntley, Shoreline
Barbara Hurst, Lynnwood
Sandra Hurtley, Birch Bay
Pam Hutchins, Bellevue
Ronald Hutger, D.V.M., Arlington
Vicki Hyde, Marysville
Eva & Robert Hynes, Edmonds
Patti Ickes, Everett
Elaine Ingraham, Lynnwood
Chuck & Ruth Ingram, Marysville
Don Irvin, Bothell
Debbie Isaacson, Vancouver
Robert Jackson, Mercer Island
Clay Jackson, Redmond
Cloyd & Barbara Jackson, Renton
Ruth Jacobson, Mercer Island
Eric Jass, Stanwood
Ann Jeffrie, Mukilteo
Vern Jenkins, Port Orchard
Tim Jennings, Edmonds
The Family Jensen, Everett
Leanne Jinneman, Mukilteo
Bob Johnson, Bothell
Si Johnson, Bothell
Rick Johnson, Edmonds
Gary Johnson, Edmonds
Val Johnson, Edmonds
Linda O. Johnson, Everett
Victor Johnson, Kirkland
Krystal Johnson, Mill Creek
Betty Johnson, Mukilteo
Dixie Johnson, Puyallup
G.L. Johnson, Seattle
Sarah Johnson, Snohomish
Bob Johnston, Lake Forrest Park
Bruce Johnston Lynnwood
Karen Johnson, Montesano
Lindy Jones, Ardenvoir
Mike Jones, Bainbridge
Melanie Jones, Spokane
Mrs. Susan Jones, Tacoma
B.Scott Jones, D.C., Mukilteo
Sherry & Keith Jongsma, Mukilteo
Lucy Jordan, Bothell
Tracy Jordan, Everett
Lori Jordan, Mukilteo
Ira Joseph, Auburn
Walid Joudi, Shoreline
Jamie & Crystal Joyce, Bothell
Lani Juett, Edmonds
Sequoya Juge, Mukilteo
Marialis Jurges, Bremerton
Laila M. Kacher, Snohomish
Chris Kain, Bremerton
Aurel J. Kajlich, MD, Edmonds

Elisabeth Kakala, Everett
Rick Kaminski, Seattle
Ken Kappel, Everett
Rick & Kay Kaps, Sequim
Lynn F. Kasel, Bellevue
Kristina Katsarus, Seattle
Daphne Kautz, Seattle
Sylvia Kawabata, Mukilteo
Wanda & David Kay, Battle Ground
Jane Kealy, Mukilteo
Bev Kegley, Everett
Carol Keleske-Weis, Edmonds
Linda & Joe Kellar, Mukilteo
Susan Kelley, Edmonds
Ilona Kellison-Bullard, Lynnwood
Rose & Lisa Kerson, Bremerton
Cindy Kessler, Everett
Kathy Kettman, Bellingham
Doug Kimball, Mukilteo
Lori King, Brush Prairie
Jan & Dick Kinnier, Edmonds
Rachel Kinzinger, Anacortes
Paulette & Gaylon Kipp, MD, Mukilteo
Victoria Kirkland, Anacortes
Norlonna Klein, Mukilteo
Peter Klika, Mercer Island
Kathleen Klotz, Bellevue
Adam Knapp, Sequim
Rietje & Rich Knapton, Lynnwood
Jay Kneib, Silverdale
Esther Knight, Everett
Patti Knight, Shoreline
Donna Knox-Rai, Lynnwood
Wally & Dale Kodis, Wenatchee
Nancy Mitchell Kofoed, Bothell
Rachel Kohr, Everett
Ed & Sharon Konarzewski, Everett
Carol Kovach, Edmonds
Milo Kramer, Mukilteo
Marla Kroll, Edmonds
Kelly Kronberg, Mukilteo
Kathy & Kelly Kuhnhausen, Marysville
Sandra Kuiken, Bothell
Judy Kurlander, Seattle
Sue Kutches, Everett
June Kuzminsky, Puyallup
Kim Lacey, Kent
Gwen Lamb, Anacordes
Earlene Lamb, Everett
John Lamb, Sequim
Robin Lamb, Shoreline
Lilo Lamerdin, Mukilteo
Jean Lance, Mountlake Terrace
Shalley Lane, Marysville
Steven Minor & Sandy Langham, Kingston
Joan Langlais, Mukilteo
Anna Langseth, Arlington
Doug Lantz, Bothell
Jack LaPoint, Everett
Connie LaPoint, Seattle
Gary Larsen, Lynnwood
Gunnar Larsen, Seattle
Anthony & Molly Larson, Bremerton

THANK YOU:

Rich Lathrope, Lynnwood
Marcus Law, Everett
Tom Lawrence, Maple Valley
Erin Lawrence, Seattle
Corey Lawson, Edmonds
Mike Le, Everett
Gary & Lorri Leach, Poulsbo
Ed & Brenda Leacock, Kent
Cheryll Leamer, Walla Walla
Bob & Lou Leduc, Shoreline
Ted P. Lehn, Friday Harbor
Dale & Karen Leible, Port Orchard
Kathleen Leikam, Auburn
Dan Stillmank & Joyce Lem, Seattle
Molly Lenaburg, Marysville
Dave Lenci, Mukilteo
Veronika Lensch, Everett
Claudia Lent, Mukilteo
Gary & Marji Leonard, Mukilteo
Keith Leonard, DDS, Arlington
Suzanne Lescantz Kirkland
Roberta Lewandowski, Mercer Island
Connie & Nick Lewis, Bothell
Kari Lewis, Marysville
Max Lewis, Mukilteo
Karen Libby, Everett
Ed & Gari Lillis, Mt. Vernon
Mona Lillis, Ritzville
Greg & Diane Lind, Mukilteo
Mark & Karen Lindem, Monroe
Karen Lindenmayer, Bothell
Faith Lingenfelter, Edmonds
Mike Linskey, Mukilteo
Nan Lippold, Anacortes
Lynda Little, Mukilteo
Barbara E. Lloyd, Friday Harbor
Richard Lockhart, Bothell
Bobbie Loeks, Edmonds
Jeanne Lofthouse, Everett
William Long, Mukilteo
Sue Ellen Longwell, Everett
Bonnie Loomis, Everett
Ted Loomis, Seattle
Cardyn Lorang, Bothell
Barbara Lord, Woodinville
Cathy Lorino, Mukilteo
Ben & Bobbi Lovelle, Edmonds
David Lowry, Bothell
The Family Loyd, Everett
Tom Luft, Orcas Island
Traci Lund, Everett
Kevin Lungren, Freeland
Sondra Lustgarten, Bellevue
Tom Lux, Camano Island
Barbara J. Lyle, Bellevue
Rebecca Lyle, Graham
Sheila Lynch, Seattle
Dale Lyski, Everett
Steve Lytle, Maple Valley
John Maas, Edmonds
Don & Mariane Macamber, Mukilteo
Dr. and Karen MacDonald, Mukilteo
Julianne Mach, Everett
Robert MacKay, Mountlake Terrace

Lori Dee MacKenzie, Lakewood
Michell MacLeod, Woodinville
Craig & Ann Madsen, Lynnwood
Sandy Mael, Seattle
Bernadine Mahar, Freeland
Beth Mahar, DDS, Marysville
Rick Mangan, Everett
Cecil E. Manley Jr., Everett
Pat Mann, Seattle
Phil Mansell, Mill Creek
Greg Marchand, Seattle
Kelly Margulies, Seattle
Morris Marleau, Everett
The Family Marshall, Colbert
Joyce Marshall, Olympia
Grace Marshall, Shoreline
John Foster & Chery St. Martin,
Lynnwood
Larry Martin, Lynwood
Jan Martin Mukilteo
Carla Martin Mukilteo
Naoma S. Martin, Sequim
Eileen Martin, Shoreline
Anjay Martinez, Mukilteo
Vassa Martushev, Mukilteo
Lois J. Mason, Lynnwood
David & Dolores Mathers, Everett
Kristi Mathisen, Brier
David Matsumoto, Bremerton
Claude Matz, Vancouver
William & Mary May, Mukilteo
John Putnam & Victoria Mayorga,
Kent
Janet McAllister, Stanwood
Christiane McAuliffe, Kirkland
Karen Mccann, Seattle
Marilyn McCanna, Veradale
Lissa McDowell, Medina
C.L. McEown, Shoreline
Phyllis McEvoy, Hoquiam
John McGeehan, Mukilteo
Cindy & Murray McIntyre, Shoreline
Sheryl McKay, Kirkland
Judy Ann McKay, Marysville
Jean McKee, Edmonds
Olga McKenna, Edmonds
Jack & Marlene McKimson, Bremerton
Beth & Mark McKinney, Mountlake
Terrace
Carol McKissick, Mukilteo
Judie McLaughlin, Belfair
Mitch & Marianna McLeod, Edmonds
Patti McLucas, Sequim
Laurie McQueen, Everett
Lois I. Meade, Marysville
Bonnie Melton, Seattle
Steve & Barb Melton, Wenatchee
June & John Mercer, Kent
Boni Merrill, Silverdale
Helen Merriman, Mukilteo
Frank Mesa, Woodinville
Rita Messina, Bothell
John W. Boothby & Karen Messo, Port
Orchard

Melanie Methven, Mukilteo
Diane Michael, Bellevue
Sid Miedema, Marysville
Lorraine & Dick Mietzner, Edmonds
Gloria Mikes, Monroe
Cecilia Miller, Everett
Anne Miller Everett
Jim & Jo Miller, Langley
Sunnie & Paul Miller, Lynnwood
Ray Miller, Palmer
Teresa Miller, Sedro Woolley
Mary Miller, Shoreline
Glen Mills, Lynnwood
Judi Mitchell, Bothell
Kelly Mitchell, Everett
John Mitchell, Yakima
Laurie Moats, Everett
Karis Moberg, Seattle
George & Lesley Moffat, Mill Creek
Nancy Monlux, Everett
Joyce Monroe, Bremerton
Barbara Montague, Snohomish
Bill Monteforte, MD, La Conner
Linda Mooney, Lynnwood
Richard E. Moore, Bainbridge Island
Tom Moore, Kennewick
Sally Moore, Lynnwood
John & Madelline Moore, Seattle
Colleen Moran, Woodinville
Mary Morgan, Seattle
Dan Moriarity, Sequim
Carol Morris, Mukilteo
Kris Morrison, Vancouver
John David Morse, Vancouver
Ione & Jack Morse, Woodway
Diana Mortensen, Everett
Greg Mosley, Hansville
Carla Motaghedi, Lynnwood
Otto F. Motal, Edmonds
Andie Murat, Machias
Chris Murdoch, Mt. Vernon
Athena Murphy, Des Moines
Suzanne Murphy, Seattle
Linda Murray, Everett
Edith C. Murray, Everett
Mike Murray, Kingston
Michelle Murray, Mukilteo
Beverly J. Murrish, Edmonds
Del Muse, Poulsbo
Mary Mutchler, Kingston
Carrie Myers, Bremerton
Kenneth & Brooke Nadeau, Everett
Maggie Naff, Lynnwood
Cathy M. Nau, Stanwood
George & Lynn Naumowicz, Spokane
Frank Neito, MD, Mukilteo
Diann Neitz, Edmonds
Beverly Nelson, Edmonds
Judy Nelson, Edmonds
Kristina Nelson, Snohomish
Bryan Nelson, Woodinville
Steven Neuhauser, Bothell
Karen Newbom, Kirkland
Ann L. Nichols, EA, Arlington

THANK YOU:

Robert Nielsen, Bellingham
Susie Niemi, Aberdeen
Roy Nishi, Walla Walla
John & Elly, Nist Everett
Susan Nixon, Seattle
Christopher Noel, MD, Bellingham
Barbara A. Nordin, Seattle
Marilyn Norris, Edmonds
Peggy Norris, Port Angeles
Norlynn Norsby, Everett
Marilyn Northern, Spokane
Geraldine Nourouzee, Mukilteo
M.J. Novak, Mill Creek
Susan November, Kirkland
Tom & Jonlee, Nunn Edmonds
Susan O'Brian, Redmond
Tom O'Dell, Issaquah
Tammy O'Reilly, Edmonds
Joyce Oates, Monroe
Ginnie Obee, Everett
Kathy Ogden, Mill Creek
Sarah Ohaks, Mukilteo
The Family Oldenburgs, Mercer Island
Beverly Olson, Edgewood
Ruth Olson, Seattle
Peggy Sue Opsahl, Everett
Betsy Ormond, Lake Forest Park
Karly & Ami Orr, Bothell
Graciela Ortega, Puyallup
Patty Osberg, Woodway
Jaci Oseguera, Shoreline
Sylvia Ostler, Mukilteo
Suzanne Simmons Othess, Greenbank
Kat Overman, Everett
Clint Owen, Belfair
Antonio & Mary Pace, Seattle
Mike Pagel, Bremerton
Barbara Paglia, Everett
Mark Pahlow, Mukilteo
Greg Paine, Duvall
Gail Painter, Mukilteo
Bernadette Pajer, Monroe
Julie Panusis, Snohomish
Karen & David Papandrew, Sequim
Alesa Parker, Bellingham
Helen Parker, Mukilteo
Jim Parker, Spokane
Barbara Parker, Ph.D, Seattle
Yvette Parks, Fairwood
Jan Parlier, Kirkland
Karen Parrish, Stanwood
Dale Partna, Bothell
Dee & Ron Parypa, Seattle
Judy H. Paskett, Everett
Margery Paterson, Issaquah
Corey Patt, Seattle
Jim Paul, Edmonds
Elaine Pauly, Lynnwood
Michele Pebley, Kent
Lone Pedersen, Edmonds
Dan Pelletier, Lynnwood
Betty Penny, Everett
Claudia Perkins, Mukilteo

Mary Ann Perley, Everett
Barbara M. Perra, Bothell
Connie Perry, Everett
Billie Jo Peterson, Bremerton
Pat & Fred Peterson, Edmonds
Karen & Bradford Peterson, Mercer Island
The Petersons, Renton
Robin Petras, Kent
Edick Petrossian, Renton
Geri Pewitt, Everett
Wayne Pflepsen, Burlington
Ilene Philbrook, Vancouver
Cheryl F. Phillips, Everett
Mara Phipps, Bothell
Glen Pickus, Mukilteo
Robert Pierce, Camano Island
Rob Pierson, Bothell
Jim & Gill Piggott, Bothell
Sue Pilarski, Seattle
David Pine, Bremerton
Chuck Pinnell, Seattle
Tom Platt, Kent
Bob & Kelli Polcha, Freeland
Stefany Pollak, Seattle
Joni Pollino, Shoreline
Bruce Pope, Renton
Laine Potter, Mill Creek
Genie Potter, Shoreline
Barbara Poulsen, Mill Creek
Mr. & Mrs. Lloyd Powell, Kirkland
Trudy Pownall, Monroe
Jamie Pratt, Seattle
Tina Pravalpott, Tacoma
Anne Presta, Spokane
Jim Price, Tacoma
Barbara Pritchett, Mukilteo
Kathy J. Proctor, Snohomish
Bill Profitt, Kingston
Bev Rademacher, Ellensburg
Bill Rall, Edmonds
Andrea Ramsauer, Sequim
Jean Ramsey, Everett
Chuck Randall, Bellingham
Mark Hamilton & Suzie Rapp, Seattle
Tammy Rasmussen, Everett
John & Dorothy Rasmussen, Seattle
Donna Rasor, Everett
Roy Ratliff, Seattle
Bill & Carol Rayborn, Friday Harbor
Steve Rayner, Freeland
Maria Red Elk, Port Angeles
Sharon Redford, Everett
Connie & Tab Redling, Friday Harbor
Lorrie Reed, Woodway
Cathy Reese, Mukilteo
Kathryn Rehfeld, Lynnwood
Patrick Reid, Mukilteo
Joy Reitan, Bellevue
Linda Reiter, Everett
Cheryl Renouard, Edmonds
Darrel Resleff, Vancouver
Jack Napolitano & Kathy Reyes, Everett

August Reyes, Kirkland
Robert & Jane Reynolds, Mukilteo
Teresa Rhoads, Anacortes
Brent Rice, Mercer Island
David & Tynia Rich, Everett
Darcy & Susanne Richardson, Mukilteo
Ron Richardson, Renton
Sondra Rick, Yelm
Donovan & Cara Rickel, Dupont
Rose Ricks, Anacortes
Amy L. Rider, Bellevue
Rhonda Rose Rieker, Port Angeles
The Riselmans, Edmonds
Teresa Ritter, Seattle
Beth Rivin, MD, MPH, Seattle
Dolores J. Robbins, Marysville
Len Roberts, Everett
Lisa Roberts, Stanwood
George & Robin Robertson, Lake Stevens
Geraldine Robinson, Freeland
Elizabeth Robinson, Lynnwood
JoAnne Robinson, Mukilteo
Brian Robison, Duvall
Ann Robison, Edmonds
Judith L. Rochelle, Snohomish
Bob & Kathy Rodgers, Mukilteo
Tony Roebuck, Arlington
Peggy Rogers, Arlington
S.E. Rogers, Mountlake Terrace
M.L. Rohrenbach, MD, Mukilteo
Bill Rohweder, Mukilteo
Mary Roop, Lynnwood
Joanne M. Rosain, Bellevue
Richard Rose, Kirkland
Barbara Rose, Mercer Island
Bill & Joan Rose, Mount Lake Terrace
Joe & Holly Rossano, Arlington
Dave & Debbie Rossi, Marysville
Robin Roth, Seattle
Allen Roth, Shelton
Lars Durbin & Marlene Roth, Snohomish
Lori Roulier, Everett
Ann Roush, Everett
Jeannine Rowbottom, Lynnwood
Bryan & Jerrien Rowe, Mukilteo
Vicki Roy, Mukilteo
Susan Ruedebusch, Port Orchard
Sharon & Wes Ruff, Edmonds
James & Roxyann Ruiz, Bremerton
Judy Runions, Shoreline
Valerie Rusch, Everett
Dick Russell, Edmonds
Willie Russell, Everett
Rindy Russell, Everett
Darren Russinger, Kent
Wilhemina Rust, Lynnwood
David Sigman & Krina Van Ry, Seattle
Carol Ryan, Kingston
Jan Sage, Edmonds
Jerry & Gina Saldis, Brier
Kelvin Sallette, Bremerton

283

THANK YOU:

Jerry & Gina Salois, Brier
Christie Samples, Mukilteo
Connie Sampson, Mukilteo
Darla Sanders, Lake Stevens
Rus Sandomire, Seattle
Jodi Sather, Silvana
Michele Saunders, Seattle
Glen Saurdiff, Kent
Patricia Sauter, Lynnwood
Linda Skugstad & Robert Savela, Mukilteo
Veronica Sayer, Mukilteo
Audrey Schafer, Mountlake Terrace
David Scheirman, Bainbridge Island
Judith Ann Scheller, Everett
Bill & Ardis Scheller, Mukilteo
Kari Schidleman, Bothell
Stan & Fran Schill, Mercer Island
Larry & Kathy Schindler, Snohomish
Mary Schmitt, Marysville
Steve Schmitz, Mt. Vernon
Jim Schmoker, Snohomish
Martin & Michelle Schneider, Everett
Eunice Schneider, Lynnwood
Bill Schoepflin, Farmington
Betty Schrier, Everett
Beverly Schuller, Edmonds
Erwynne Schumann, Lynnwood
John Schwartz, Renton
Mike Schwarz, Federal Way
Colleen & Gary Schwarz, Sultan
Susan Scoby, Edmonds
Ruth Scollan, Lynnwood
Mike Scott, Suquamish
Jim Seaman, Mukilteo
Andy Seaver, Edmonds
Wendy Sedlacek, Mercer Island
Andi Seets, Suquamish
Julia L. Seibert, Clyde Hill
Brent Seidel, Mukilteo
Jody Serl, Everett
Frances Sevela, Alderwood Manor
Liz & Bill Shackelford, Brier
Tracy Shaffer, Arlington
Richard Sharick, Snohomish
Kathleen Shaw, Mukilteo
Vicki Shaw, Seattle
Brad Sheneman, Kirkland
Toogy Shepard, Bellevue
Sheila Sherwin, Edmonds
Robyn Sherwood, Snohomish
Tim & Mary Shields, Bothell
Chuck Shifren, Edmonds
Nori Shoji, Seattle
Pam Shuart, Ellensburg
David & Carol Siebert, Mercer Island
Sue Silberman, Edmonds
Tom Simmons, Camas
Karen Simons, Mukilteo
Cindy Simonsen, Snohomish
Sherry Simpson, Everett
Michael & Paulette Skinner, Lynnwood
Walt & Nancy Slater, Mukilteo
Jane R. Smilowicz, Bellevue

Warren Smith, Bellevue
Carolyn Smith, Bothell
Michael Smith, Clinton
Rene K. Smith, Issaquah
Walter Smith, Lynnwood
Rebecca Smith, Mountlake Terrace
Art Smith, Mukilteo
Lorie Smith, Oak Harbor
Cris & Craig Smith, Redmond
John & Susan Smythe, Everett
Tom Snodgrass, Mukilteo
Norma Snow, Port Orchard
Susan Somes, Kirkland
Shari Sommerfeld, Edmonds
Douglas Hansen & Diane Sorensen, Mercer Island
Marilyn M. Southern, Bellevue
Tom Sovay, Everett
Denzil & Leona Space, Bremerton
Jackie Specht, Mukilteo
Nathan Spencer, Bremerton
Devin & Shannon Spooner, Marysville
Stephen and Jean Sprinkle, Kirkland
Maggie Sprouse, Marysville
Anne Spruance, Lynnwood
Deanna Stach, Woodinville
Ginger Stackpole, Monroe
Mark Stanton, Shoreline
JaAnn Starck, Marysville
Denise Startin, Mt. Vernon
Juanita Stave, Seattle
Al Stearns, Edmonds
Wendee Steele, Arlington
Laurie Steele, Edmonds
Judith Stein, Clinton
Nancy Stein, Kirkland
Sonya Steiner, Anacortes
Art & Kay Stendal, Mt. Vernon
Eileen Stevenson, Everett
Jennifer Stewart, Mukilteo
Cynthia Stewart, Seattle
Sue Stine, Bremerton
Margaret & Lee Stoltz, Lynnwood
Karley Stoltz, Mountlake Terrace
Micheline & Charles Stone, Mukilteo
Cash & Dorothy Stone, Spokane
Jacie Storme, Kirkland
Mary Stovel, Edmonds
George Stratton, Port Angeles
Ken Strauss, Marysville
Alice Striegel, Marysville
Richard Striker, Edmonds
Sally Strom, Monroe
Scott & Vicki Strong, Lynnwood
Lis & Roy Stubbs, Edmonds
Juli Sturgeon-Taggart, Kirkland
Pat Sturtz, Everett
Dick Sugiyama, Shoreline
Stephen & Melissa Sullivan, Bothell
Brian Sullivan, Mukilteo
LaVonne Sunde, Bothell
Shirley Suttles, Friday Harbor
Paul & Linda Suzman, Seattle
Art & Ann Swanson, Bellevue

Linda M. Swanson, Mukilteo
Marie & Skip Swanson, Mukilteo
Bobbie Swanson, Spokane
Florice Swanson, Woodinville
Celia Sweeten, Lynnwood
Elaine Swift, Brier
Charlotte Swift, Edmonds
Julie Systad, Shoreline
Nannette Tallman, Mill Creek
Debra Taniguchi-Sumaoang, Seattle
Sue Taninecz, Mukilteo
Matt Taormina, Bremerton
Debbie Tapia, Everett
Larry Tate, Seattle
Perry & Ella Tate, Tacoma
J.B. Taylor, Bothell
Darryl Taylor, Coupeville
Susan Taylor, Mercer Island
Ed Taylor, Mukilteo
Steve Taylor, Winthrop
Janet R. Taylor-Phillips, Bothell
Brad Teigen Snohomish
Hunter Terry, Friday Harbor
Eddie Tews, Redmond
George & Suzanne Thomas, Bremerton
Gene & Bev Thomas, Edmonds
Frances Jean Thomas, Friday Harbor
Helen Thomas, Kent
Joyce Thomason, Lake Stevens
Tom & Brooke Thompson, Bainbridge Island
Nettie Thompson, Bellevue
Ruth M. Thompson, Bothell
Sally Thompson, Kirkland
Margee Thompson, Shelton
Marilyn & Ken Thorn, Mukilteo
Nero & Deborah Threet, Mill Creek
Charles & Judy Thurman, Port Ludlow
Ted R. Tidd, Woodinville
Robert M. Timonen, Mukilteo
Dee Tindall, Mukilteo
George Tinker, Bothell
Jamie Card & Isaiah Tinsley, Lake Stevens
Brett Tolpin, Seattle
Teresa Tonnemaker, Mukilteo
Cheryl & Brian Torbet, Mukilteo
Jim Torres, Everett
Piper Travis-Beck, Clinton
Virginia Treche, Sequim
Eileen Trentman, Bothell
Lillian Trimble, Bothell
Robert Trimble, Mukilteo
Shelby Triplett, Edmonds
Donald R. Trombley, Marysville
Janet Turner, Arlington
Launce Turner, Bremerton
Gary Turner, Edmonds
M. Susan Turner, Mill Creek
Marit & Michael, Turner Seattle
Tom & Min Tussing, Astoria
Richard & Dora Twedt, Bothell
Pat Tyson, Spokane

THANK YOU:

Shane Umbrell, Redmond
Karen Vail, Marysville
Mark Valentine, MD, Mukilteo
Cynthia Van Cleave, Edmonds
Eve Van Kleeck, Indianola
Heather Van Mullem, Pullman
Lauren Vanderhoof, Bellevue
"Sal" VanGuilder, Everett
Marilyn VanVolkenburg, Everett
Dianna Varner, Lynnwood
Al Varness, Kirkland
Brett Vaughan, Everett
Lynne Vea, Seattle
Bobby Vegas, Edmonds
Tibor Verebi, Everett
Carolee Vergeer, Silverdale
Rosina Vertz, Port Orchard
Monica Vessell, Seattle
Ben & Susan Vining, Stanwood
Maureen & Steve Vis, Hansville
Evangeline & Paul Visocky, Silverdale
Carol, Jeff, John, Connor Vogan,
Lynnwood
Yvonne Vogele, Kirkland
Jim Voght, Renton
Lonnie Van Volkenburg, Lake Stevens
Gary Volkman, Everett
Mary Vollbrecht ,Edmonds
Joyce Von Borstel, Mukilteo
Francis & Audrey Von Feldt, Redmond
Giacinta Vosika, Mukilteo
Marcia Waddell, Renton
Tracy & Adriann Wade, Mukilteo
Zoe Waggoner, Everett
Brian Wagner, Everett
Katie Waite, Bothell
Susan Walker, Belfair
Jim Walker, Bremerton
Sherry Walker, Kirland
Marquita Walker, Maple Valley
Johnny Walker, Monroe
Readene Wallace, Bellingham
Toph Wallace, Green Bank
Max & Jim Waller, Mukilteo
Bill & Sue Walters, Mukilteo
Brenda & Damian Walters, Redmond
Mia Walterson, Lynnwood
Lee and Cathy Wangerin, Kirkland
Lawrence Wanichek, Seattle
Cathy Warren, Friday Harbor
Karen E. Watkins, Mukilteo
Fern Webber, Mukilteo
Dan Weber, Aberdeen
Connie Webster, Lynnwood
Susan & Craig Weckesser, Olympia
Christopher Wedtke, Everett
Jack Weed, Marysville
George Weed, Sedro-Woolley
Gloria Wegener, Mill Creek
Eva-Marie Weisenberger, Silverdale
Judy Werther, Everett
Nick Westerberg, Veradale
Candace Whedon, Everett
Bobbi White, Bellevue

David White, Everett
Chuck White, Tacoma
Mike & Joy Whiteis Mukilteo
Lori Whitney, Kirkland
Harry & Donna Whittaker, Bothell
Daniel Whornham, Mukilteo
Marilyn Whyte, Mountlake Terrace
Derrell Widner, Shelton
Rolf Wielick, Mukilteo
Janice Wilbur, Mountlake Terrace
Rob Wilcox, Everett
Jack Wiley, Seattle
Phil Wilkerson, Everett
Joe Williams, Blaine
Mark Williams, Kingston
Andrea Williams, Mukilteo
Janet Williams, Mukilteo
Carrie Williams, Seattle
Donna Williams, Shoreline
Brent & Suzanne, Williams Tacoma
Virginia Williams, MD, Edmonds
Pete Williamson, Seattle
Dale Wilson, Everett
Chris Wilson, Mukilteo
Barbara Wilson, Seattle
Dianne Wilson, Tracyton
Gary Wise, Everett
Ray Witham, Edmonds
Michael Woelke, Bellevue
Pete & Ann Wohl, Mukilteo
David Wohrman, Renton
Nikki Wolff, Puyallup
Remmert Wolters, Redmond
John Wong, Mukilteo
Agnes Wong, MD, Edmonds
Jeannette Wood, Woodway
Gene Woodwick, Ocean Shores
Madeline Woolworth, Everett
James Wootton, Renton
Richard Worden, Seatac
Ron Wright, Everett
Antje C. Wyatt, Tacoma
Zane Wyll, Lake Stevens
Yvonne Wyngaard, Bellevue
Debbie Yardley, Bellevue
Jan Ybarra, Mukilteo
Gary Yeager, Cheney
David Yocom Jr., Lynnwood
Donna Youman, Kirkland
Marty Young, Centralia
Rose Zimmer, Mercer Island
Roxanne & Dale Zlock, Spanaway
Jay Zorich, Mukilteo
Mollie Zrust, Mukilteo
Lee Weinstein, Mercer Island

Wisconsin
Phyllis Brillowski, Sheboygan
Cindy Esser, Milwaukee
Mary Genske, Sheboygan
Pat Reilly, Milwaukee
Pat & Laura Stack, Madison

West Virginia
Joyce Cook, Daniels
Wyoming
Blanch Cox, Newcastle